GEISHA

E I S H A

© yoko yamamoto

Beyond

the

Painted

Smile

edited by the
Peabody Essex
Museum

published by

George Braziller, Inc.

in association with the

Peabody Essex Museum

Published in conjunction with the exhibition *Geisha: Beyond the Pained Smile*, organized by the Peabody Essex Museum, Salem, MA, (February 14–May 9, 2004) and presented at the Asian Art Museum—Chong-Moon Lee Center for Asian Art and Culture, San Francisco (June 25–September 26, 2004).

ISBN: 0-87577-200-5 (paperback)
ISBN: 0-8076-1545-5 (hardcover)

www.pem.org
www.georgebraziller.com

Notes to the Reader

Japanese names in this publication are listed in Japanese order with the family name first, unless the person is better known by or has chosen the western order of surname last. Romanized versions of Japanese words are italicized and defined or explained at their first appearance in each essay. Japanese words that have entered the English lexicon are not italicized.

Japanese words are pronounced with vowels as in Italian (roughly, a = ah, i = ee, u = oo, e = eh, o = oh), with each syllable given approximately the same length. The dipthong ei = ay, as in geisha [gay-sha]. Vowels with macrons (ō, ū) indicate that the vowel sound is to be held twice the length of the sound of the same vowel without a macron.

Japanese historical periods referenced in this volume are:
Edo period: 1615–1867
Meiji period: 1868–1912

Contents

Women of the Kyoto Entertainment District, Mihata Jōryū, 1830–1850.

This pair of six-fold screens (see also pp. 14–15) shows a selection of twelve women who populated the Kyoto pleasure quarters around 1840. The women (left—right) in positions one, three, five, and six on each screen are likely *geiko* (Kyoto geisha) or *maiko* (Kyoto apprentice geisha), while the women in the second panels are older women, probably matrons who act as managers. Although the exact status of many of these women is not clear, the fourth figure from the left in each screen is a *tayu*, an elite prostitute of the Kyoto/Osaka region.

6

Director's Foreword

THE PEABODY ESSEX MUSEUM—home to one of the world's largest collections of Japanese works of art and culture outside of Japan—owes this outstanding legacy to Edward Sylvester Morse (1838–1925), the museum's director from 1880 to 1916. Morse was nothing short of a Renaissance man in the breadth and depth of his interests, from science, cultural studies, and folklore to art, architecture, and technology, all of which he pursued with a distinctive predisposition toward exploring relationships and influences in ways that, today, would be considered interdisciplinary.

Three periods of residency in Japan between 1879 and 1883 moved Morse from his early focus on zoology to a lifelong study of traditional Japanese culture, an experience so profound that he asserted, "It seems as if the Japanese were the greatest lovers of nature and the greatest artists in the world," in his still widely regarded 1917 book, *Japan Day by Day*. The results of his access, scholarship, and understanding were considerable, yielding most of the museum's nearly 20,000 Japanese works and inspiring an upsurge of interest in Japanese art and culture, particularly in the Boston area. Morse's protégé was Salem's Ernest Fenollosa, who became a preeminent authority on Asian art, while the pioneering collections of Japanese art formed by Bostonians William Sturgis Bigelow and Charles G. Weld—now in the Museum of Fine Arts in Boston and the Peabody Essex Museum—also reflect his influence.

Incorporating a merger as well as an exponential expansion of program, staff, and facilities over the past decade, the Peabody Essex Museum has entered the twenty-first century not just as America's oldest continually operating museum but also as an international museum vigorously committed to presenting and interpreting art and the world in which it is made in innovative and humanistic ways. These two facets are mutually inclusive, for the museum's collections, in representing often this country's first efforts to introduce America to the art and culture of Africa, Asia, India, Native America, New England, and Oceania, provide the foundation on which we now base our efforts to forge relationships between the past and present, traditional and experimental, familiar and unfamiliar. Through interwoven threads of art, history, and culture, we see the fabric of the human spirit in all of its richness and complexity, qualities that are at the heart of our exhibitions, interpretive strategies, and programming.

The Peabody Essex Museum is pleased to present *Geisha: Beyond the Painted Smile*, the first major exhibition and scholarly publication to consider the artistic accomplishments of this uniquely Japanese tradition against the backdrop of a gamut of cultural perceptions. A contemporary audience, western and Asian, could well assume that the past decade's proliferation of fiction, non-fiction, and documentaries about geisha represents a singular fascination. In fact, geisha have enjoyed admiration and endured curiosity and compromising circumstances, first in Japan since their rise to prominence after 1760, and then in the West following the opening of Japan in 1853. Across this arc of time and cultural geography, geisha have become icons of performance and sensuality, although exalted for very different reasons in Japan and in the West.

To describe an artwork or a person as an icon is to assert singular symbolic and presumably lasting status, worthy of veneration originally associated with devotional imagery. An icon is neither solely image nor reality, but rather a duality based on both. How and why iconic status is conferred, sustained, eroded, or even transmuted into misperception and stereotype is a complex evolutionary process, one shaped as much by the forces of history, culture, and money as by the human psyche and the erratic yet cyclical nature of taste. Even more than an exquisite kimono or an elaborate, codified hairstyle, the painted smile has become the visual cue that elicits the iconic melange of refinement and hedonism identified with geisha. This contained yet expressive silhouette—lush red punctuating stark white—also encapsulates the challenge of characterizing geisha as a whole, for they represent both centuries of tradition in the performing and entertaining arts and real women dedicated to a contemporary profession, both recurring characters in history and art and a lightning rod in the interpretation of feminine and national identity.

Geisha: Beyond the Painted Smile has taken as its challenge the duality of image and reality. Both the exhibition and book examine Japanese and western perceptions of geisha, particularly the themes of exoticism and the interplay of high and popular culture, as well as the geisha culture in which their aesthetics of performance, entertainment, and companionship have evolved and been perfected. The historical and contemporary artworks selected for the exhibition and the constellation of topics in the publication explore the inherent dynamic tension between perceptions of geisha—some prurient, many contradictory, others well-founded—and the indisputable impact of geisha not just on Japan's performing, visual, and decorative arts, but also on Japanese and western definitions of beauty and character.

The museum has been most fortunate in securing a broad range of expertise, support, and access to realize this study of a complex subject, one that epitomizes our interest in the nexus of art, culture, and history. Dr. Andrew L. Maske, the museum's curator of Japanese art, developed the exhibition and book, based on the conviction that geisha today are exemplars of Japan's traditional arts. I would like to second his generous acknowledgments of the many individuals and organizations in Japan, the United States, and Europe who have so kindly provided their knowledge, resources, time, and good will. To the lenders of precious artworks and objects intimately connected to the geisha world, the latter infrequently available, we are especially grateful for this privilege.

I extend additional deep appreciation to the book's distinguished authors. Anthropologist Liza Dalby, journalist Lesley Downer, novelist Arthur Golden, Boston's Japan Society President and filmmaker Peter M. Grilli, Japanese art history scholar Money L. Hickman, and Asian art historian Allen Hockley have joined Andrew Maske in contributing thoughtful essays reflecting these diverse disciplines, in concert with the sensitive photographic essay by contemporary Japanese artist Yoko Yamamoto. The collaboration between PEM Chief Curator Lynda Roscoe Hartigan, the project director, and Letitia Burns O'Connor and Dana Levy, editor and designer respectively of Perpetua Press, was critical to bringing the book to its considered and elegant fruition. We are most fortunate in copublishing this book with George Braziller.

The exhibition has benefited considerably from the talents and dedication of the museum's staff, in particular Deputy Director of Exhibitions Fred Johnson, Deputy Director of Interpretation and Education Vas Prabhu, Head Registrar Claudine Scoville, Project Manager Priscilla Danforth, and Exhibition Coordinator Christine Bertoni.

The museum gratefully acknowledges the generous support of the E. Rhodes and Leona B. Carpenter Foundation for this exhibition, and thanks San Francisco's Asian Art Museum—Chong-Moon Lee Center for Asian Art and Culture and its distinguished director Dr. Emily J. Sano for joining the Peabody Essex Museum in presenting *Geisha: Beyond the Painted Smile* to a national audience.

DAN L. MONROE
Executive Director
The Peabody Essex Museum

Acknowledgments

IN THE FALL OF 1988, while I was living and working in Fukuoka, Japan, I met Mrs. Takahashi Fumi. Introduced to the eighty-one–year-old lady because I wanted to find out about geisha ditties known as *kouta* (little songs), I eventually took lessons from her and later rented the upper floor of her house. I learned that Mrs. Takahashi had been the geisha "Kotsune" during the 1920s and 1930s in the Mizuchaya geisha district of Fukuoka. Mizuchaya was the premier geisha district in Kyūshū from the late nineteenth century through the post–World War II period, and as a geisha there she had entertained nationally prominent politicians and company presidents. Mrs. Takahashi (whom I came to call *Obaachan* [Grandma]) was an independent spirit who had an insatiable desire for novelty, a taste whetted, no doubt, by her experiences as a geisha in her youth. She and I got on famously, and it was a unique experience to share her dwelling, one of the last remaining Mizuchaya geisha lodging houses (*okiya*). Our relationship was in some ways like a real grandmother and her adult grandson, in other ways different. But it was her life as a geisha that I found most fascinating and I think she felt reaffirmed that I considered the experiences of her youth as interesting as she did. Though generally easygoing, she insisted on proper ceremony when it was appropriate, and she was intimidated by no one, no matter their status or position. I have found these same characteristics in many other geisha I have met since.

Although I left Fukuoka for graduate school in 1990 and Mrs. Takahashi passed away in 1998, knowing her was the single most important influence on my decision to pursue this book and an exhibition on the topic of geisha. My study of *kouta*, and later, Japanese dance, instilled in me a respect and appreciation for the artistic accomplishments of geisha, a theme that I address in detail in this volume. I dedicate my work on this book to the memory of Mrs. Takahashi Fumi (1907–1998).

In preparation for this book I talked with dozens of practicing geisha, retired geisha, and members of their families. All of them were enthusiastic about a project intended to dispel incorrect notions about the role of geisha in Japan; they understandably wanted themselves and their profession to be seen in the best possible light. Geisha associations, registration offices, and teahouses see the protection of the geisha image in general and of the rights of the geisha connected to them in particular as their most important responsibilities. These bodies act as agents for the geisha and as clearing houses for requests to interview, photograph or film them. Because of their roles in determining the access that outsiders have to geisha in their districts, these organizations are faced with a dilemma: how to promote geisha entertainment to an audience unfamiliar with its world, while preventing the appropriation of the geisha image in ways that they feel are inappropriate or might impinge on the privacy of the geisha they represent. The general sense of dissatisfaction in the geisha world with the focus of many of the books and films on geisha produced in recent years has increased the difficulty of dealing with geisha organizations, who insist on ever-stricter control over access to and representations of their members. I consider myself extremely fortunate to have received a tremendous amount of cooperation from many individuals and organizations associated with geisha, as well as from geisha themselves, in Tokyo, Kyoto, Kanazawa, and Fukuoka.

In Tokyo, each of the five principal geisha associations (*kumiai*) gave their permission for use of photographs taken by Yoko Yamamoto of their members: Shinbashi, Akasaka, Kagurazaka, Asakusa, and Yoshichō. I was kindly allowed access to other geisha communities and/or their facilities by the geisha registration offices of Nagasaki *kenban* (Nagasaki City) and Hakata *kenban* (Fukuoka City). My understanding of the environments in which geisha entertain was expanded immeasurably by the following establishments: Kanetanaka, Shinbashi, Tokyo; Shinkiraku, Shinbashi, Tokyo; Ichirikitei, Gion, Kyoto; Masuume, Gion, Kyoto; Itō, Gion, Kyoto; Gion Kanikakuni, Kyoto, Masunoya, Pontochō, Kyoto; Nakazato, Kamishichiken, Kyoto; Nakanoya, Kazuemachi, Kanazawa; Mine, Nishichayamachi, Kanazawa; Yamatomi, Higashichayamachi, Kanazawa; Shima, Higashichayamachi, Kanazawa; Miyakodori, Asakusa, Tokyo; Yayoi, Hakata, Fukuoka; Kagetsu, Nagasaki.

I am particularly indebted to Yoko Yamamoto, whose deep understanding and sensitive photographs of the geisha world have both informed and inspired me, and this volume. I have benefited greatly from her long experience of living and working with geisha in Tokyo, and admire her passion for presenting geisha in an honest yet evocative way.

I am also deeply indebted to R. Scott Drayer (Sōzan), whose profound knowledge of geisha in Kanazawa opened for me an entirely new and fascinating world. His dedication to preserving the culture of geisha and ensuring that they are presented with truth and dignity echoes some of the core objectives of this project.

Also in Japan, Hata Masataka of Shōeidō Incense, Kyoto, and Noguchi Yoshio provided me with essential insights into the geisha world from customers' perspectives. Tanimura Susumu kindly sent tapes of geisha programs broadcast on NHK television in Japan, while Nakahara Noriko provided extensive research material in Japanese that otherwise would have been difficult to access. Mr. Itō Genjirō, whom I have not yet had the pleasure of meeting in person, made valuable suggestions regarding sources of research and assisted with connections in Japan.

Mayor Nishino Yoshio of Ōta City, Tokyo, furnished useful introductions and encouragement. Others in Tokyo to whom I am indebted include Sakuma Yukiko, Kamata Chizuru, Shibuya Shinichirō, and Asai Kazuharu of Aoyama Gakuin University. Mizushima Takayoshi and Kamitsu Mamoru of Hakubi Kyoto Kimono School and its foundation, Friends of the World, as well as employees Yamada Sachiko, Kajiwara Kikuyo, Iijima Tomoko, and Tomioka Kuniko who contributed greatly to my understanding of how geisha kimono are worn.

In Kyoto, the following people provided special access to events or environments associated with geisha or information about the *geiko* (geisha) of that city, or assisted with research projects carried out there: Endō Atsuhiko, Fujisawa Haruko, Itō Jun, Ōtsuki Tadao, Sakai Hiroaki, Tanaka Hiroko, Tanaka Ichiko, Tsuji Kōko, and Yasuda Hiroki.

In Kanazawa, my preparations were greatly assisted by: Tanada Keiko, photographer Noca (Noka) Wakihiko; Wakayagi Kazuo, master dance teacher of the Wakayagi school; Ichizuka Mamoru of the Association for the Promotion of Kaga-dyeing (*Kaga-zome Shinkōkai*); Kineya, instructor of shamisen and singing, Kazuemachi; and Fukushima Mitsukazu, expert restorer of traditional Japanese musical instruments. Further assistance was rendered in Kanazawa by Nakamura Eiichirō, filmmaker, and Bruce Wilson, entertainer extraordinaire.

In Fukuoka, I am indebted to Watabe Miyo, Fukushima Mieko, Fukushima Hiroko, Shibayama Miyoko, and Yamao Yosoichi. In Nagasaki, Harada Hiroji, Director of the Nagasaki City Museum, Ōta Yuki of Nagasaki Broadcasting Corporation, and Katō Takayuki gave me valuable assistance in understanding geisha of that city.

A very special word of appreciation is due to the individuals and institutions who so kindly agreed to lend works to the exhibition and to allow their reproductions in this book. I am grateful to colleagues

The Geisha Kotsune
(Mrs. Takahashi Fumi)

at museums where I investigated collections: Amy Poster, Brooklyn Museum of Art; Matthew Welch, Minneapolis Institute of Arts; Anne Morse, Midori Oka, Angie Simonds, and Masaru Shima, Museum of Fine Arts, Boston; Barbara Ford, Miyeko Murase, and Sondra Castile, Metropolitan Museum of Art; Matthi Forrer and Ken Vos of the Rijksmuseum voor Volkenkunde, Leiden, the Netherlands, and Menno Fitski of the Rijksmuseum, Amsterdam; Kobayashi Jun'ichi, Nitta Tarō, and Koyama Shūko of the Edo Tokyo Museum; Dainobu Yūji, Kanba Nobuyuki, Matsubara Shigeru, Matsumoto Nobuyuki, and Tamamushi Reiko of the Tokyo National Museum. I would also like to express my appreciation to Julia White, Honolulu Academy of Arts, and to Sebastian Izzard, René Scholten, Katherine Martin, Tara Adrian, and Leighton Longi. I am also indebted to Barry Till, Curator of Asian Art at the Art Gallery of Greater Victoria, who inspired me with his own exhibition on the geisha/diva Ichimaru. I deeply appreciate the efforts of all members of the collections, conservation, and photographic reproductions staffs of the institutions listed above.

I have been assisted with important groundwork, research, and preparation for this book by the following interns and volunteers: Kristen Bengsten, Wataru Fujiwara, Megumu Mabuchi, Rie Suzawa, Katja Triplett, and Akiko Takata Walley. In April 2002, the Edwin O. Reischauer Institute of Japanese Studies at Harvard University generously supported and hosted a roundtable discussion on the topic of geisha, attended by scholars including Andrew Gordon, Roger Keyes, Adam Kern, Timon Screech, Elizabeth de Sabato Swinton, and Merry White. Several of these researchers, joined by Amy Poster of the Brooklyn Museum of Art, gave me continued advice in the preparation and execution of this project.

I also want to thank the other contributors to this volume, Liza Dalby, Lesley Downer, Arthur Golden, Peter Grilli, Money Hickman, and Allen Hockley, all of whom made sacrifices to meet the demands of our schedule, and who have brought stimulating and varied perspectives to bear on the subject of geisha. Sincere thanks are also due to designer Dana Levy and editor Letitia B. O'Connor, ably assisted by Jane Oliver, of Perpetua Press, Santa Barbara, who believed in this project even when it looked as if it might never happen. This book is a tribute to your talent, hard work, and tenacity.

I would like to express my appreciation to the Peabody Essex Museum staff who assisted with this project, especially Chief Curator Lynda Roscoe Hartigan, curatorial assistant for Japanese art Gerald Marsella, and departmental assistant Keiko Thayer, all of whom contributed time and energy to this project that went far beyond the normal call of duty. I thank Susan Bean, PEM curator for South Asian and Korean art, for her kind advice and support, as well as her curatorial assistant, Alyssa Langlais Dodge, who assisted me in the early stages of planning this project.

I also thank my wife Huajing and our children Angela and Angus for their patience and support during the nearly five years it has taken to bring this project to fruition. Your smiles have made the tremendous challenges all worthwhile.

Despite my best efforts, I have surely missed some people who have provided information or other material that have proved useful to this book. To you I offer my apologies, but assure you that your contributions have helped to make this a better volume. Thank you.

ANDREW L. MASKE
Curator, Japanese Art
Peabody Essex Museum

Lenders

Art Gallery of Greater Victoria, Victoria, British Columbia

Mary and Jackson Burke Foundation

Carole Davenport

R. Scott Drayer (Sōzan), Yamahatsu, Kazuemachi, Kanazawa, Japan

Robert and Betsy Feinberg

Mr. and Mrs. Richard Fishbein

Peter M. Grilli and Diana Grilli

Tom Haar

Harvard University Art Museums

Honolulu Academy of Arts

Masunoya, Pontochō, Kyoto, Japan

The Metropolitan Museum of Art

Minneapolis Institute of Arts

Montreal Museum of Art

Museum of Fine Arts, Boston

National Galleries of Scotland

The Nelson Atkins Museum of Art, Kansas City, Missouri

Peabody Essex Museum, Salem, Massachusetts

René Scholten

Shibayama Miyoko, Fukuoka, Japan

Tokyo National Museum

Tsuruta Eitarō, Tokyo, Japan

Yoko Yamamoto, Japan

Yamao Yosoichi, Japan

and several anonymous lenders

15

Why Do Geisha Exist?

Arthur Golden

IT'S NO WONDER GEISHA HAVE BEEN POORLY UNDERSTOOD in the West. We have nothing even remotely like them here. They are trained in the performing arts, and so we sometimes view geisha as artists; and yet if we learn that their jobs may in certain circumstances involve sex, we tend instead to view them as prostitutes. In fact, a woman working as a geisha in one of the renowned districts of Tokyo or Kyoto is neither an artist nor a prostitute. She is instead something unfamiliar to us, a kind of professional who makes her living through social engagements. She entertains clients by telling stories, pouring drinks, and laughing at jokes. Sometimes she'll perform songs or dances, which she may have mastered at a very high artistic level. On occasion she may stay up late into the night chatting with an old familiar customer as if they have been friends for years—and indeed, perhaps they have. It is a job that seems almost incomprehensible to us here in the West. Why then does it exist in Japan?

It is an often-cited fact about the Japanese language that the honorific title for a married woman translates as "revered interior," while the somewhat plainer word used to refer to one's own wife means simply "within the house." The roles suggested by words like these may have changed dramatically over the past fifty years, but still, such words tell us everything we need to know about social norms many generations ago when geisha came into being. In the past, or at least in a common, sepia-toned view of the past, a newly married woman was expected to spend each evening waiting at the front door until her husband came home for dinner. Sometimes his work responsibilities, entertaining customers or perhaps simply drinking with colleagues, kept him out until the early morning hours. From this we derive one of the iconic images of newlyweds in traditional Japanese society: the young wife asleep on her knees with dinner still uneaten on the table.

Although it's possible for us to imagine a culture in which men go out together for the evening without any expectation that women should be present, this is certainly not the way things turned out in Japan. That doesn't mean Japanese men never do such things. Close friends certainly do. In business-related entertainment, however, the hierarchical relationships between bosses and their employees, or even between colleagues whose seniority differs a bit, can be very restricting. Relaxing in such circumstances is a good deal easier with the benefit of alcohol, but the presence of women offers something even more important: it makes the men simply men. Most of the women hired as entertainers in these circumstances aren't geisha at all but bar hostesses, who wear western-style clothing and have no special training in the arts. Nevertheless, their roles are much the same. Senior department heads and recently-hired college graduates, who in the office treat one another about like kings and sub-

17

jects, can join in laughter together when the bar hostess who has entertained them for the past hour begins ribbing the boss. The bantering that takes place during relaxed evenings of this sort often veers well into the realm of innuendo; usually the more alcohol, the more innuendo. But sex is not by any means a part of the agenda, at least not in reputable clubs or bars. A man who goes out for a few drinks in Tokyo with a colleague will almost certainly hire a woman to sit with them, but neither the men nor the woman will have any expectation of leaving the club together or slipping away to a back room. To tell the truth, using the word "hire" makes the arrangement sound more contractual than it really is. No Japanese man will enter such a bar in the first place unless he expects that a bar hostess will come and join him. Nor will he expect to pay her fee outright. He will pay only for his drinks, but at the rate of perhaps $50 or even $100 for a couple of beers. It is a concept westerners don't easily grasp, which is why bar owners in the expensive districts of Tokyo block the door when an American tourist wearing a fanny pack and with his wife behind him on the stairs tries to enter. The Americans will enjoy the karaoke and the amusing mime-like efforts at communicating with the bar hostesses. They'll enjoy the beer or the scotch too. But when the bill comes they'll be outraged, and they may well refuse to pay it.

Things in Japan have changed a good bit in recent years, so we might expect Japanese men and women to socialize together more now than ever before. That is indeed the case, and yet even so, the old ways haven't by any means disappeared. Although it's possible in almost any restaurant in Tokyo to stumble on two couples having dinner together or a group of women out for a night of fun, male colleagues still go to restaurants and bars just as they always have. As long as they continue to do so, the presence of women will very likely remain the surest way to keep them from spending their evenings staring bleary eyed across the table at one another with nothing much to say.

But explaining why bar hostesses still exist goes only partway toward explaining geisha. Geisha are in many ways the bar hostesses of several hundred years ago. A bar hostess wears a skirt or a dress, sometimes a slightly provocative one, while a geisha wears kimono in a provocative way—though "provocative" in a kimono is still far from risqué. A bar hostess joins her customers singing popular songs with a karaoke machine, while a geisha plays a *shamisen* and sings old folk songs, most of which were first popular at least a hundred years ago and probably more. Geisha do bring to their profession a number of skills bar hostesses lack, such as various elegant forms of dance that differ from one district to another. But even if they are highly trained and their modern-day counterparts are not, geisha originally came into being to fill very much the same role. Nowadays their clothing, their hairstyles, and their formal makeup are no more modern than the powdered wigs worn by members of the British judiciary. And yet these professional entertainers have managed to survive into the modern era not as museum pieces but as desirable companions—and this despite the extraordinary cost of a few hours of their time.

How have geisha managed to achieve this feat of historical endurance, seemingly against the odds?

The existence of geisha in the modern era makes sense most readily when we regard their survival as merely one aspect of a much larger mechanism in Japanese culture. All around the world customs and institutions outlive their expected lifetimes, but in Japan anachronisms are something of a defining cultural trait. I believe there exists within Japanese culture a deep-rooted mechanism of protectiveness that arose not only naturally but inevitably as a result of historical circumstance.

In the first four or five centuries of the Christian era the Japanese were a relatively primitive people. They had no written language, or at least, none that has survived; and although many of the unique aspects of their culture must undoubtedly have put down roots by this time, the monuments visited and admired by tourists today didn't exist at all. Nor did the cities, except perhaps as rudimentary settlements.

All this changed with the spread of Buddhism, first brought to Japan by monks from Korea and China during the sixth century. The scriptures were written mostly in Chinese, and over the course of a few hundred years the Japanese undertook a very

Maiko in Stands at Sumo *Basho* (tournament), Tokyo. Dana Levy, 1977. Geisha, like sumo wrestlers, have attained iconic status for their distinctive appearance and preservation of Japan's traditional culture.

earnest study of the language and used its forms to develop a written language of their own. Because of its isolation, Japan was never overrun by China like many other Asian cultures, but along with the Chinese language and the religion of Buddhism came a great many new ideas the Japanese were happy to adopt. Soon they were dressing in Chinese-style robes, living in Chinese-style cities, and practicing forms of government modeled closely on those of China. For various ideas and institutions they'd never known before, they adopted Chinese words, pronounced in ways the Chinese themselves would have found unintelligible—and bear in mind that the Japanese and Chinese languages are no more fundamentally alike than Japanese and English.

This involvement with China on the part of the early Japanese was an intense and prolonged cultural homage. It lasted hundreds of years and transformed Japan from a preliterate society into a pre-modern one. It would be wrong to say that Japanese culture is based on the culture of China; at the same time, Chinese culture is for the Japanese more or less what Greco-Roman culture is for us.

Such profound cultural change could obviously never have been possible if the introduction of foreign ideas had seemed threatening to the early Japanese. Different cultures react in very different ways to such influences, and the Japanese must obviously have developed at that time, or must already have had, some secure sense that their essential Japanese-ness could not be undermined even as foreign influences remade their language, their system of government, their dress, and their religion—that is to say, those things most fundamental to their understanding of themselves.

An analogy in the realm of architecture might help to point out just how astonishingly curious such a remaking really is. Imagine turning a small house into a palace, vastly expanding and remodeling its most basic spaces, but without altering the original support structure that allowed it to stand in the first place. In architecture such a feat would of course be impossible or at the very least totally impractical, but in the realm of reordering the human mind and the ideas and institutions that are its out-

Geisha Playing Party Game, 1890s
Eight geisha and apprentices demonstrate the *ozashiki* game "Konkonchiki," the objective of which is to reach through the loop and grab an object (here, a sake cup) before the loop is pulled closed.

growth, what often matters most is simply what we believe to be true. The Japanese are able to adopt foreign ways so readily (they have done so again in the modern era under influence from the West) precisely because they carefully protect institutions which—whether significant to their wellbeing or not—they regard as uniquely Japanese.

Examples of this protectiveness are not hard to find. We can start at the very highest level, politically at least, by contrasting the Japanese emperor with the English monarchy. In England the monarchy has been without meaningful power for perhaps a few hundred years at most. During that time its value to the English people has degraded so much that tabloids ridicule and humiliate the royal family whenever possible. In Japan the imperial family has been without meaningful political power for more than one thousand years. And yet few Japanese would regard the emperor as a meaningless symbol. His survival doesn't appear to be in doubt.

Or consider traditional dress. It's true that in the West our most formal clothing, probably white tie and tails, has come down to us from an earlier era. But in Japan, traditional dress is far more impractical, many times more expensive, and vastly more widely used. Young Japanese women buy reference books and even attend special schools to learn how to wear kimono; otherwise they probably wouldn't know how to walk becomingly with the legs so uncomfortably restricted, or match the robes and their accessories in a elegant fashion, or—most troublesome of all—tie the obi properly. And yet the Japanese, who wear western clothing for work and for play, take out their terribly expensive and impractical kimono whenever one of life's defining moments comes along, such as a wedding, a funeral, or an important ceremony.

In the arts, the Japanese have actually institutionalized a method for protecting those who practice traditional arts at the highest level by designating them as Living National Treasures and offering them special benefits and attention. In sports, non-Japanese sumo wrestlers, now a relatively common sight, still seem very curious to many Japanese; sumo is, after all, something native to Japan.

There can be little doubt that other nations, ours included, often go to exaggerated lengths to define themselves as unique. What is unusual about the Japanese is their extraordinary ability to preserve what might be called "cultural artifacts" and define themselves by reference to those artifacts in order that new ideas and institutions can readily be absorbed. To some extent we might almost say, at grave risk of overstatement, that bar hostesses can exist in modern Japan only because geisha still exist. It is through confidence in the old traditional ways, after all, that the Japanese feel so accepting of the modern.

The geisha is a complex character within Japan. For some she is a source of shame because of widely held misconceptions abroad that she is nothing more than an exotic prostitute. For others she is a source of pride because of her beauty and elegance, her uniqueness in the world, and her mastery of dance. Those who know her through long experience of evenings in teahouses see her differently still, as a trusted companion. Whether she will still exist in another hundred years is anyone's guess. Only one thing is certain: her survival will be more likely if the Japanese continue to regard her as a meaningful symbol of their past.

Arthur Golden's critically acclaimed novel, *Memoirs of a Geisha*, was published in 1997. He holds an undergraduate degree in art history, with a specialty in Japanese art, from Harvard College, and advanced degrees in Japanese history from Columbia University, where he also studied Mandarin Chinese, and English from Boston University. He has also studied in Beijing and lived in Tokyo.

PART I understanding geisha

A World Behind Closed Doors

LESLEY DOWNER

A hole in the paper wall,
Who has been so guilty?
Through it I hear the breaking of a shamisen string,
Meaning bad luck.

Yet the prediction-seller says
That mine is excellent.

Geisha song[1]

GEISHA LIVE OUTSIDE MAINSTREAM SOCIETY and so prefer to maintain a certain secrecy, to shield themselves from prying eyes. Life in the geisha districts goes on behind closed doors. Most Japanese have never seen, let alone met, a geisha, and have as many false conceptions of them as do Westerners. This very mystery enhances their allure.

Geisha refer to themselves and the world they inhabit as the *karyūkai*, the "flower-and-willow world." In the past it was the Japanese equivalent of the demimonde. The courtesans were the colorful "flowers," glamorous and enchanting, while geisha were "willows," modest and demure but resilient, able to bend with the winds of fate. The courtesans have long since disappeared, to be replaced by more garish ladies of the night. But the willows endure.

In the evenings geisha spirit their wealthy customers into a delightful alternative universe, a world of dreams where they can forget their domestic and business lives, though the price for such pleasures is high. The customers may even forget that the geisha are working. In the daytime, away from the public gaze, geisha dedicate themselves to practicing and perfecting classical Japanese dancing, singing, and music, comparable in standing and seriousness to western ballet and opera. This is their art (*gei*). *Sha* means "person." A geisha is thus a "person of art," an artiste.

At present there are five communities where geisha work, or *hanamachi* (flower towns), in Kyoto: Gion, Gion Higashi, Pontochō, Kamishichiken, and Miyagawa-chō; and five in Tokyo: Shinbashi, Akasaka, Kagurazaka, Yoshichō, and Asakusa, plus some unofficial ones; together with varying numbers in Japan's other major cities. Each has its own history and traditions, and there are subtle and not-so-subtle differences in dialects and in the styles of dance and music geisha perform.

***Maiko* Dancing, Pontochō, Kyoto**, Francis Haar, c. 1954
The primary skill of *maiko*, which today means an apprentice geisha in Kyoto, is revealed in the literal meaning of the term, "dancing girls." In the past, *maiko* began their apprenticeships as early as age thirteen; today, they must complete mandatory education and begin at age sixteen or later.

OPPOSITE
***Maiko* and *Geiko* Leaving the Gion Kaburenjō Theater**, Tom Haar, 1993
To allow ordinary people an opportunity to see geisha perform, many geisha districts present public stage performances in such theaters as the Gion *kaburenjō* in Kyoto. *Geiko* is the term used for geisha in the Kansai region of Japan.

Standing Courtesan, attributed to Kaigetsudō Dōshin, c. 1700–16
The zenith of popularity of high-class courtesans of the pleasure districts occurred in the first half of the eighteenth century. They eclipsed all others in beauty, fashion, and elegant accomplishments. By the end of that century, they were overshadowed by the chic and understated geisha.

In Gion, the *maiko*, apprentice geisha, flit along the streets like butterflies in their vivid regalia. In Tokyo, only an aficionado can tell whether an elegant woman in a kimono is actually a geisha. In his essay "Identifying Geisha in Art and Life," curator Andrew Maske provides clues to elucidate these distinctions.

In the course of their two hundred fifty-year history, geisha have played many parts. Today they have re-created themselves for the modern age. The seven essayists in this book examine different aspects of geisha—their arts, lives, history, and the complex question of their image—without, we hope, dispelling their mystique.

The Glittering Evening Face

Imagine yourself transported to the Gion district of Kyoto. It is evening. One by one, white lanterns begin to glimmer along the darkened street. Suddenly you hear the clacking of wood on stone. Approaching on high clogs is an extraordinary vision. Painted, powdered, and coiffed, wrapped in layer upon layer of richly patterned silks, she is as out of place in modern Japan as a lady of Louis XIV's court would be in modern Paris. But this is not modern Japan. Here time, at least partially, stands still.

This magical creature is a *maiko*. More of a painted doll than a woman, her oval face is painted lustrous white. Her eyes are outlined in black, her eyebrows etched in brown, and her lips a tiny pout of cherry red. At the front, her brilliantly colored kimono is tightly crossed and covers her to the throat. At the back it is tugged daringly low, revealing a breathtaking expanse of exquisitely white-painted back. At the nape of the neck, which Japanese men find especially provocative, is a lick of naked, unpainted flesh.

She is not so much a woman as a walking work of art, a compilation of symbols and erotic markers. She is an actress, done up to play a role. This applies particularly to *maiko*, whose hair is teased, combed, and oiled, and festooned with hanging ornaments. Wherever she goes, she is visibly a *maiko*. But unlike a professional actress who removes her makeup in the evening and returns to ordinary life, a geisha regards her life as a calling. Once she joins the ranks of geisha, she is a geisha twenty-four hours a day.

Andrew Maske unravels the iconography of geisha, for the geisha world is all about appearances. As he points out, the way a woman wears her kimono, her hair, and her accessories has been a code for centuries that communicates the age, wealth, social status, and sometimes even the occupation of the wearer.

A Woman's World

Who are the women who choose to become geisha in twenty-first–century Japan? In 1999, I lived for several months in geisha areas of Kyoto and Tokyo to research my book, *Women of the Pleasure Quarters*, and little by little was accepted by the community. It was rather like slipping into a parallel universe. I sat in coffee shops and walked the Kyoto streets with my new friends who, in skirts and blouses, were indistinguishable from ordinary women. No one seeing them would ever have guessed that they took on very different personas in the evening.

In the nineteenth and early twentieth centuries, the heyday of the geisha, women did not take up the profession by choice. They were indentured by their families at the age of five or six, or became geisha at an older age to escape poverty. Today things are very different. Geisha such as Kyōha, from the Shinbashi "flower town" in Tokyo are brilliant, independent-minded women who have chosen a career rather than marriage or children. A glamorous thirty-seven-year-old, Kyōha became a geisha in order to pursue her study of Kiyomoto-style classical singing professionally. Off-duty she enjoys flying to Paris and wearing French couture. The only thing missing in her life, she says, is a lover. She does not regret that she is not married.

Many of the young women I met in Kyoto had fallen in love with the geisha life when they first saw *maiko* on school trips to Kyoto. Much like a young woman

yearning to be a model or a ballerina, they longed to become one of these ravishing butterflies.

Harumi, the daughter of a carpenter, was an exquisite, poised young woman. She had wished so fervently to become a *maiko* that her mother, a taxi driver, arranged for her to be interviewed by the *okamisan*, the house mother, of an *okiya*. (The *okiya* is the "geisha house" where *maiko* live, as opposed to the teahouse or restaurant where they work. It is their private residence, strictly off-limits to guests.) In theory, a would-be *maiko* has to complete her secondary education by fifteen before entering the "flower-and-willow" world. Harumi, however, left home at thirteen. She took on a new name—Harumi is her *maiko* name, akin to a stage name—and thinks of the house mother as her own. Her friends are other *maiko*. She has little in common with her old school friends.

New entrants to the community first learn to speak with the distinctive Kyoto lilt and to use the special geisha vocabulary, some of which only cognoscenti can understand. Apprentices quickly learn their places in the hierarchy. If a senior geisha tells a *maiko* that grass is black, she agrees.

For the first few months, the novice does errands, has her first dancing lessons, and learns by watching her seniors. Later she has her face painted, puts on the lavish *maiko* kimono, and sees herself transformed for the first time. The house mothers and teachers are strict, and for young women, the life is harder than expected. Many leave after a few months.

An Elite Courtesan, 1880s–90s
Top courtesans were highly admired for their beauty, which was further enhanced by gorgeous apparel, elaborate coiffures, and cosmetics. They were known for having refined speech and handwriting. Unlike geisha, who entertained in groups, the highest courtesans were the center of attention whenever present.

The young woman who perseveres goes through a ceremony called *misedashi*, or "opening the shop." She then begins five years of training. Unlike the old days, she has not been sold and has no debt to repay. She may leave if she likes, though it is considered poor form not to put some years into her dancing and music studies when the house mother has invested so much money, time, and trouble to train her. She learns how to put on makeup and to choose a kimono for each season and occasion.

Harumi spends her mornings in the *kaburenjō*, the heart of her geisha community and a kind of geisha "union," housing offices, classrooms, and a public theater where regular displays of geisha dancing take place. There she takes lessons in classical Japanese singing, the shoulder drum (*tsuzumi*), the floor drum (*taiko*), the *shamisen*, and the flute (*yokobue*). For *maiko* the most important skill to acquire is dancing. Even a beginner can still look charming when she moves or performs a simple dance.

But Harumi is still an ordinary Japanese teenager. In her room in the *okiya*, she has posters of Japanese heartthrobs and of Leonardo di Caprio. The difference is that as a *maiko*, she is able to meet and entertain her heartthrobs when they visit Kyoto. Becoming a geisha has opened doors for her into worlds that she could otherwise never dream of entering.

Sliding Back the Paper Doors

For most people, Japanese as well as western, seeing a *maiko* on a Gion street is the closest they will ever get to a geisha. Only the wealthy and privileged are able to meet geisha close-up at a teahouse party, and then only if they have the right connections. (Geisha call the parties over which they preside *ozashiki*, "the honorable room"; customers call them *enkai*, "a banquet.") The guests at a party are almost always exclusively men, although some occasionally bring their wives. Geisha do not encourage this. The point of a geisha party is to enter a separate reality, away from the everyday concerns of work and family, in much the same way as townsmen of the eighteenth and nineteenth centuries found respite in the pleasure quarters.

In "Performance and Play: Arts and Accomplishments of Geisha," Andrew Maske explores the many arts of the geisha. He reminds us that the term "person of art" does not refer only to the geisha's skills in dancing and music. Whether she is participating in teahouse parties or walking along a Gion street, the geisha's total being is a work of art. Her makeup, dress, skills at conversation, and entertainment are equal parts of her geisha persona, learned directly or indirectly from senior geisha. All these, of course, she colors with her personality.

The *Niwaka* Festival in the New Yoshiwara, from the series *Famous Places in Edo*, Utagawa Hiroshige, poem by Kōgetsu-an Kisetsu, 1850s
The main gate of the Yoshiwara district is depicted with the trappings of a popular festival. The teahouse Ōsaka-ya is seen on the left; on the right is the Echizen-ya.

The evening starts out rather quietly. Like perfect dinner party hostesses, geisha top up the guests' sake cups and make sure that every guest is talking, laughing, and having a good time. The host almost certainly has been entertaining at this teahouse for years. He knows the proprietress and will have asked for particular geisha by name. A few teenage *maiko* join in to add variety and laughter to the proceedings.

At first the guests are rather subdued. Maids bring tiny dishes of food each arranged like a miniature work of art—glistening slices of sashimi resemble fish swimming through the sea; vegetables are sculpted into butterflies or flowers—on fine stoneware or porcelain chosen to complement the season and the delicacies. Only the guests eat, never geisha; they have dined before arriving for work. The purpose of their evening is not the cuisine.

Geisha and *maiko* take their places on their knees beside each guest. After a while one of the senior geisha will rise gracefully. This signals all the geisha to rise and move like a swarm of butterflies to the next place so that every guest has a chance to chat with each geisha. As Maske writes, the "effect of beautifully kimono-clad women rising at once and shifting one position to the right or left can look like a dance in itself" (p. 116).

Geisha keep the conversation light. Far from showing off their charm and humor, their job is to make their customers, no matter how old or infirm, feel that they are the most attractive men alive. Rather than remembering the beauty and charm of the geisha, the customers should feel as one American told me he had felt at a geisha party, "I'd never realized before what an incredibly witty and fascinating conversationalist I am!"

The same rule applies when geisha play golf. Modern geisha are sometimes invited to spend the day at an exclusive golf club with a client. A geisha has to be subtle. She has to be a very good player while losing convincingly so that the customer can take pride in his brilliance at defeating such an opponent. Anathema though it may be to feminists, geisha swear by the axiom that, "A clever woman never lets a man know how clever she is."

As Maske remarks, flirtation is one of the geisha arts. Far from being an invitation to sex, it is a game to be played with skill. When a geisha kisses a gnarled company chairman on the cheek and jokes that he is the most handsome man she has ever met and that she is faint for love of him, he is well aware that she is acting. He plays along with the game; he probably enjoys it. But ultimately he knows perfectly well that she tells the same story to every man she meets at a geisha party. She is not being insincere: she is doing her job.

Once the guests have dined, geisha provide formal entertainment. One, usually older, twangs out rhythmic melodies on the banjo-like *shamisen*, a geisha's trademark instrument, and sings. First the *maiko* dance coyly, one by one, to much applause. Then older geisha demonstrate their prowess. These are professional dancers who have spent many years perfecting one or another form of dance. It is like being treated to a private performance by a ballerina accompanied by first-rank musicians.

In the past, guests were assumed to be connoisseurs and often performed themselves. A teahouse party was a participatory event. One man, then another, would rise to his feet to dance, sing, or perform on the *shamisen*, rather like a modern-day karaoke evening. There are still men who are aficionados of the geisha arts and see a teahouse party as a musical evening where they can show off their skills and enjoy the usually superior skills of geisha. Others find this part of the pleasure of the evening.

As more sake is consumed, the evening becomes more and more rowdy. Geisha are adept at games. Some can be to western sensibilities eye-poppingly risqué, full of innuendo and horseplay. But in the end they are only games. The guests stagger off into the night.

After that, as at a western party, the hostesses may do as they please. Some geisha will have known the customers for years and may have formed attachments. Some may have a *danna*, a patron who provides them with an income, an apartment, and covers their expenses—their lavish kimonos, dance classes, and the fees for public performances that they have to pay to participate in. Even if a *maiko* wished to slip away with a client, it would be virtually impossible to do so. The *okiya* where they live communally is rather like a dormitory at a girls' boarding school and the house mother keeps a tight rein.

Sex is a private matter and is certainly not part of the job. Geisha today are well paid, independent women and have no need to sell themselves. They are well aware that they would be foolish to devalue themselves for money. Their lives revolve around developing their performance skills in music and dance and navigating the complex relationships within the geisha hierarchy.

Behind the Scenes

At work a geisha provides an enchanted escape for men. Offstage her daily life is far more down-to-earth. In the daytime *maiko* flutter around the geisha district

Young Geisha with a *Shamisen*,
Tōgensai Eijū, late 1790s
Geisha were forbidden by law to practice prostitution, a fact that inevitably made them all the more sexually attractive to visitors of the pleasure districts. Eijū depicts a young geisha rather worse for wear after an evening of entertaining. Her kimono disheveled, she adjusts a hair ornament.

in *yukata* (simple cotton kimono) on their way to classes or the hairdresser. Their faces scrubbed clean, they look like ballet students. Like professionals worldwide, geisha continue to develop their dancing and performance arts throughout their careers. They train, they rehearse, they learn new skills. From time to time a famous performer of Nō dancing or *kyōgen*, a form of Japanese comic drama, may visit one of the geisha districts to hold master classes. Geisha—some in their fifties, very accomplished dancers and musicians—flock to the workshops.

On the surface the geisha districts are the mirror image of establishment Japan. The lives of geisha share little with the values and daily experience of wives. In the "real world," even the wealthiest Japanese wives pride themselves on doing their own housework, and prefer not to employ a cleaner, nanny, or baby-sitter. In the parallel universe of the "flower towns," geisha boast that they have no idea how to cook or clean. Wives start their families when still in their twenties and tend to mix mainly with other women. Geisha often do not have children. Not only are they at ease in the company of men, some may be the confidantes of the most brilliant and powerful men in the country.

But behind the scenes in the *kenban*, the geisha unions from which each district is administered, elderly men in suits mostly pull the strings. For all its shimmer, in the end the whole enterprise is commercial. Geishas' time and company—though not their bodies—are for sale, and at a very high price. As Money L. Hickman reveals in "Geisha to the Fore: *Niwaka* Festivals and the New Luminaries of Edo," profit has been at the center of the geisha's act for two hundred and fifty years.

Yoko Yamamoto has spent the last twenty years living among the geisha of the Kagurazaka "flower town" in Tokyo. Her insightful photo essay, "The Floating World Today," presents geisha from an insider's perspective. Geisha are consummate performers, accustomed to posing for photographs. But Yamamoto has also caught their private faces. She photographs them when they are relaxed, off-guard and off-duty, emerging from a doorway or rushing to a teahouse party through the snow, sheltering under an umbrella. She has created an invaluable record of daily life in one community of geisha.

Balm for the Soul

Wine and women
Balm for the soul,
This floating world is
Women and wine.

Geisha song [2]

Like the hetaerae of ancient Greece and the courtesans of Renaissance Venice and Belle-Epoque Paris, geisha originated in a culture where marriage was a union of families arranged by one's parents. Decent girls were assigned a husband. Love had nothing to do with it. Girls' educations tended to the womanly skills, primarily sewing. Wives were not expected to be brilliant conversationalists or witty companions; beauty and education were irrelevant. After marriage women spent their lives largely indoors, where they became matriarchs, taking care of the children and household affairs.

Courtesans and geisha were trained to be the charming companions of powerful, brilliant men. Witty, sophisticated, skilled at singing, dancing, and such other arts as poetry writing, they were often beautiful and the best educated women in their societies. The most successful became wealthy, celebrated, and influential. Unlike in Greece, Venice, and Paris, in Japan the sexual and entertainment elements of the job became separated. Geisha arose to provide entertainment for the men who waited hours, days, or even weeks in the hopes of spending a night with the most sought-after courtesans. But their skills, cool elegance, and sheer novelty eventually made them draws in their own rights.

Long before the word "geisha" was coined, their precursors in the seventeenth century were strutting their stuff on stages set up in the dry bed of the River Kamo in Kyoto. The most original, a woman named Izumo no Okuni, electrified her public by cross-dressing. Wearing brocade trousers and an animal-skin jacket and sporting a sword like a dashing young man about town, or dressed as a Christian priest with a cross around her neck, she performed erotic dances and saucy sketches. Her *kabuki* (wild and outrageous) performances were the origin of Kabuki theater.

Until the end of the nineteenth century, the line between acting and prostitution was thin, as it was in England in Shakespeare's time and well into the reign of Queen Victoria. Soon troupes of courtesans were performing risqué dances around the country and selling sexual favors after the show. The shogun's government was not at all worried about morality, but greatly concerned over threats to public order. In 1647, women were banned from the public stage after unseemly squabbles between samurai over particularly desirable women.

The government had already rounded up as many courtesans and prostitutes as possible and installed them in government-sponsored pleasure quarters to maintain order. It was easier to keep an eye on potential troublemakers who haunted the red-light districts if they were all gathered in one place. The quarters were primarily patronized by wealthy merchants and, in Edo, the shogun's capital, by the samurai retainers of the feudal lords who were required by law to spend alternate years there away from their fiefdoms.

The quarters were a huge success. They offered far more than sex. From their sordid beginnings they quickly turned into sparkling entertainment hubs where a man could spend days enjoying side shows, Kabuki and puppet theater, as well as music, dancing, fine food, conversation, and fun. Many ruined themselves in pursuit of the most desirable courtesans. Unlike the indentured prostitutes, courtesans had the right of refusal; courtesans only shared their luxurious beds when they felt like it.

The first entertainers to call themselves "geisha," early in the eighteenth century, were men. Like Shakespeare's fools, their repertoires included bawdy conversation, song, and dance. Women began to join their ranks around 1760 and so quickly outnumbered them that the word geisha was soon used primarily for women. Among the crowds of jugglers, acrobats, montebanks, performing monkeys, child dancers, puppeteers, and actors, geisha stood out. Like the much desired but too often unavailable courtesans, they too were attractive women with an air of distinctive chic.

In this world nothing was what it seemed. A courtesan played the role of a high-class lady while a geisha portrayed herself as an artiste. Some were prepared to sell sexual favors for extra cash. Profit motivated every aspect of the pleasure quarters. Money L. Hickman's essay looks at this colorful world and at the earliest days of the geisha profession. He evokes the brilliant and boisterous *niwaka* festivities, as thrilling as a western Mardis Gras, as the platform on which geisha stepped to the fore. Crowds packed the streets of the Yoshiwara district in Edo (Tokyo), the largest and grandest of the pleasure districts, to gawk at the fantastic spectacles. Decorative floats wound their way through the mobs, borne on people's shoulders or on wheels, decked out like treasure ships or fanciful peacock-prowed boats, and loaded with dancing geisha.

Until then events in the pleasure quarters had always starred courtesans. But the *niwaka* festivals featured mainly up-and-coming geisha. There were geisha sporting splendid costumes with swinging gold and silver fringes; geisha dancing in formation or carrying a huge lion mask and performing the Lion Dance; geisha disguised as monkey trainers, sumo wrestlers, peddlers, or troubadours; and yet more geisha acting out skits and mini-dramas on portable stages (see pp. 124–131). Thus this exciting new profession made its debut before the general public. Soon artists were depicting not only courtesans but geisha in their woodblock prints, transforming

Sake Cup with Decoration of Pine Needles,
20th century
This sumptuous sake cup with scattered gold-leaf pine needles was used at the Tokiwakan restaurant in Fukuoka. The pine needle (*matsuba*) motif is an auspicious design.

Tokiwakan Restaurant, Fukuoka, 1920s–30s
The Tokiwakan, among the finest traditional restaurants (*ryōtei*) in western Japan, hosted elite parties from throughout Japan during the early twentieth century. The drama of international politics played within its walls when Sun Yatsen, founder of the Chinese Republic, hid here from Qing authorities before the Revolution of 1911.

Table Setting from Tokiwakan Restaurant,
1840s–1920s

Interior of the Tokiwakan Restaurant, 1920s–30s

the most glamorous into celebrities. The lovely Tomimoto Toyohina (see p. 137) was among the first geisha to achieve such fame: renowned for her beauty, she was also an artiste, skilled at singing and playing the *shamisen*.

The chic, intelligent geisha—not just pretty faces but able to sing, dance and converse as well—soon became the toast of fashionable Japan, both inside and outside the pleasure quarters. By the late eighteenth century the courtesans with their ornate hairstyles and heavy multilayered kimono had come to seem overdressed, over made-up, and passé.

The 1860s were marked by the civil war that led to the fall of the shogun's government and its replacement by a government of provincial samurai with the emperor as figurehead. In the battles and skirmishes that swept through Kyoto and Edo, geisha on both sides risked their lives to protect their samurai lovers. Some of the samurai married the geisha who had saved them. When these samurai later took high office in the new government, geisha who had started out as lowly entertainers rose to become aristocrats. The dashing Itō Hirobumi was one of the most famous of the samurai leaders. His geisha lover, Umeko, risked death to hide him from the shogun's troops when they hammered on her door, asking if he was there. After the Meiji Restoration he married her. He rose to Count, then to Prince, and became prime minister four times. Umeko, who had started life as a geisha despised by the upper classes, became First Lady.

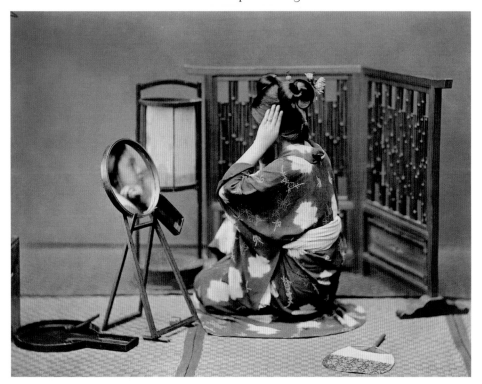

Arranging Hair, 1880s

The excuse of ethnographic documentation gave western photographers the opportunity to show Japanese women in private situations: arranging their hair, applying make up or simply relaxing, sometimes only partially clothed. Photographs like this one were purchased by visitors to Japan singly or in albums.

Barbarians at the Gate

By then the first Westerners had begun to arrive. For two hundred and fifty years Japan had been in self-imposed isolation, closed to foreigners except for a few Dutch and Chinese traders confined to a small island in the port of Nagasaki. Then, in 1853, the American Commodore Matthew Perry's Black Ships dropped anchor in Shimoda demanding that the country open its doors to trade and commerce with the west. He was quickly followed by diplomats, sailors, missionaries, and adventurers, then by curious travelers eager to "understand" this extraordinary, seductive society.

In "First Encounters—Emerging Stereotypes," Allen Hockley explores the origins of the western preoccupation with geisha. Of the Westerners who visited Japan, some prided themselves as connoisseurs, assessing the looks and dancing skills of Tokyo geisha against those of Osaka and Kyoto. Others, such as Baron Raimund von Stillfried, had no compunction against cashing in back home on the image of geisha as sex objects. In the 1870s, Hockley asserts, Stillfried's photographs of bare-breasted Japanese women, some of them geisha, circulated as soft porn.

Word of the mysterious geisha soon spread to the West and was eagerly picked up. Westerners fantasized the geisha as everything their western sisters were not: "exotic," seductive, soft, submissive and—amazingly—sexually available.

As Japanese arts and crafts flooded the West, Europeans and Americans were swept up in the craze for all things Japanese, dubbed "Japonaiserie." They hung woodblock prints of women, whom they took to be geisha, on their walls. Pierre Loti's 1887 novella *Madame Chrysanthème*, the story of how he purchased a "wife"

GEISHA: BEYOND THE PAINTED SMILE

in Nagasaki for six months and set up house with her, was a best seller. Stories such as this reinforced western notions of the geishas' easy-going morality. Geisha came to epitomize the "exotic east" as it burgeoned in western imaginings.

The first Japanese to perform as a professional actress in the west was a former geisha named Sadayakko. Her plays, notably *The Geisha and the Knight*, were smash hits across America, then in London, Paris, and throughout Europe. Astutely playing to western stereotypes, she vamped up the romanticized image of old Japan. In 1902, her tour took her to Italy, where Giacomo Puccini was working on his opera, *Madama Butterfly*. He based his plot on a short story by John Luther Long, but, given the enormous interest in Japan, he was eager to make his Cho-Cho San as "authentic" as possible. He rushed to Milan to see Sadayakko, went to all her performances there, and—as well as borrowing some of her music— modeled his Madame Butterfly on her. This melodrama of the betrayed and hopeless Japanese woman who kills herself for love of a western man struck a powerful chord with western audiences. The image of a geisha as prostitute and plaything for men seemed set in stone forever.

For Japanese too, geisha have been a source of inspiration and curiosity for centuries. As Peter Grilli

The Apprentice Geisha Toyochiyo Making Up, Francis Haar, c. 1954
The traditional hairstyle and white makeup of geisha have been among their most conspicuous features. *Maiko* in Kyoto are now the only women who habitually wear their hair in a traditional Japanese style. Toyochiyo was an apprentice in Kyoto's Pontochō district.

points out in "Geisha on Screen and Stage," geisha are seen as living lives of heightened intensity that makes them natural subjects for novels, drama, and film. Geisha are performers—that is the core of their work—and there is a natural bond between them and other performers, such as Kabuki actors. They are eternally playing a role. No matter what private pain or sadness they feel, they must always conceal it, putting on a cheerful face to entertain their guests. As Grilli writes, "Their lives have been depicted as colorful and glamorous, but the glamour usually masks tragedy or moments of pain and unhappiness." Since Japanese literature has traditionally taken special pleasure in portraying the subtle nuances of loneliness and melancholy, it is not at all difficult to understand why novelists and playwrights might find rich material for melodrama and tragedy in true stories about geisha."(p. 141)

In his essay Grilli gives a fascinating account of some of the best-known Kabuki plays and films, which revolve around geisha and their dramas, both public and private. Geisha, he reminds us, are all different, vulnerable human beings: "Beneath the artifice of their magnificently created exteriors beat some hearts that are tough and bitter and others that are soft and pitiable."(p. 142) Plays and movies give a heightened and sometimes idealized view of the geisha world but convey some idea of the complexity of their lives and feelings.

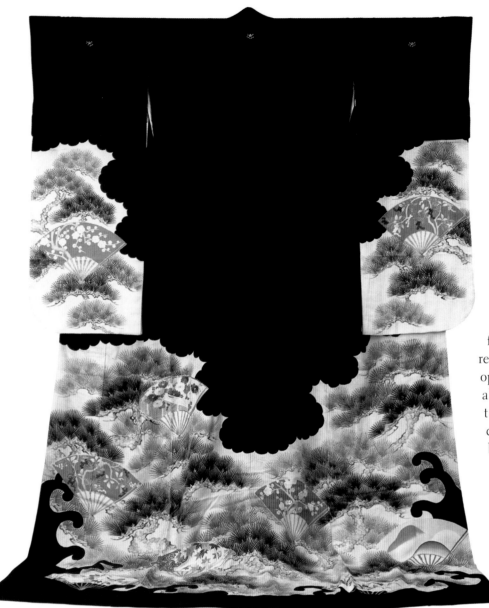

Formal Kimono (*Hon'ishō*) for *Maiko*, Pontochō district, Kyoto, 20th century
Each January, geisha dress in their most formal kimono, known in Kyoto as *hon'ishō* (true garments). Always black with a decoration on the lower area only, *hon'ishō* are adorned with auspicious New Year's emblems. These robes are often a geisha's most valuable kimono.

The Paper Doors Slide Shut

In late nineteenth and early twentieth-century Japan, the highest level of geisha had become celebrities. As famous and adored as the actresses of the Victorian West, they were stars whose names were on everyone's lips. Woodblock prints and hand-tinted albumen photographs of them sold instantly. They were trendsetters and fashion icons. When Japanese started experimenting with western fashions, geisha were the first to be seen in bustles and bonnets. Townswomen emulated their styles and everyone avidly followed their exploits, endlessly recorded in gossip columns. At theater openings and first nights, they were always invited. An evening's entertainment would not have been complete without a bevy of geisha to bring sparkle and glitter to the occasion.

But as Japan entered the modern world, and especially after World War II transformed their environment, a geisha's role became more uncertain. Geisha themselves point to the banning of prostitution in 1958 as the real watershed, after which they needed to reinvent themselves and their image to fit the new age. They proclaimed themselves artistes whose work had nothing to do with sex.

In modern Japan, women have many options other than to be a wife or an artist, like a geisha, living outside the mainstream. Wealthy men who would once have prided themselves on their familiarity with the Gion teahouses, now choose to spend their money in Paris or the ski resorts of Switzerland. Connoisseurs of classical Japanese dance and music are also growing fewer.

A geisha's life too is very different. Modern *maiko* no longer begin their training at the tender age of six but at fourteen or fifteen, when they have completed their basic schooling. Far from being sold, they usually want desperately to become geisha, and they may leave whenever they like.

But despite all these changes, and although they may seem anachronistic in twenty-first century Japan, there is something so enthralling about geisha that they continue to endure, even to thrive. Their numbers have declined, but they continue to occupy a place right at the heart of Japanese culture.

In his commentary, novelist Arthur Golden poses the intriguing question, "Why Do Geisha Exist?" Geisha, he argues, fulfill a role that has no parallel in the West: they are professional entertainers who attend small, all-male gatherings, ensuring that the guests are happy and conversation runs smoothly. In this respect they are like contemporary bar hostesses in expensive clubs. But unlike bar hostesses, geisha dress in a style that is resolutely traditional with erotic subtleties alien to modern taste. Golden suggests that the reason why geisha prevail is because they are so uniquely Japanese in a culture that venerates its traditions while equally embracing the new. Geisha are one of those institutions that the Japanese lovingly preserve as "a meaningful symbol of the past," synonymous with Japan and with being Japanese and requiring all the more to be preserved as Japan gradually becomes indistinguishable from the rest of the modern world.

To western fancies too, the concept of "geisha" continues to fill a niche. More than a courtesan or any other profession, a geisha is a potent symbol of the "erotic other." In "The Exotic Geisha," Liza Dalby takes a long and compelling look at the place geisha occupy in the imaginations of virtually everyone who has never encountered one. Ever since the nineteenth century, writers familiar with Japan have asserted again and again that geisha are not prostitutes. Yet Westerners continue to cling stubbornly to the belief in an imagined Orient populated by sweet, feminine, submissive women selflessly devoted to fulfilling a man's every requirement. No doubt this refusal to give up the daydream of a lotusland Japan answers some kind of secret need for a woman who will cosset them rather than demand equal rights. For women too, she writes, geisha provide a fantasy, an "image of mythic femininity, holding men in thrall."

Geisha are now rare birds in Japan too. Modern Japanese girls and women pay large sums to be made up and costumed as geisha to be photographed at Kyoto landmarks. Troupes of mock geisha, who (to the untrained eye, at least) look the part but lack the training, add color at social gatherings. And the tourists who fill the streets of Gion anxiously looking for *maiko* to photograph are mainly Japanese.

As Dalby points out, the feudal regime of the shoguns under which geisha arose has long since disappeared and they can no longer rely on a single wealthy patron to support them. In this demanding new world, they have chosen to focus on their role as guardians of Japanese artistic heritage. They are, as we have seen, adept at the traditional performing arts of music and dance, closely akin to those of the Kabuki theatre. But the geisha experience is all-encompassing. For geisha, theirs is not a job but a calling. They maintain and preserve the culture of a world quickly disappearing, where men gather to enjoy music, dance, and witty conversation in the company of brilliant, elegant women who have dedicated their lives to honing themselves and their art.

Geisha wisely continue to hide their world behind closed doors. As a result they have succeeded in keeping their secrets and perpetuating their allure.

NOTES:

1. Ihara Saikaku, *Comrade Loves of the Samurai and Songs of the Geishas*, translated by E. Powys Mathers (Rutland, VT and Tokyo: Charles E. Tuttle Company, Inc., 1972) [first edition 1928], p. 107, poem no. 8.

2. Liza Crihfield Dalby, *Ko-uta: "Little Songs" of the Geisha World* (Rutland, VT and Tokyo: Charles E. Tuttle Company, Inc., 1979), p. 87, poem no. 23.

Leslie Downer has regularly lived and studied in Japan since 1978, including a period among the geisha of Kyoto and Tokyo. She is the author of *On the Narrow Road: Journey Into a Lost Japan* (1989), *The Brothers: The Hidden World of Japan's Richest Family* (1994), *Women of the Pleasure Quarters: The Secret History of the Geisha* (2000), and *Madame Sadayakko: The Geisha Who Bewitched the West* (2003).

當世風俗通
芸者風

哥麿筆

The Geisha Style (Geisha fū), from the series
*Present-Day Aficionados of the Pleasure
Districts (Tōsei fūzoku tsū),* Kitagawa Utamaro,
c. 1795

In this print, Utamaro, the foremost artist of beautiful
women of his time, depicts what was to become the
classic geisha style. The *shimada* hairstyle and a
kimono of restrained color and pattern are elements
that still comprise the formal geisha look.

Identifying Geisha in Art and Life

Is She Really a Geisha?

Andrew L. Maske

H OW CAN ONE TELL IF A WOMAN IS A GEISHA? Today's visitor to Japan can find it difficult, since most geisha wear kimono and hairstyles very similar to other Japanese women except on the most formal occasions. Yet, for those with an eye for it, the understated elegance of a geisha's dress is readily apparent, as Liza Dalby explains in her essay, "The Exotic Geisha." In every culture, personal appearance contains important clues to an individual's identity within that culture. In a brief film scene described by Peter Grilli in "Geisha on Screen and Stage," a woman is revealed as a geisha by a shot of her embroidered hem and her heels. Such sensitivity to dress detail and its implications is intrinsic to Japan, where strict societal structure has been a part of life for hundreds, if not thousands, of years. The type of kimono, the accessories that accompany it, and even the manner in which they are worn indicate the age, wealth, social status, and sometimes even occupation of the wearer.[1] A foreign visitor to Tokyo sees a Japanese woman in a kimono, while a person attuned to the details of dress sees the wife of a wealthy businessman, a tea-ceremony instructor, a stage entertainer—or a geisha.

Prior to Japan's gradual opening to the outside world in the 1850s and 60s, geisha were depicted in art wearing only a limited array of garments and styles. In his *Ukiyo gafu* (Painting Manual of the Floating World), a set of three printed books published around 1830, Keisai Eisen (1790–1848) includes six labeled illustrations of geisha (see p. 47). Eisen also pictures other women who would have been seen in and around the pleasure quarters such as *geiko,* youngish geisha, dancing girls and courtesans.[2] From his illustrations it is possible to identify the essential characteristics of geisha at that time. Earlier portrayals in woodblock prints during the 1780s and 1790s included portraits of geisha and scenes from selected performances, as Money Hickman discusses in "Geisha to the Fore: *Niwaka* Festivals and the New Luminaries of Edo." Since the most formal geisha style has not changed greatly during the past two hundred years, some of these examples resonate today.

Attributes of a Classic Geisha

A painting of a Nagasaki geisha, circa 1800 (see p. 41), is the earliest documented illustration of a geisha in an American collection.[3] The painting shows the dress and hairstyle of geisha around the time that their formal attire was codified. Today this style, worn for formal public appearances and certain other occasions, is known as *denoishō* (literally, "going-out outfit").

In the painting the kimono is black with minimal decoration below the sash

Maiko, c. 1925
This beautifully printed, early full-color postcard shows the elaborate hairstyle, as well as gorgeous kimono and obi in which *maiko* dressed.

Geisha Looking in a Mirror, Tsukioka
Yoshitoshi, 1860s
A chic, sophisticated geisha pauses to
check her appearance in a small mirror
while in the garden of a wealthy and
important client.

OPPOSITE
Kimono with Chinese Bellflower Design,
c. 1930
Kimono are identified with specific seasons
by fabric and motif. This unlined garment of
semitranslucent *komarō*-type silk was
owned by the geisha Tsunaji of Kanazawa
during the 1930s and would have been
worn in July, a time of year also symbolized
by the Chinese bellflower (*kikyō*) design.

The Former Kanazawa Geisha Tsunaji,
c. 1940
In the late 1930s the geisha Tsunaji retired from geisha life to take over the operation of the family teahouse. She had her hair cut short in a fashionable western style, but continued to wear beautiful kimono. At right is the open-weave (*rō*) summer kimono she wore for this photograph.

Kimono with Decoration of Pinks, c. 1935
The delicate blossoms of the *nadeshiko* (pinks, or Japanese carnations) depicted in three shades on this garment, invoke a feeling of freshness welcome during the warm months when this kimono was to be worn. The term *Yamato nadeshiko* (carnation of Japan) is used to describe a Japanese young woman of unsullied beauty.

in front and just above the rear hem. The white crest (*mon*) of the house with which the geisha was registered appears on the front of each shoulder and in the center of the garment's back. A blue-edged padded train (*hikizuri*) trails on the floor. When walking outside, geisha gathered the front of their robes to chest height, which lifted the long train enough to prevent the train from being soiled.[4] The underside of the kimono train (*fuki*) is thus positioned to reveal a pattern of young bamboo. At the neck and hem are two layers of underkimono, one red (with a white detachable collar) and the innermost white. Creating a vivid contrast, the yellow obi sash overlaps in a crisscross fashion and is tied so it hangs to the knees in the back, in the so-called "willow" (*yanagi*) style. Her feet are bare, a style made popular in the eighteenth century by geisha of the Fukagawa district in Edo.

Although two rather than three layers of robes are usually worn today, the components and overall style of the dress of the Nagasaki geisha have remained unchanged for more than two hundred years. The dress of traditional geisha as shown here was generally simple and restrained compared to women of the upper classes.

When Eisen's painting manuals were published, typical geisha in Edo still wore kimono of a single hue, with little or no decoration. Sometimes a kimono with an overall vertical pattern of narrow stripes was worn, with the plain collar of a single underkimono showing around the neck. The obi was tied then as later in the "willow-style," cascading from the waist down (see p. 47).

The Nagasaki geisha wears her hair in a style that would have been rather demodé to a geisha in the shogun's capital of Edo. Known as the *katsuyama*, it was worn by Edo geisha during the 1780s, but apparently remained fashionable among Nagasaki geisha into the early nineteenth century. The principal hairdo of Edo geisha of the 1790s was the *shimada*,[5] which remains the representative style for geisha, though both the *katsuyama* and *shimada* styles had any number of variations. Compared to other traditional hairstyles, the *shimada* is a simple but elegant coiffure in which the side locks are stiffened with camellia nut oil (*tsubaki abura*) and pulled to the back. The hair is raised above the crown and gathered behind in a large loop that is secured at two or three points.

Dressing the Hair, Felice Beato, 1860s
Scenes of personal toilette were among the most popular depictions of women in nineteenth-century photography. The elaborate hairstyles of Japanese women fascinated western visitors and images of dressing the hair helped spread the fame of geisha around the world.

A Nagasaki Geisha, c. 1800
The dress and hairstyle of this geisha of two hundred years ago differs little from the formal appearance of geisha today. The elegant yet seductive beauty of a flowing black robe lined with red and white has a timeless appeal.

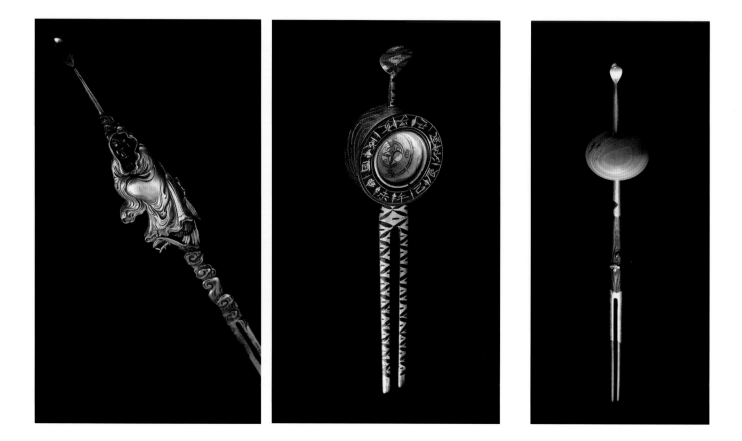

**Hair Ornament with Design of
Bodhidharma**, 19th century

The pinlike *kanzashi* hair ornament is made
of various materials. This nineteenth-
century metal example bears a depiction
of Bodhidharma crossing the Yangtze on a
reed, a reference in the entertainment
districts for the pleasure a woman can
bring a man.

CENTER

Hair Ornament with Compass, c. 1780–
1820

The compass was introduced to Japan by
the Dutch. By the late eighteenth century,
when this example was made, domestic
production of compasses had been
developed. This ornament was a conversation piece, featuring a type of exotic
technology that identified geisha as
trendsetters.

RIGHT

**Hair Ornament with Mother-of-Pearl
Bead**, 1840s–1890s

Hair ornaments, whether simple or
elaborate, are made of rare or finely
crafted materials. A moonlike bead of shell
is pierced by a silver shaft on which a tiny
Japanese iris blossom is depicted in gold.

A few pinlike hair ornaments (*kanzashi*) of tortoiseshell, lacquered wood, precious metal or other fine materials enhance an ensemble that is appropriate to both the season of the year and the specific occasion. The geisha selects them according to her own taste, but normally includes a single comb placed vertically above the forehead to separate the front hair from the loop in the back. The comb is also the principal decorative motif. In the early twentieth century, the comb was omitted to create a larger puff of hair on top. Apprentice geisha (*maiko*) in Kyoto take seasonality to the extreme by changing their dangling *hana kanzashi* (flower hair ornaments) every month.

Geisha throughout Japan wear white makeup called *oshiroi* (white, with the honorific *o*), since a white complexion was highly prized until the recent preference for tanned skin. A rouge known as *beni* (vermillion) highlights the lips and eyes, and adds blush to the face. Entertainers of all kinds, including courtesans, common prostitutes, and Kabuki actors, wore white makeup until the early twentieth century, although the applications depended on the profession, status, locale or an actor's role. Today, only geisha and Kabuki actors continue to wear *oshiroi*, and do so only on stage or on other special occasions such as parades and processions.

Props and Settings

Certain accoutrements identify geisha on stage or in paintings, prints, photographs, or films. Principal among these is the *shamisen*, similar to a banjo with three strings. Though today a geisha is either a singer, musician, or dancer, originally geisha were probably *shamisen* player-singers. Many woodblock prints show them walking to engagements, usually accompanied by a servant known as a *hakoya* who carries her *shamisen* in a long box of black lacquered or plain wood. Other props associated with geisha include rather large, folding dance fans, the hourglass-shaped drums called *tsuzumi*, and oiled-paper umbrellas printed with the emblems of their houses. Geisha still use all these objects today.

Geisha have been represented often in particular situations or environments

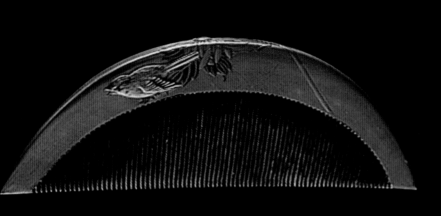

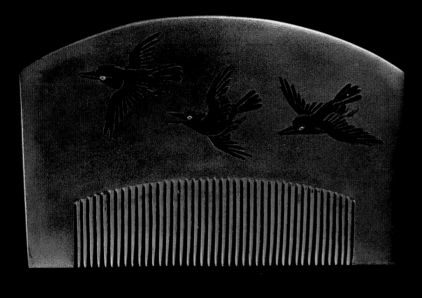

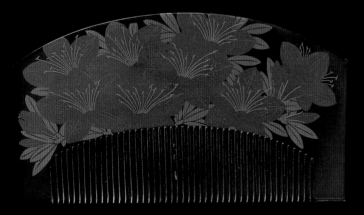

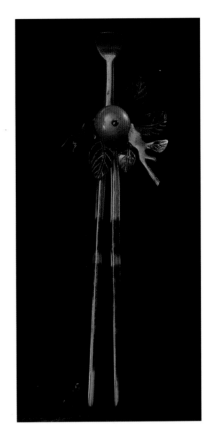

Hair Ornament of Tortoiseshell in Cherry Branch Design, 19th century

Forms from nature are frequently seen in the designs for hair ornaments. The coral bead in the center of this nineteenth-century example represents a cherry fruit, creating an ornament suitable for use in summer. This motif is unusual, as most artworks featuring the cherry depict the blossom, symbolic of spring.

Decorative Comb with Design of Sparrow and Chrysanthemum, 19th century

Combs, usually of wood with finely crafted lacquer decoration, ornament elaborate Japanese coiffures. With its delicate design of a sparrow and chrysanthemum in raised gold lacquer, this piece is suitable for wearing in autumn.

Decorative Comb with Design of Crows, first half, 19th century

Lacquer artists appear to have relished the challenge presented by women's hair combs. Here, the artist has chosen to depict glossy black crows on a matte black background. Gold lacquer eyes complete the striking effect.

Decorative Comb with Design of Azaleas, mid-19th century

Women change their hair ornaments and combs according to the season. This comb with lacquer azalea decoration was made to be worn in early summer.

43

妙玉屋内
春日野
ささち
うらく

The *Oiran* **Kasugano of the Sumidamaya and Her Retinue**, Hosoda Eishi, c. 1790
The elegant courtesan Kasugano is flanked by her two child attendants (*kamuro*) and her teenage atttendant (*shinzō*). The green obi sash of Kasugano and the orange sash of her older attendant are both tied in front as required by law for registered prostitutes and their postpubescent trainees.

<small>OPPOSITE</small>
Geisha and Attendant in Snow,
Kitagawa Utamaro, 1790s
Attendants called *hakoya* (box porters) served not only to carry a geisha's boxed *shamisen* but also to see a geisha safely to her destination and back home again. The picturesque pair of figures was instantly recognizable from a distance, and therefore made an evocative theme for *ukiyo-e* paintings and prints.

such as preparing for or entertaining at teahouse or restaurant parties. Woodblock prints portray them performing in public festivals or in the audience of a Kabuki play. From the Meiji period on there are photographs of their stage performances. More rarely, geisha are shown at home, putting on makeup, having their hair done, or otherwise preparing to go out.

When Is a Geisha Not a Geisha?

There are women who are part of the geisha profession who are not strictly "geisha." The apprentice geisha, or *maiko*, seldom appear in Edo-period documents, but came to specifically mean "an apprentice geisha dancer," usually from Kyoto, in the Meiji period (1868–1912). A *maiko*-to-be, essentially an errand girl just beginning her training, is known as a *shikomi* (trainee). The rough equivalent of a *maiko* in the geisha districts of Tokyo, Kanazawa, and elsewhere is an *akaeri* (red collar) or *hangyoku* (half-fee), though it is now rare for geisha in those areas to go through a formal apprenticeship. Ostensible virgins in their teens, apprentices go about in brightly colored kimono with long swinging sleeves and embroidered red collars as well as flowery hair ornaments reminiscent of those worn by merchant-class unmarried teenagers of the Edo and Meiji periods.

Dancing girls (*odoriko*) were popular entertainers beginning in the 1680s.[6] Originally they were teenage performers of dance who appeared in the entertainment districts and even before domain lords. *Odoriko* gained notoriety in the mid-eighteenth century as illicit freelance prostitutes who used their performances to engage in prostitution without government oversight. Records note that numerous women calling themselves *odoriko* were arrested at various times and sent to work without pay in the licensed brothels of the Yoshiwara in Edo.[7] Unlike the geisha, who were recognized as the principal female performing artists of the pleasure quarters, the eighteenth-century *odoriko* never established a legitimate occupation, since they operated in a largely unregulated arena and their activities straddled the line between performance and prostitution. Today the term *odoriko* is sometimes used in geisha areas of Tokyo to distinguish a geisha whose specialty is dance from one whose specialty is *shamisen* playing and singing.

Mistakable Misses

During the Edo period (1615–1867), the pleasure quarters, not the upper echelons of society, were the primary source for visual representations of attractive and fashionably dressed women. Government-enforced restrictions on subject matter and scope made plebian artists hesitant to portray women of the ruling samurai class in media such as paintings, prints, and books for popular consumption.[8] When such portrayals became more common in the middle of the nineteenth century, it was necessary to cast aristocratic women as characters from history, legend, or literature,

though in contemporary dress. Top level courtesans in the pleasure districts were the stars of popular acclaim, admired for their beauty and gorgeous dress, until the end of the eighteenth century when geisha began to usurp their position.

Courtesans, or elite prostitutes, usually appear in prints, paintings, or books with a virtual spray of ornaments framing the face. When parading in public, they wore multiple robes, many of them sumptuously embroidered. *Oiran* and other courtesans were required by law to tie their sashes in the front, a practice that both readily identified them to clients and placed the magnificent obi material front and center. While most other women, including geisha, would have found that a sash tied in front interfered with their activities, tying the obi in front made perfect sense for prostitutes since it made disrobing all the easier. Not all women who wore their sashes tied in front were prostitutes, however, since some matrons also tied their obi in front on occasion. In woodblock prints and other illustrations these women may be differentiated from courtesans by their shaved eyebrows. Married women wear costumes, hairstyles, and accessories of restrained design and subdued hue.

The highest-ranking courtesans had several types of apprentices, who were trained to conduct themselves in a manner that would enhance the courtesan's

The *Oiran* Michitose of the Miuraya with Her Child Attendants, Keisai Eisen, c. 1825
In the early nineteenth century, the dress and hairstyles of top Edo courtesans (*oiran*) became almost unbelievably elaborate, as layer upon layer of kimono and numerous tortoiseshell hair ornaments were added.

beauty, not compete with it. Part of this training included acting as part of the retinue of an *oiran* as she paraded down the main street of the Yoshiwara to her meeting with a wealthy client (see left). *Shinzō* (newly made) were young apprentices who accompanied an *oiran*, the younger virginal ones wearing kimono with long sleeves known as *furisode* (swinging sleeves). For this reason they are also sometimes referred to as *furi-shin* (a contraction of *furisode shinzō*). Older apprentices wore shorter sleeves and were called *bantō shinzō* (attendant *shinzō*) because they were expected to wait on and possibly even sleep with clients while the courtesan was entertaining someone else. In prints showing an *oiran* retinue, there may be either one or two *shinzō* walking in front of a courtesan. *Kamuro* (literally "balds") were pre-adolescent girls who were also trained by an *oiran*. Usually in pairs, *kamuro* are identifiable by their very elaborate dress and hairstyle, as well as their small stature. One in a pair of *kamuro* often sported a closely shorn head.

Ordinary prostitutes of the pleasure quarters wore their sashes tied in front like their higher class sisters, but their kimono and hair decoration were much less ornate. Illicit prostitutes who conducted their business outside the pleasure quarters were known by numerous suggestive names, like "night hawk," and can be distinguished in illustrations by the hand towels worn over their heads and faces, and sometimes by a roll of thin straw matting they carry under one arm.

Teenage girls who were not part of the pleasure districts were known as *musume* (maidens). Those from wealthier merchant families dressed quite fashionably and can be mistaken for geisha or geisha apprentices. Younger *musume* wore more brightly colored kimono than older women, and their hair commonly was adorned with ornaments made in imitation of flowers. Like the geisha apprentices known as *akaeri*, *hangyoku*, and *maiko*, *musume* wore kimono with long sleeves and collars of embroidered silk or velvet.

Finally, it must be recognized that many of the ostensibly female figures shown in prints and paintings are in fact *onnagata*, male Kabuki actors playing female roles. Because the most popular Kabuki plays were written at a time when courtesans, not geisha, held the popular imagination, there are fewer roles portraying geisha than might be expected. Ukiyo-e prints of the Kabuki stage feature actors in other female roles as well, including wives of all segments of society, girls and unmarried young women (*musume*), teahouse waitresses and maids, aristocratic women (always cast as historic personages), and women from legend and fantasy. Without the ability to read the Japanese inscriptions on prints that give the name of the actor, the play, and the role, it can be difficult to distinguish between a print of a geisha and one showing a Kabuki actor in a geisha role. Suffice it to say that print depictions of *onnagata* actors display more angular faces, sharper noses, and more bulging eyes than do prints depicting actual women, especially prints dating from the nineteenth century.

Floating World Characters, Keisai Eisen, c. 1830

In the three volumes of *Drawing Manual of the Floating World* (*Ukiyo gafu*), Eisen depicts a wide variety of pleasure-quarter inhabitants, from elite courtesans to teahouse managers to geisha. The illustrations are labeled to identify women of various types.

In the page at left, Eisen shows an overstuffed courtesan walking with her child attendants, along with a coy, sleekly dressed geisha. A frame of a customer accompanied by a high-class courtesan is surrounded by men and women who administrate brothel business.

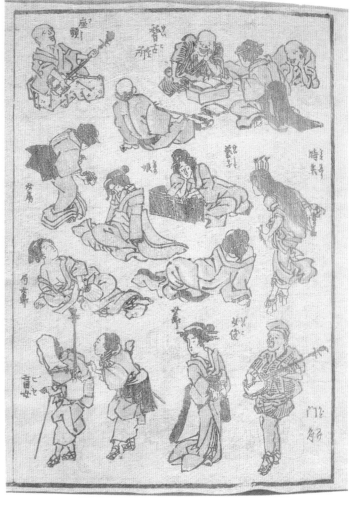

The high-class Edo courtesan (*oiran*) shown
here wears her hair in the striking *yoko hyōgo*
style, popular in the late eighteenth to early
nineteenth centuries. She exudes an air of
fashionable elegance, an attribute that soon
was to be usurped by geisha. During the
nineteenth century, the attire of *oiran* became
increasingly burdened with a profusion of
decorative elements.

Reclining Courtesan, Katsushika Hokusai,
calligraphy by Santō Kyōden, c. 1802

Enduring Geisha Style

The classic *denoishō* geisha outfit consists of a black, trailing kimono with
minimal decoration, an obi that crisscrosses in front and hangs low in the back,
white facial makeup with pink highlights, and hair done in the *shimada* hairstyle.
Since this attire was and is reserved for only the most formal occasions, it remains
a challenge to identify geisha dressed differently in prints, paintings, and old
photographs. Although the frequency with which geisha appear in woodblock
prints increased steadily from the 1780s on, reflecting their growing popularity
within the pleasure quarters, the number of prints featuring geisha never exceeds
that of prints showing other types of women, especially courtesans. The reasons
for this are not yet fully understood, but it is evident that geisha had not yet achieved
the iconic status that they would in the latter nineteenth century. In the Meiji
period, geisha were the first choice for models in studio photographs,[9] and as Allen
Hockley points out in his essay "First Encounters—Emerging Stereotypes:
Westerners and Geisha in the Late Nineteenth Century," many photographers
went out of their way to blur distinctions between geisha and other Japanese women.
Identifying geisha in early photographs is particularly tricky, since geisha in the
late nineteenth century were eagerly trying out new styles and fashions, some of
them European in origin.

Geisha are most often shown wearing a kimono of a single color ground,
often with a padded hem and with minimal, but elegant decoration; an obi worn
crisscrossed in front and hanging long in the back, a sheaf of *kaishi* paper protruding
from the top left front; a hair style of the *shimada* type, with a comb in front and
no more than a handful of hair ornaments; and musical instruments, especially

shamisen, somewhere in the scene. The greater the number of these attributes in any one work, the greater the possibility that it is a geisha who is represented.

The ability to identify the visual attributes of geisha in paintings, prints, and photographs helps to clarify the role these women played in Japanese culture. Understanding the differences between geisha and other women makes them all more real, more alive, more human. After all, geisha are not just pictures, but real women, immortalized in an artistic medium as those who live their lives for art.

NOTES:

1. Liza Dalby sets forth six distinctions used in determining the appropriateness of a kimono to a wearer or an occasion in *Kimono: Fashioning Culture* (New Haven: Yale University Press, 1993), p. 165.

2. The term *geiko* continues to be used today but only for fully mature geisha in western Japan, particularly Kyoto and Osaka. In this sense, it is an alternative word for geisha.

3. The painting was given to the East India Marine Society collection (now the Peabody Essex Museum) in 1826 by Salem, Massachusetts, ship captain Henry King; it undoubtedly had come to America via either the *Franklin* or the *Margaret*, Salem merchant vessels that traded at Nagasaki in 1799 and 1801, respectively. See *Worlds Revealed: The Dawn of Japanese and American Exchange* (Tokyo: Edo Tokyo Museum, 1999).

4. In the late nineteenth century, the term *hidarizuma* (left-holding hem) became a sobriquet for geisha, who were the only remaining women commonly wearing kimono with trailing skirts. Dalby (1993), p. 332.

5. The origin of the name is uncertain, but it is likely derived either from a hairstyle worn by prostitutes in the town of Shimada in the seventeenth century, or from a style favored by the Kabuki actor Shimada Bankichi during the Kan'ei era (1624–48). Another explanation is that the term is a variant of *shimeta*, or "tied-up."

6. Cecilia Segawa Seigle, *Yoshiwara: The Glittering World of the Japanese Courtesan* (Honolulu: University of Hawaii Press, 1993), p. 171.

7. Ibid., p. 172.

8. The *ukiyo-e* print artist Kitagawa Utamaro was jailed for three days and forced to wear handcuffs for fifty days in 1804 for designing prints that offended the shogunal authorities. For Utamaro's portrayals of geisha, see Money L. Hickman's essay, this volume.

9. Joseph I.C. Clarke, *Japan At First Hand* (New York: Dodd and Mead Co., 1918), pp. 204–05.

The Geisha Apprentice Tsunaji of Kanazawa, c. 1926
Apprentice geisha dancers in Kyoto are called *maiko*, but elsewhere they are known as *akaeri* (red-collars) for the red-collared under robes they wear. This teenage apprentice is shown in her traditional dress holding the novelty of the time—a hand-held camera.

Andrew Maske, PhD. in Japanese art from Oxford University, has organized *Geisha: Beyond the Painted Smile* as the Curator of Japanese Art at the Peabody Essex Museum since 1999. His publications include articles in *Orientations, Journal of Japanese Studies, Archaeometry,* and *Transactions of the Asiatic Society of Japan.*

PART II confronting the image

First Encounters—Emerging Stereotypes

Westerners and Geisha in the
Late Nineteenth Century

ALLEN HOCKLEY

WRITING IN 1901 FOR A WESTERN AUDIENCE reaching the height of its fascination with all things Japanese, the British theater historian and critic Osman Edwards took up the subject of geisha with the intent of describing the intricacies of the profession and the characters of women attracted to it. His opening remarks address an entirely different issue, however: "Nothing is more difficult to eradicate than a British misconception of foreign defects. French lubricity, German clumsiness, Russian cruelty, are quite as much as articles of faith on this side of the Channel as Albion's perfidy on the other. Similarly, it is useless to controvert the popular opinion that the geisha is generally pretty and always improper."[1]

Evidently Edwards felt the need to dispel some popular misconceptions about geisha. After discussing a geisha's apprenticeship, the nature of her employment, and the arts for which by then she was well known in the West, he addressed the stereotypes with more specificity: "To return to the question of the social status of geisha, I should say that it corresponds more exactly with that of a Parisian actress than of an Athenian *hetaira* [*sic*]. Convention having banished the actress from the Japanese stage, the geisha takes her place as the natural recipient of masculine homage. She is much courted, and sometimes makes a brilliant match. There are a large number who make the profession an excuse for attracting rich admirers, just as the name of "actress" in more Puritan climes will cover a multitude of sins. But a professional courtesan she is not: her favors are not always for sale to the highest bidder."[2] Analogies made across the vastly different cultures Edwards cites could never be precise, but his implications with regard to their common element, the demimonde, are clear: Westerners thought geisha were prostitutes. This is the misconception Edwards felt compelled to address.

In documenting a history of Westerners' earliest contacts with geisha, this essay explores the circumstances that led to Edwards's concerns. It traces their gradual acquisition of knowledge about geisha from the 1860s to the early twentieth century. It also examines the means by which representations of geisha were disseminated to

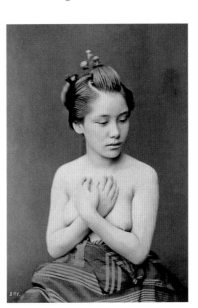

broader audiences in Europe and America through a wide variety of media. Travel narratives, in which Westerners describe their firsthand experiences with geisha, are explored in some detail as they provide an important means to measure what Westerners knew about geisha. These accounts imply authenticity because their authors actually visited Japan. But travel narratives were motivated by commercial gain, and as such, they tended to focus on subjects that would interest potential readers. Geisha were one such subject. Accordingly, travel narratives need to be approached with a critical eye and an awareness of their potential, intentional or otherwise, to enhance misconceptions. News periodicals, in particular the *Illustrated London News*, the most widely read publication of its type at the time, provide another source of documentation of Westerners' interactions with geisha.[3] Like travel narratives, the *Illustrated London News* was a commercial newspaper with a vested interest in expanding its circulation. Its reportage has the feel of a factual account, but it was not above pandering to readers' interest in the exotic and sensational. Commercially produced tourist photographs, theatrical productions, and fiction are also considered because they fueled the West's fascination with geisha, while often perpetuating misconceptions.

Authoritative Accounts, Travel Narratives, and Guidebooks

Edicts passed by the Japanese government in the early seventeenth century prohibited interaction with all but the Dutch, the only western nationals permitted to trade with Japan. Confined to a small man-made island in Nagasaki harbor, diplomatic and trade negotiations occasioned most of the contact between the Dutch and individual Japanese. The Dutch were permitted to engage the services of Japanese prostitutes, however. Written reports of this practice, which circulated widely in Europe and America in the mid-nineteenth century, piqued Westerners' interest in Japanese women in general, but not in geisha specifically.

Westerners began to encounter geisha in the late 1850s, shortly after diplomatic negotiations facilitated the creation of five treaty ports. Of these, Yokohama was the most important because of its proximity to the capital Edo (renamed Tokyo in 1868).[4] Laws confining foreign residents to the immediate vicinity of the ports severely limited contact until 1868, when a new administration, seeking to modernize Japan's infrastructure, industries, and education system, encouraged more open engagement with the West. Western expertise was necessary to make Japan more competitive in the world economy and laws restricting foreigners to the treaty ports were an impediment to this goal. In the early 1870s as employment opportunities for Westerners opened up in government ministries, schools, and private industry, restrictions on the activities of foreigners, both resident and tourist, were relaxed. As more of the country was made accessible to visitors a new tourist industry began to emerge.

Westerners exhibited a progressively fuller understanding of geisha as contact increased. For example, accounts from the 1860s record numerous interactions with entertainers who were surely geisha, although Westerners did not recognize them as such. By the 1880s, Westerners were capable of distinguishing the nuances between Tokyo, Kyoto, and Osaka geisha. J. E. De Becker's turn-of-the-century publication, *The Nightless City* (1899), reveals how rapidly Westerners acquired a full understanding of geisha. It offered a credible history of the profession, one detailed enough to include a lengthy discussion of male geisha—an esoteric topic by any measure.[5] But while the West's general understanding of geisha gradually improved as contacts increased over the late nineteenth century, the following examples demonstrate that the level of detail and degree of accuracy in written accounts, including diplomatic narratives, travelogues, and guidebooks, not only varied widely but also reflected the interests and disposition of the authors of these texts.

Most of the occasions when early foreign residents of the treaty ports were

Entertainments in the Tenth Month, from the series *Edo Customs of the Twelve Months*, Yōshū Chikanobu, 1889
This woodcut triptych shows a nostalgic view of a pleasure-quarter restaurant prior to the opening of Japan to western influence. Geisha entertain at parties on the second floor, while on the ground floor merchants celebrate the Festival of Ebisu (*Ebisukō*) held on the twentieth day of the tenth month.

entertained by singers and dancers took place in Ōji, a district of Edo (now Tokyo) with relatively high-class teahouses and restaurants. Many Westerners also saw what were surely geisha performing at local festivals in the treaty ports.[6] They failed to recognize that these teahouse and festival performers had been exhaustively trained in their respective arts. Westerners referred to these women as "entertainers"; the word "geisha" does not appear in western accounts of Japan until the mid-1870s.

Perceptions of geisha began to sharpen by the late 1860s as foreign diplomats and their staffs stationed in Japan started to publish accounts of their impressions of Japan. The lengths of their residencies made their accounts more detailed and reliable. These books became references for the tourists who would be arriving in ever-greater numbers in the 1870s. Easily the most influential text of the time, Aimé Humbert's *Japan and the Japanese Illustrated* (1874) was the first to demonstrate an understanding of geisha as a distinct class of entertainer subject to legal and behavioral codes. Humbert described the singers, "guitar" (*shamisen*) players, and dancers employed as entertainers in teahouses. He referred to them as professionals and noted that "they never set their feet in such establishments, unless they are expressly sent for." As to their deportment, he stated: "By the correctness of their behavior, they are distinguished from the street musicians and dancers at fairs. The law does not permit them to come into private houses; they can only be asked for in places subject to police regulation."[7] Although he does not use the term "geisha," Humbert, a Swiss diplomat stationed in Japan from the mid-to-late 1860s, focused the West's attention on the profession. His accounts, which first appeared in serialized form in French-language newspapers, were collected into a single volume, published in 1870. The English language edition, released four years later, was widely quoted in the accounts of later visitors to Japan, likely because it was recommended in tourist guidebooks as a reliable source of information on Japanese culture.

Humbert's authoritative text was superceded by William Griffis's *The Mikado's Empire*, published in 1876. Like Humbert, Griffis had extensive contact with Japan. He taught several Japanese students visiting America in the late 1860s and was subsequently invited to Japan and employed as a teacher, first in the province of Echizen and later at the University of Tokyo. Griffis's four-year residence, from 1870–1874, his facility with the Japanese language, and his scholarly inclinations made him a respected authority on Japanese history and culture. If not the first, he was

Teahouse at Ōji, 1880s
Ōji, on the outskirts of Tokyo, featured a lovely setting away from the bustle of the city. Teahouses there featured geisha entertainment that was less sophisticated than at the top metropolitan geisha districts like Yanagibashi, but the contrast was a pleasant change of pace for geisha connoisseurs.

Young Woman at Home, attributed to Raimund or Franz von Stillfried, c. 1879–82
With her ordinary clothing and hairstyle typical of unmarried young women, this attractive girl is probably not a geisha. By placing a *shamisen* in the scene, however, the photographer gives the impression that she is an entertainer.

certainly one of the earliest, foreigners to use the word "geisha." His descriptions of their skills reveal a level of familiarity with the profession not seen in the writings of Humbert and other earlier writers. "In all the large cities there are geisha, noted for their wit, beauty, skill in playing the three-stringed banjo. The daughters of Kioto and Tokio do excellently, but those of Ozaka excel them all."[8]

Humbert's *Japan and the Japanese Illustrated* and Griffis's *The Mikado's Empire* were important resources for western tourists who began visiting Japan in ever greater numbers in the 1870s. Visitors to Japan arrived in either Yokohama or Nagasaki and made day trips to local sites in the vicinity of these ports. For example, visitors disembarking at Yokohama typically toured the many Buddhist monasteries in Kamakura or made day trips into scenic places in Tokyo. Three to four-day excursions were common, Nikkō and the Fuji-Hakone area being popular destinations. Longer trips, along the Tōkaidō or Nakasendō, for example, required passports issued by representatives of the Japanese government stationed in the treaty ports. Visits to Kyoto from Kobe required similar documentation. Guidebooks frequently recommended Humbert's and Griffis's texts as references and sometimes quoted from them directly. In 1870 W. E. L. Keeling's *Tourists' Guide to Yokohama, Tokio . . .* remarked, in a description of the amusements one might find in Japan, that the traveler "may call an unlimited number of singing and posturing girls (geisha) to entertain him and his friends during their repast."[9] Keeling also noted that hiring geisha was especially popular among foreigners who visit Kyoto. Douglas Sladen, in his *Club Hotel Guide to Japan* (1892), mentions the availability of geisha for hire through teahouses at a cost of "under a couple of yen each" (roughly the cost of a night's lodging) and seconded the appraisal articulated by Griffis: "Osaka is full of geisha girls, said to be the prettiest in Japan."[10]

With guidebooks recommending the experience to travelers, accounts of geisha in travel memoirs of the 1880s and 1890s increased to the point that even Basil Hall Chamberlain, regarded at the time as one of the foremost authorities on Japan, deferred to popular accounts in *Things Japanese* (1890), a text that superseded Humbert and Griffis: "The charms of the Japanese singing-girl, or geisha, as the Japanese term her, have been dwelt on so often that we gladly leave them to her more ardent admirers."[11]

The accounts to which Chamberlain refers describe lavish dinners in expensive restaurants with geisha entertaining. Discussions of the geisha's training and lifestyle, most of which were drawn from the authoritative reference texts noted above, were often added to these accounts. Dresser's *Japan: Its Architecture,*

Art, and Art Manufactures (1881) includes one of the earliest examples of this practice.[12] Sir Edwin Arnold's *Seas and Lands* (1891) and Douglas Sladen's *The Japs At Home* (1892) typify the more extensively detailed accounts of the 1890s.[13] Lengthy descriptions of geishas' costumes, coiffures, powdered faces and painted lips, and their performances, specifically their dances, dominate these narratives. Westerners invariably found geisha highly entertaining but the formulaic character of their accounts—they appear to copy each other in their content and structure—elicits an important question: how well did Westerners actually understand the subtleties of the geisha's art? Gilbert Watson, a British tourist who visited Japan in the late 1890s, provides a good example of a typical account and the likely answer to this question:

Geisha on Charles' Veranda, Felice Beato, 1872

The son of Henry Wadsworth Longfellow, Charles lived in Japan for twenty months in 1871–72. He purchased a house in Tokyo, where he had photographs taken of several geisha with whom he had become acquainted. The standing geisha is unidentified, but seated left to right are Sokuhe(i), the apprentice Matahe(i), and Metama.

> They were worth watching, these little visitors of ours; such quaint fantasies in paint and powder, such comical creations in silk and satin, such whimsical artificiality in voice and gesture, could not be seen every day. We thought of the long hours before the silver looking-glasses necessary to compose these wonderful complexions, to arrange these fantastic coiffures, to drape these girlish figures; of the difficulties overcome in the crowded geisha quarter; of the cheerless night journey; of the anxiety lest some bold, intruding raindrop should fleck the dainty dress or mar the painted face; and so thinking, for once we agreed with Jiutei [Watson's guide] that they were cheap – yes, 'dam' cheap.
>
> 'What are they doing know?' whispered Kingston.
>
> 'Sh-h-h! Play has begun!' reproved Jiutei.
>
> That comedy was incomprehensible, but infinitely amusing. There appeared to be three heroines, but a decided lack of heroes, and as for the inevitable marriage, it was not even thought of! The plot of the little story lay deep in a maze of dainty gesture, decipherable only to critics versed in the strange geisha atmosphere of faint suggestiveness. Words were few and far between, but words were not required to express the feelings of these Oriental oddities: the lifting of an eyebrow seemed freighted with mighty meaning, the voluptuous undulation of a rounded arm appeared to be an entire act in itself.
>
> We felt our ignorance deeply.[14]

Although common, travelers' accounts of the sort noted here do not fully represent all Westerners' attitudes toward geisha. Long-term residents of Japan had more opportunities to engage the services of geisha, but as most Westerners in such positions either were Christian missionaries or were attached to the diplomatic corps or were employed by the Japanese in some official capacity, their social statuses prohibited them from writing on subjects deemed risqué. Missionaries, in particular, avoided topics that hinted at impropriety. On rare occasions when they did broach the subject of geisha, their comments tended to moralize. Accounts written by women—teachers and missionaries as well as tourists—are particularly revealing. Travel in the late nineteenth century was a liminal experience for most women. It allowed them to escape, although not entirely, the social structures and domestic duties that otherwise would have restricted the occasions and manner in which they could express their opinions. Their gender, in other words, gave them a unique perspective on geisha.

Some wrote enthusiastically about their experiences. The American traveler Eliza Scidmore, for example, indulged what seems to be a budding connoisseur's interest in the subject. In *Jinrikisha Days in Japan* (1891) she recalls in vivid detail her encounters with geisha in Nagoya, Kyoto, and Osaka. Of the former, she wrote:

"Nagoya *maiko* and geisha are celebrated throughout Japan for their beauty, grace, and taste in dress, and a geisha dinner is as much a property of Nagoya as the golden dolphins on the old castle." She then took in one of the great geisha spectacles of Kyoto: "Kioto's *maiko* and geisha performances are, of course, more splendid than those of any other city. The great training-school of *maiko* conforms to the classic tradition, and critics and connoisseurs assemble at the *kaburenjo* theatre each spring when the famous Kioto dance, the Miakodori is given by troops of *maiko*." By the time she reached Osaka she felt she had the expertise to make the following claim: "The *maiko* and geisha of this southern capital are renowned for their grace, beauty, and wit; their taste in arranging the obi and dressing the hair; their cleverness in inventing new dances; and the entertainments in which they figure, under the lanterned awnings of the house-boats as they float up and down the river at night, are unique among such fêtes."[15]

But Scidmore was an exception. Most women avoided the subject of geisha altogether while others treated it in a cursory fashion. Mrs. Hugh Fraser, the wife of a British diplomat, mentions geisha only in a brief footnote to her two-volume *Letters From Japan* (1899).[16] *Present Day Japan*, authored in 1904 by Augusta M. Campbell Davidson, a British tourist, referred to geisha briefly in a general discussion on women's fashion: "As for what Japanese dress is as worn in Japan, if your ideas of it are derived from fans and screens and the garments you see for sale at home, you are probably under quite a false impression. Gorgeous embroideries and brilliant colors are things of the past; they are worn only by geishas when professionally engaged."[17]

Alice Bacon provides the most detailed account of geisha written by a woman, but her perspective, formed by many years teaching in Japan in missionary schools for young women, clarifies to some extent why some women avoided the subject. Her treatise, *Japanese Girls and Women* (1891), arranges Japanese women according to class and profession, and in her hierarchy geisha were positioned only one step above professional courtesans. She prefaced her descriptions of a geisha's training and arts with a suggestion that such employment is "not always regarded as wholly respectable by either Japanese or foreigners." She then elaborated:

> The geishas unfortunately, though fair, are frail. In their system of education, manners stand higher than morals, and many a geisha gladly leaves the dancing in the tea houses to become the concubine of some wealthy Japanese or foreigner, thinking none the worse of herself for such a business arrangement, and going cheerfully back to her regular work, should her contract be unexpectedly ended. The geisha is not necessarily bad; but there is in her life much temptation to evil, and little stimulus to do right, so that, where one lives blameless, many go wrong and drop below the margin of respectability altogether. Yet so fascinating, bright, and lively are these geishas that many of them have been taken by men of good position as wives, and are now the heads of the most respectable homes.[18]

Bacon was as curious about geisha as any Westerner. Her fascination extended to the geisha's social mobility, but that mobility, and the ends to which it was applied, ran counter to her moral sensibilities—and to those of most of her western contemporaries. Her sensitivity to this issue was societal as well as moral. She concludes: "If the wives of the leaders of Japan are to come from among such a class of women, something must be done, and done quickly, for the sake of the future of Japan."[19] Morality aside, Bacon's Eurocentric views could not accommodate the idea that women of low social status became wives of the elite.

The fact that Westerners indulged in the extra-curricular services geisha offered made the subject even more contentious for some writers—Bacon included foreign men among those who took geisha as concubines, for example. Other writers disparagingly suggest that these relationships were relatively common. Osman Edwards reinforced the very stereotype he set out to correct when he mentioned a young Frenchman who came to Japan to learn the language and was advised to seek a "pillow dictionary," a Japanese lover, in other words. Apparently "the geisha of the capital did not attract him: they were too openly venal or brightly conspicuous for his quiet taste, which desired gentle companionship without such publicity as the appropriation of a Tokyo geisha would involve."[20] In 1904 Geo. H. Rittner's criticisms were broader in their sweep but nonetheless pointed:

> "[T]he geisha who are trotted out to perform be-fore the average European might shock even many women who call themselves broad-minded; they coquette, flirt, and fling themselves about. They are little better, in fact, than the European music-hall people who profane the world by call-ing themselves artists; still, they are better, and they act in that way merely because Europeans have taught them to do it. The European man has ruined the morality of the Japa-nese, and they will probably never regain it."[21]

The Yoshiwara, Tokyo, 1880s–90s
In 1872, following a great fire in which two-thirds of the Yoshiwara was burned, the main street was widened and many of the buildings were rebuilt in western style. Despite the curiosity of many non-Japanese about the famous pleasure district, there are remarkably few first-hand accounts of visits by foreigners.

The comments of Bacon, Edwards and Rittner suggest that by the early twentieth century Westerners with firsthand experience of Japan had come to recognize and openly question what they regarded as the more unsavory aspects of the geisha's profession. But the criticisms these authors expressed were directed as much at their compatriots as the geisha themselves. In their view Westerners in Japan who took geisha as sexual partners were partly responsible for misconceptions about the profession. This practice, and especially western perceptions of it, needed to be clarified. By the strictest definition, geisha were entertainers, not prostitutes. Nonetheless, geisha often took lovers and these relationships involved the exchange of financial support for sexual intimacy. *Danna-san*, the term used for men in these relationships, conveyed the sense of "patron" rather than "customer" or "client," terms more appropriate to those who purchased prostitutes. Westerners who took geisha as lovers in the late nineteenth century assumed the role of *danna-san*, whether they understood its implications or not. However, geisha varied widely in their training, skills, and level of professionalism. Moreover, women with minimal training often posed as geisha as a front for prostitution—a problem that can be traced back to the earliest years of the profession. It is unlikely the geisha Westerners took as lovers in the late nineteenth century came from the upper echelons of the profession, if indeed they were geisha at all. There was, in other words, some confusion among Westerners as to the true nature of the geisha profession and this contributed to emerging stereotypes that tended to over-sexualize geisha. Popular media furthered this process.

Popular Media: The Geisha Goes Abroad

Commercial photographs produced in the treaty ports provided many in Europe and America with their first introductions to the entertainers they would later come to know as geisha. Felice Beato, the most prolific of early commercial photographers in Japan, is important in this regard. Beato, an Italian by birth, had a long career as a war photographer prior to his arrival in Yokohama in 1863. He was commissioned by the British military to photograph the Crimean war in 1855. In 1858 he documented the aftermath of the British reprisals in India, and in 1860 Lord Elgin's sacking of Beijing. While in China he met Charles Wirgman, a reporter and sketch artist for the *Illustrated London News*. Wirgman was posted to Yokohama in the early 1860s to document the opening of diplomatic relations between England

and Japan. Beato came to Japan on Wirgman's invitation to partner in a photography business.

As one of the earliest commercial photographers in Japan, Beato established many precedents that later Japanese photographers would follow. His photo albums were particularly important in this respect. Typically they contained twenty-five to fifty images in small or large formats, which, according to an advertisement Beato issued in 1865, were priced at fifty dollars.[22] Half to two-thirds of the images in Beato's albums were views of scenic places: Mount Fuji, the Buddhist monasteries of Kama-kura, the port of Yokohama, for

Instrumentalists, Felice Beato, 1860s
Scenes of "daily life" were among the popular themes in early photography of Japan. These four women are featured in the improbable situation of playing music while having tea around a brazier. Their dress and hairstyles indicate that they are ordinary women, not geisha.

example. The rest, most of which were posed in Beato's studio, focused on the costumes worn by Japanese of various classes and occupations. It is among these studio-posed photographs that we find many images of women playing *shamisen* and other instruments associated with geisha performances. Wirgman, who wrote captions for Beato's photographs, labeled these images as "entertainers," "singers," and "dancers." As noted above, Westerners were not using the term geisha at this time. Beato sold his albums to residents of the treaty ports and to tourists who passed through his Yokohama studio. His albums traveled the world as souvenirs, shown to family and friends when these voyagers returned home. Although the paths of their dispersals are difficult to trace, the great number of extant examples in foreign collections suggests that Beato's albums played an important role in introducing geisha to the West.

Beato's photographs were also distributed in Europe and America by other means. One of Wirgman's duties as a correspondent for the *Illustrated London News* was to secure images that could be reproduced as engravings for publication. Often these were his sketches. Most Westerners, regardless of whether they actually visited Japan, were exposed to geisha primarily through this medium. The January 3, 1874 issue, for example, featured Wirgman's full-page illustration showing geisha entertaining Westerners and their Japanese hosts at a party in the Gion district of Kyoto (p. 59). His lively and humorous report accompanying the image recounted the entire evening's events, culminating in a description of the geishas' performances. Because of his long residency in Japan, Wirgman was familiar enough with Japanese culture to note the subtle differences in dress and speech between geisha he had encountered in Tokyo and those Kyoto women entertaining at this event:

Young Woman Playing *Shamisen,*
attributed to Raimund or Franz von Stillfried, c. 1879–82
Western visitors to Yokohama recorded that geisha commonly acted as models in photographic studios. This girl playing the *shamisen* has her hair done in the *itchō-gaeshi* (ginko leaf) style that was worn by some geisha as well as other young women.

> Presently I became aware that seated at the table with us were some gorgeously-dressed singing and dancing girls; their face painted ghastly white, their lips green, and their teeth black, they were indeed lovely. The style of dress was quite distinct from that of the same girls in Jeddo [Edo, Tokyo]; their language, too, was that of Kyoto, a soft and beautiful speech, different in accent from that of the provinces near Jeddo. This was very pleasant.[23]

Wirgman's awareness of differences between Kyoto and Tokyo geisha coincides with that of William Griffis, noted above. The expatriate community being as small as it was, and most of its diplomatic corps attending the same social functions, information of this sort easily passed among its members. The result was a tendency

to repeat and thereby emphasize highly specific characterizations of Japanese culture, geisha included. The formulaic nature of later travel narratives was one result of this tendency. Wirgman's account would have been well known in the West owing to the large circulation of the *Illustrated London News*. The authors of travel narratives would not have missed the opportunity to capitalize on the popularity of Wirgman's precedent.

As with all popular media, the *Illustrated London News* constantly monitored the response of its market. Lavishly illustrated special supplements designed to boost sales by returning to popular themes were often added to some issues. Evidently, Wirgman's sketch and story about Kyoto geisha were popular enough among the paper's readers for the editors to revisit the theme four months later. An engraving of two geisha, "Japanese Dancing Girls Practising," was featured prominently in the supplement added to the April 11, 1874 issue (see p. 61). The November 15, 1890 issue included yet another full-page illustration, in this case R. Homphrey Moore's portrait of the geisha who visited the 1889 Paris Universal Exhibition (see p. 62). This image is certainly indicative of the continued popularity of geisha among *Illustrated London News* readers, but it responds to a later phenomenon—the presence of geisha in Europe and America around the turn of the century, discussed more fully below.

Many of the reports Wirgman filed for the *Illustrated London News* utilized Beato's photographs as visual sources, which were easily converted to engravings by artists and technicians employed by the press in London. The image for the April 11, 1874 supplement, for example, may be a composite of two Beato photographs. Beato's photographs were often sent in bunches and filed for future use in London, sometimes resulting in a considerable time lag between the making of the original and its publication in the *Illustrated London News*. Images made in the 1860s were sometimes still in circulation in the 1890s. In other words, Beato had little control over the context in which his photographs appeared in the paper. Commercial publishers also used Beato's photographs to illustrate books authored by visitors to Japan. Beato's image of entertainers, for example, appeared on page 191 in Humbert's *Japan and the Japanese Illustrated*.

Through Beato's agency, photographs, in the original or in reproduction, quickly became a powerful medium for dispensing information about Japan in general and geisha in particular. But the fact that geisha images were posed in a studio and

A Japanese Dinner Party, Charles Wirgman, 1874
This scene, published in the *Illustrated London News* on January 3, 1874, illustrates a remarkable scene in Kyoto in the 1870s: geisha and their guests seated, not on the floor in front of individual trays, but in chairs around a large table. The atmosphere was likely as novel for the geisha as it was for their western guests.

Netsuke of Geisha and European, Tomochika III, late 19th century
This decorative ivory toggle, used for securing small items hung from the kimono sash. It shows a geisha pouring foreign liquor for a European, possibly Russian, man. Geisha accustomed to entertaining foreigners were found in such treaty ports as Nagasaki, Yokohama, and Kobe.

Young Women Posed for "Workmen's Holiday," attributed to Raimund or Franz von Stillfried, c. 1879–82
Both men and women of the lower classes customarily removed the upper part of the kimono during the summer's heat in the nineteenth century. Photographers seized upon this habit, incorporating it into scenes of women relaxing at home, or even, as here, women in the guise of workmen on their day off.

could subsequently be recontextualized with captioning suggests the very real possibility of misrepresentation. Even Beato and Wirgman indulged in creative reinterpretations of this sort, sometimes recasting their images of Japanese women in a sexually suggestive manner. But for the most part, they were reasonably truthful in the way they posed and characterized the models they employed for their studio-created images.[24] The same could not be said for other photographers.

The Austrian Baron Raimund von Stillfried, Beato's chief competitor, operated a number of commercial studios in Yokohama under different names from 1871 to 1881. Stillfried eventually purchased Beato's studio and stock of negatives in 1877. Following the precedents set by Beato, Stillfried often made photographs of the same themes, knowing that market demand for certain subjects was relatively constant. The restrictions placed on foreigners traveling in Japan and the expectations of the market did not prevent commercial photographers from pursuing their own predilections or catering to the tastes of specific clientele. Public nudity was common in late nineteenth-century Japan. Foreign travelers often commented on women, stripped to the waist, working in the fields. Communal bathing, judging from travel accounts, was another common Japanese practice that either intrigued or offended Westerners depending on their sensibilities. It is easy to understand, then, why photographs of people bathing, for example, were highly popular commodities. Although these represented a practice Westerners actually saw, most of these photographs were posed in studios and all depict women—never men.

Stillfried purposefully indulged Westerners' general fascination with Japanese women by producing erotically charged portraits. He often posed his models seated or reclining in a manner that exposed their breasts. His remarkable skill as a portrait photographer resulted in highly sensual images that invited the prurient. His photographs move well beyond simple documentation of what may have been a relatively common sight Westerners encountered. These evocative images conveyed a sexuality that sets them apart from Beato's portraits and the general aesthetic of commercial photography in Japan. They were, in this author's assessment, some of the earliest examples of what would become by the 1880s a minor industry in soft-core pornography.

Perhaps it is important to question Stillfried's motivations for producing sexualized portraits. As a commercial photographer, he must have based many of his decisions on what he felt the market would accept. In the context of the treaty ports where prostitution was rampant and foreign men often engaged Japanese women for sexual servitude in what were euphemistically termed "temporary marriages," Stillfried's eroticized images of Japanese women were not entirely out of place. In fact, Stillfried may have been directly involved in this libidinal economy. He arranged, at his own expense, the construction of a Japanese teahouse at the 1873 Vienna Exposition for which he employed three Japanese geisha to serve tea, sing, and dance. Rumors circulating at the time suggested that Stillfried's teahouse was actually a front for a brothel. Given the highly eroticized nature of his photographs, this is perhaps understandable. The exhibition organizers forced him to move his pavilion off the exhibition grounds.[25]

Stillfried's role in promoting the sexuality of geisha, although perhaps indirect, cannot be understated. Props carefully arranged in his studio-posed portrait photographs, such as teahouse furnishings and musical instruments, implied that his models were geisha. He would sometimes replicate well-known Beato photographs. But Stillfried's versions would add an entirely new nuance. As with many of his portraits of Japanese women, he arranged the garments of the models he employed to expose their breasts (see p. 58). Westerners who resided or traveled to Japan may have understood the lack of veracity in this photograph. Or perhaps they would have viewed these women as low-class geisha or prostitutes fronting as geisha. But what would an image like this convey about geisha to foreigners with little or no direct experience in Japan, especially if they had seen the reproduction of Beato's image in Humbert's authoritative text? Is it images like this that gave rise to popular misconceptions of the sort addressed by Edwards, Bacon, and Rittner at the turn of the century?

Geisha and Their Imitators on Western Stages

R. Homphrey Moore's engraving of geisha performing at the 1889 Paris Universal Exhibition, which appeared in the November 15, 1890 issue of the *Illustrated London News*, highlights another means by which Westerners were introduced to geisha. Theatrical performances of geisha who traveled to Europe and America and later, of western women playing the role of geisha, were highly popular attractions at the turn of the century. These productions were pitched to audiences with preconceived notions about geisha that they had acquired through various literary and popular media. Many of these theatrical productions, moreover, were based on popular fiction authored by westerners with little or no firsthand experience of Japan. Although far removed from their Japanese context, these stage productions significantly influenced western conceptions of geisha.

International exhibitions, as Moore's engraving suggests, were important venues for Japan to present itself to the western world. Accordingly, participation at these exhibitions was organized at the upper levels of government. The intention was to put the best foot forward, primarily because these exhibitions provided an opportunity to promote Japanese industries. This meant, in some respects, playing to the expectations of the patrons who visited these fairs. It was not uncommon for the Japanese delegation to reconstruct architectural edifices representing the temples and shrines that had always attracted the attention of tourists, for example. Exhibits in these structures typically focused on Japan's pottery, bronzes, and lacquerware because these products sold in tremendous quantities to western travelers visiting the treaty ports. Live performances were de rigueur as they drew crowds to the pavilions in ways that static displays could not.

Undoubtedly it was an acquired taste, but by the 1880s Westerners who visited Japan began expressing an interest in the bombast and spectacle of Kabuki performances.[26] For this reason the Japanese government commissioned the famous actor Kawakami Otojirō to organize a theater troupe for the 1900 Paris Exhibition. In Paris Kawakami's wife, Sadayakko, quickly emerged as the star of the troupe. A former geisha, she danced and sang in elaborately beautiful costumes. Her performances often ended in tragically staged ritual suicides—another Japanese practice, which, if travel narratives and Wirgman's reports are any indication, enthralled Westerners as much as geisha. Sadayakko followed up her Paris success with a tour of Europe, England, and America where she continued to perform to great acclaim. Her performances, extensively reviewed in the popular press, captivated widespread public interest including that of several artists, notably Pablo Picasso, who made sketches of her, and William Nicholson, who featured her in his woodblock prints.

Japanese Dancing-Girls Practising,
Charles Wirgman, 1874
The stiffly posed scene, which appeared in the *London Illustrated News*, April 11, 1874, is highly improbable in its composition. It was likely popular with readers because it includes many of the motifs Europeans associated with Asia: fans, porcelain, lacquerware, and silk, plus it adds one that was soon to join the others as a symbol of Japan: the geisha.

Japanese Musicians, R. Homphrey
Moore, 1889

Although the woman playing the *taiko*
drum is documented as a geisha, the title
of the image, which was published on
November 15, 1890 in the *Illustrated London
News*, does not include that word. By the
latter part of the 1890s, however, the term
"geisha" had become more widely
recognized.

Sadayakko was certainly the most successful and well-known Japanese geisha to tour Europe and America at the turn of the century, but she was not the only one. Like Sadayakko, Ōta Hisa, better known by her stage name Hanako, trained as a geisha before she came to Europe in 1901 at the age of thirty-seven to perform with a troupe organized by the American impresario and dancer Loie Fuller. Hanako, who specialized in geisha roles much like those pioneered by Sadayakko, had a similar effect on the artists who attended her performances. Sculptor Auguste Rodin saw her in Marseilles in 1906. Shortly thereafter she agreed to pose for a series of sketches and figure studies. Confessing a fascination with Hanako's body and acting style, Rodin was especially taken by a role in which Hanako performed a death scene. Several of the fifty-three surviving busts Rodin made of Hanako show her with the anguished grimace she used to convey the climax of that scene. Rodin sculpted Hanako in clay and bronze, two media for which he is well known. One wax model conveys the stark whiteness of the makeup traditionally used by geisha.[27]

The extent of Westerners' enthusiasm for geisha is truly revealed in theatrical productions of their own making. It is in these that geisha stereotypes take their most potent forms. Osman Edwards's comparisons to Parisian actresses were very deliberate—and perceptive in this regard. He recognized that the theatrical medium was the source of much misunderstanding of geisha: "Her detractors have seen an English opera bearing her name and traducing her character: it is enough; they know."[28] In fact, there were many plays and musicals that contributed to Westerners' misconceptions of geisha. While Gilbert and Sullivan's light opera *The Mikado*(1885) had no geisha per se, its three female roles, best described as charmingly girlish, conveyed the sensibilities Westerners often associated with geisha. The term "geisha girl," which remained popular until the 1960s, came into widespread use at this time. With nearly one thousand performances in the first year after its debut in 1885, its impact on Westerners' conception of Japanese women was considerable.

Charles Wilmott's *The Geisha*, another English musical play that debuted in 1896 at George Edwarde's Gaitey Theatre, catered more specifically to emerging western stereotypes of geisha. The title song included the following lyrics:

> Ev'ry little Jappy chappie's gone upon the Geisha –
> Trickiest little Geisha ever seen in Asia!
> I've made things hum a bit, you know, since I became a Geisha,
> Japanesey, free and easy Tea house girl.

The last line, in particular, hints at the accessibility and sexuality Westerners were beginning to imagine for geisha. Equating geisha with teahouse girls reveals a misunderstanding that can be traced back to the earliest narratives written by Westerners in Japan. Most inns and teahouses employed women who could sing, dance, and play *shamisen*. These were the "entertainers" frequently depicted in Beato's photographs. But in less reputable inns these women were also available as sexual partners. Few Westerners engaged them as such, but they were certainly aware of this practice. Rittner addresses this misconception, though it appears to contradict his lamentation of geisha morals expressed above: "In Europe the name Geisha has, I think, been wrongly interpreted. People often imagine that every tea-house girl is a Geisha; they imagine, in fact, that a Geisha is a person who merely ogles the men, flirts, and behaves like most European barmaids. They are wrong."[29] Westerners who had visited Japan certainly knew the difference between a teahouse waitress (*chaya musume*) and a geisha, and many visitors delighted in pointing out the differences as a display of their expertise. But these distinctions, perhaps because of photographs like Stillfried's, disappeared as geisha roles became popular on the stages of Europe and America.

Two Geisha Apprentices, 1885
The large, flowery hair ornaments identify these girls as geisha apprentices, probably *akaeri* (red collars) from Tokyo rather than Kyoto *maiko*. Geisha rarely played the *koto* (zither), so its presence here could indicate simply the photographer's desire to incorporate it into the picture.

David Belasco's *Madame Butterfly*, by far the most famous turn-of-the century geisha theatrical spectacle, blurred another important distinction. The exploits of Lieutenant Pinkerton are well known and need only be summarized here. He takes as his wife the geisha Cho-Cho San who bears him a child. She dutifully waits three years while he visits America but commits suicide when Pinkerton returns with his American wife. Cho-Cho San's devotion and her tragic death make for a compelling narrative, one that western audiences found difficult to resist, but what exactly did it convey? Certainly the practice of taking "temporary" wives was widespread among western men who visited Japan in the nineteenth century. Marriage brokers managed these arrangements, matching women of poor families who needed the income with foreigners who desired sex with no demands other than a down payment and monthly fee. These women were returned to their families, often with their mixed-race children, when the men departed for home. Temporary wives were not geisha, but to theater patrons who misunderstood the differences between teahouse waitresses and geisha, Cho-Cho San simply represented another sexualized Japanese female. In effect, *Madame Butterfly* lowered geisha to a form of prostitute that even the euphemism "temporary wife" could not hide.

Theatrical productions of the early twentieth century gave geisha stereotypes a remarkably high public profile. The highly successful stage version of *Madame Butterfly* was eclipsed by Giacomo Puccini's operatic version, which premiered with great success at La Scala in 1904. Two years earlier John Luther Long and David Belasco, author and producer of *Madame Butterfly* respectively, had collaborated on *The Darling of The Gods*, a five-act stage spectacular that revolved around a tragic female role embodied in its heroine Yo-san. The play was performed two hundred times after its debut in New York in 1902 and traveled to six more venues in the northeast and midwest.

The librettos for *The Geisha* and *Madame Butterfly* were drawn from an extensive repertoire of popular fiction that pandered to the same misconceptions about geisha. John Luther Long's short story on which *Madame Butterfly* was based first appeared in 1898 in both a collection of short stories and the January issue of *The Century Illustrated Magazine*. Long had also written a novel, *Miss Cherry Blossom of Tokyo*, conceived along similar lines in 1895. Its popularity prepared the ground for *Madame Butterfly's* astounding success. Slightly later, Winnifred Eaton, a Chinese-American author, penned several novels that also took up the theme of "temporary marriages." The most notable of these, *A Japanese Nightingale*, enjoyed considerable acclaim. Even Mrs. Hugh Fraser, the diplomat's wife who so judiciously avoided the subject of geisha in her *Letters From Japan*, couldn't resist the phenomenon that so captivated Westerners. In 1908 she authored her own novel, *Heart of a Geisha*.

Pierre Loti's popular novella, *Madame Chrysanthème*, written in 1887, was the likely prototype for the entire genre of geisha fiction and contemporary stage productions. Loti recounted his six-month temporary marriage to a Nagasaki woman that began by interviewing prospective "brides." His first encounter conveys many of the assumptions Westerners brought to their understanding of Japanese women:

> Suddenly enters, like a night butterfly awakened in broad daylight, like a rare and surprising moth, the dancing girl from the other compartment. No doubt she wishes to have a look at me. She rolls her eyes like a timid kitten, and then all at once tamed, nestles against me, with a coaxing air of childishness, which is a delightfully transparent assumption. She is slim, elegant, delicate, and smells sweet; she is drolly painted, white as plaster, with a little circle of rouge marked very precisely in the middle of each cheek, the mouth reddened with a touch of gilding outlining the outer lip. As they could not whiten the back of her neck on account of all the delicate little curls of hair growing there, they had, in their love of exactitude, stopped the white plaster in a straight line, which might have been cut with a knife, and in consequence at the nape appears a square of natural skin of a deep yellow.
>
> An imperious note sounds on the guitar, evidently a summons! Crac! Away she goes, the little fairy, to rejoice the driveling fools on the other side of the screens. Supposing I marry this one, without seeking any further. I should respect her as a child committed to my care; I should take her for what she is: a fantastic and charming plaything.[30]

First encounters between vastly different cultures seldom leave a complete picture in the minds of their participants. Even the most sincere attempts to see completely and understand fully are thwarted by the circumstances of the encounter and, more often, by the assumptions—personal, societal, or otherwise—that people bring to the experience. The impressions of "the other" acquired under such circumstances and constraints lend themselves to stereotyping. This is seldom through conscious malice, rather because of gaps in understanding that are invariably filled with inexact analogies and faulty comparisons. The encounters with geisha in nineteenth-century travel narratives exhibit these characteristics. They reveal an earnest and innocent curiosity about a remarkably different culture of which geisha became, by the beginning of the twentieth century, one of its widely recognized icons. Their many errors reveal the limitations of their authors, but not any deliberate pattern of misinformation and deceit.

Those with commercial motivation to entertain the public are not so easily excused. The misrepresentations of geisha that developed as a result of their efforts varied from one medium to the next, as the desire for popular success and the potential profit of such ventures often overrode the need to be truthful. While few of the stereotypes thus created were intended to harm the world they depicted, many have persisted. Perhaps these always incomplete and increasingly outmoded misconceptions of geisha can finally be righted.

NOTES:

1. Osman Edwards, *Japanese Plays and Playfellows* (New York: John Lane, 1901), p. 101.

2. Ibid., pp. 102–03.

3. The *Illustrated London News* provided the most thorough coverage of late nineteenth-century Japan, hence its choice as the primary example of its type for this essay. There were, however, several similar publications issued in a variety of languages that convey similar accounts and impressions of geisha.

4. The other treaty ports were Nagasaki, Hakodate, Hyōgo, and Niigata. Nagasaki and Hakodate opened immediately after the negotiations. Hyōgo (now Kobe) opened in the early 1860s. Niigata was never opened.

5. J. E. DeBecker, *The Nightless City* (Rutland, VT and Tokyo: Charles E. Tuttle, 1971) [reprinted from the 1899 edition], pp. 76–84.

6. F. G. Notehefler, *Japan Through American Eyes: The Journal of Francis Hall, Kanagawa and Yokohama 1859–1866* (Princeton: Princeton University Press, 1992), pp. 200–01; 265–66.

7. Aimé Humbert, *Japan and the Japanese Illustrated*, translated by Cashel Hoey, edited by H. W. Bates (New York: D. Appleton and Co., 1874), p. 295.

8. William Elliot Griffis, *The Mikado's Empire* (New York: Harper and Brothers, 1876), p. 408.

9. W. E. L. Keeling, *Tourists' Guide to Yokohama, Tokio, Hakone, Fujiyama, Kamakura, Yokosuka, Kanozan, Narita, Nikko, Kioto, Osaka, etc., etc.* (Yokohama: A. Farsari, 1880), pp. 23; 79–80.

10. Douglas Sladen, *Club Hotel Guide to Japan* (n.p., 1892), pp. 33; 104.

11. Basil Hall Chamberlain, *Things Japanese*, fifth edition (London: Kegan, Paul, Trench, Trubner and Co., 1905), p. 433.

12. Christopher Dresser, *Japan: Its Architecture, Art, and Art Manufactures* (London, New York, Bahrain: Kegan Paul, 2001) [reprinted from the 1881 edition], pp. 23–24.

13. Sir Edwin Arnold, *Seas and Lands* (New York: Longmans, Green and Co., 1891), pp. 230–38; Douglas Sladen, *The Japs At Home* (London: Hutchinson, 1892), pp. 43–48.

14. Gilbert Watson, *Three Rolling Stones in Japan* (London: Edward Arnold, 1904), pp. 105–06.

15. Eliza Ruhamah Scidmore, *Jinriksha Days in Japan* (New York: Harper and Brothers, 1891), pp. 213; 300; 338.

16. Mrs. Hugh Fraser, *Letters From Japan*, 2 vols. (New York and London: MacMillan, 1899), p. 204.

17. Augusta M. Campbell Davidson, *Present-Day Japan* (London: T. Fisher Unwin, 1904), 288-89.

18. Alice Mabel Bacon, *Japanese Girls and Women* (Boston and New York: Houghton Mifflin, 1891), pp. 286; 288–89.

19. Ibid., p. 289.

20. Edwards (1901), p. 211.

21. Geo. H. Rittner, *Impressions of Japan* (London: John Murray, 1904), 115.

22. For a reproduction of this advertisement see John Clark, *Japanese Exchanges in Art 1850s-1930s* (Sydney: Powerhouse Publications, 2001), fig. 8.

23. *Illustrated London News*: Jan. 13, 1874, p. 13.

24. Allen Hockley, "Expectation and Authenticity in Meiji Tourist Photography," in *Challenging Past and Present: The Metamorphosis of Japanese Art in the Meiji Era, 1868-1912* (Honolulu: University of Hawai'i Press, forthcoming).

25. Luke Gartlan, a graduate student from Australia, recently uncovered these unsavory aspects of Stillfried's participation in the Vienna Exposition.

26. *Chūshingura*, a samurai vendetta tale, was by far the most popular. The graves of the forty-seven samurai that avenged the death of their lord were located near the British consulate in Tokyo and became a favorite stop on tours. Ogawa Kazumasa, one of Japan's most prolific early photographers, made several images of Kabuki actors performing important scenes from this play. Tourists with interests in Kabuki were a good market for these images.

27. The author wishes to acknowledge David Getsy for alerting him to Rodin's busts of Hanako. For reproductions see Albert E. Elsen, *Rodin's Art* (London: Oxford University Press, 2003), p. 427. This publication also includes a photograph of Hanako.

28. Edwards (1901), p. 101.

29. Rittner (1904), p. 126.

30. Pierre Loti, *Madame Chrysanthème*, translated by Laura Ensor (New York: Boni and Liveright, 1887), pp. 26–27.

Allen Hockley, PhD. in East Asian Studies from the University of Toronto, is Associate Professor in Art History at Dartmouth College. His books include *The Prints of Isoda Koryusai: Floating World Culture and Its Consumers in Eighteenth-Century Japan* (2003) and *Inside the Floating World: Japanese Prints from the Lenoir C. Wright Collection* (2003). Among his research specialties is early Japanese photography.

The Exotic Geisha

Liza Dalby

EXOTICISM IS A GEISHA'S STOCK IN TRADE. The western fascination with geisha harks back to images from the first woodblock prints that fluttered out of a newly opened Japan to a curious Europe and United States from the 1860s onward. To a Westerner, then and now, a geisha is about as different as it is possible to be from the familiar girl-next-door. Racially, linguistically, and culturally foreign, geisha have always been sexually charged emblems and objects of western male erotic fantasy.

More recently, geisha are now exotic in their homeland Japan as well. Mystery and glamour have become a vital part of the geisha's raison d'être from the latter half of the twentieth century up to the present. Rare if not endangered, available only to an initiated and wealthy elite, following a career that seems the antithesis of what a modern woman would choose, geisha nowadays find themselves gawked at by Japanese as well as by foreign tourists. Yet the nature of geisha's exoticism within Japanese culture is not the same as the fascination they evoke in the West.

Westerners have always been curious about geisha, and most Americans recognize this foreign word, if not always its pronunciation (*gay-sha* not *ghee-sha*). Like sushi, "geisha" has made its way into the English language, with a few contortions along the way. The seemingly indelible definition, "a Japanese prostitute," has finally faded from newer English dictionaries, replaced by "artists" and "traditional entertainers." Yet while the latter are in several senses more accurate, we would be foolish to assume that the question of the sexual availability of the geisha does not still lie just below the surface. Thus the portrait of the geisha as sexual toy, groomed in ornate traditional fashion, trained in the arts of pleasing men, remains firmly framed in the western gallery of female icons.

When I wrote my doctoral thesis, *The Institution of the Geisha in Modern Japanese Society*, (1978) and subsequent book *Geisha* (1983), I aimed to explore the historical question of how this profession arose, and the cultural question of why it continues to exist. My main interest was how the geisha fit into Japanese society. Thinking, perhaps naïvely, that the only meaning of the geisha was to be sought in the cultural context that produced them, I did not even touch upon the issue of western

OPPOSITE

Maiko **(Apprentice Geisha)**, Kuroda Seiki, 1893
Painted shortly after he returned to Japan from nine years of study in France, *Maiko* reflects the artist's new perspective on his own traditional culture under the influence of Impressionism. This work has been designated an Important Cultural Property by the Japanese government.

A New *Maiko* Facing the Cameras, Tom Haar, 1993
Shyly emerging from the shadows of her doorway, a *maiko* (Kyoto apprentice geisha) is confronted by a battery of cameramen on the day of her debut. With the number of *maiko* decreasing, such opportunities to photograph new apprentices are becoming increasingly rare.

A Bowling Geisha Apprentice, *Life Magazine* cover, September 11, 1964
The great rise in interest in geisha following the U.S.-led occupation of Japan after World War II gave birth to numerous popular articles, books, and movies during the 1950s and 1960s.

TOP RIGHT

Lobby Card for *The Barbarian and the Geisha*, 1958
Townsend Harris, the first American consul to Japan, and his supposed geisha mistress Okichi caught the imagination of Hollywood in the postwar period. Starring John Wayne, the movie served to reinforce romanticized ideas about Japan and geisha.

RIGHT

Cry For Happy, 1961
The popular notion of the "geisha house," a term with no equivalent in Japanese, created the impression that geisha were confined to specific buildings where they lived, partied, and dallied with men. This led to the confusion of geisha with the old-style prostitutes (*yūjo*) who were indeed confined to their quarters.

misperceptions. But as the only Westerner to have temporarily joined the geisha ranks, I have always found that I need to respond to this deeper issue back home. Sometimes with amusement, sometimes dismay, I have taken note over the years of numerous manifestations of the intense western interest in geisha. The seed of this fascination may lie in the real women, but its flower has long since branched into fantasy, saying more about the yearnings of Westerners than about geisha themselves.

At the same time, fantasy, wishful thinking, and plain misconceptions are still bound together with threads of fact. Geisha have the odd distinction of being both legendary and real. They are not make-believe like nymphs or mermaids, for we know that—like playmates-of-the-month—they actually do exist somewhere. Yet if we try to reconcile the myth with reality, they match up only sporadically. Myth by nature transcends history and individuals. Real geisha live and work in a variety of communities in different areas of Japan, remaining acutely aware of hierarchies of status among their communities, and, of course, exhibiting an extraordinary range of personality differences among themselves.

The Western Fascination with Geisha

Three separate threads of implied meaning are woven together when the word "geisha" is used in English. The first is mysterious secret knowledge. When critical fans called Yoko Ono "John Lennon's geisha," they insinuated that she was holding him in enigmatic Oriental thrall against which he was helpless to resist. The second element is sex. Treating the internet as a proxy for common opinion, I can type in the word "geisha" and bring up thousands of English-language sites, of which about two-thirds are pornographic. No one can doubt that the connection between geisha and sex remains strong in the common western perception. The third overtone in English usage is subservience. When people are likened to geisha, the comparison generally means that they are outwardly servile to the

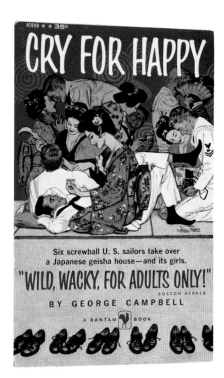

Three New Geisha Apprentices of Gion,
Tom Haar, 1981
The gorgeous costume, white makeup, and elaborate hairstyle of *maiko* make them more like living dolls. Although today they begin their training as ordinary teenage girls, new *maiko* must learn to reconcile themselves to life in a world of centuries-old custom and etiquette.

vanishing point. Ego effaced, their only desire is to please their master, albeit with strange powers of submissive attraction. During a presidential election year, my ear was caught by a radio editorial referring to Al Gore as "Bill Clinton's geisha."

The Western Male Fantasy

Evoking mystery, subservience, and secret sexual skills, the classic geisha image consists of an impassive white face and impossibly red lips, body wrapped in an intricate black kimono revealing nothing except a vulnerable nape. The colors are primal: white (face and neck), black (kimono), and slivers of red (lips, kimono lining). It is no accident that the covers of several recent photo essay books on geisha have used the close-up image of the red-painted mouth against white skin.[1] Neither is it coincidence that we don't even see the woman's entire face. A face indicates a real, individual person, not the abstract erotic ideal we are proffered.

To an average western male, geisha embody femininity at its most seductive. The particular fantasy reflected in this myth is that of a beautiful, selfless doll who has been trained in the art of pleasing men, but who makes no demands of her own. Her happiness is that her master of the moment be happy. This dream geisha-girl doesn't speak English, and, mute, is incapable of being a bitch. Even the sunniest, most self-reliant man could be susceptible to this fantasy. Imagine someone who dotes upon your every whim, satisfying desires you may not even have known you had, whose personal needs are taken care of by some vague and arcane system you need not bother about, who will obligingly melt into the background, like Madame Butterfly, stifling inconvenient emotions if need be, in order not to disturb your peace of mind. This is a fantasy that is exceedingly difficult to project onto a real woman or a long-term relationship, but it has been a remarkably durable daydream.

Historical circumstance has also had a huge influence on western perceptions of geisha. During the Allied Occupation (1945–52), when thousands of American GIs descended on Japan, every lady of the night they encountered seems to have called herself a "geisha girl"—or allowed herself to be referred to as such. Undoubtedly some soldiers were aware that the woman in the bar was not exactly a *geisha*, but the word suddenly gained broad usage in English nevertheless. For just these reasons, when they regrouped after the war, the true geisha of the venerable and prestigious community of Shinbashi in Tokyo even considered dropping the name "geisha" altogether. For lack of an alternative, they ended up keeping the word, but their indignation indicates its linguistic promiscuity at the time. Meanwhile,

Geisha and Attendant in the Rain,
Kitagawa Utamaro, 1790s
Box-carrying attendants known as *hakoya*
could be either male or female. In this
beautifully colored print, the rather staid-
looking geisha seems cowed by the storm,
while the vivacious girl carrying her
shamisen box as well as a lantern looks
positively delighted.

soldiers came home with memories of the
"geisha-girls" they had enjoyed during their
Japanese sojourn, and the cross-cultural fantasy
proliferated.

The Western Female Fantasy

Added to these peculiarities is the
curious fact that geisha are a source of fantasy
for some western women as well as men,
although as birds of another feather.

Since my book *Geisha* first came out in
1983, I have received dozens of letters and
phone calls from American women convinced
that they had been geisha in a previous
existence. To this day I get letters and emails
from others wanting advice on how to become
geisha themselves. Even pop star Madonna
went through a geisha phase several years ago,
dressing up in a classic black/white/red
Gaultier "geisha-esque" leather kimono. What
we see here is an idealized geisha, excised from
its Japanese context to float culture-free in the
global imagination.

What do I advise these would-be geisha?
First, I recommend that they learn the Japanese
language, and practice sitting for hours on
folded legs. Next I stress that it is imperative
that they like Japanese men, who are, for many,
off-putting or worse. Only then could they even
begin to study the performing arts in which
the geisha must be proficient. All this would
seem to be obvious, but not one person has
followed my advice. They seem to have had
something else in mind. Western female
admirers of geisha also focus on the geisha
myth described above, but from the opposite
side of desire. That is, they seem to identify
with the image of mythic femininity, holding men in thrall, and living aestheticized
lives for the sake of art. What appeals to these women is the fact that geisha do not
marry, that they are not under the thumb of a husband, that they live in communities
of women, dress elegantly, and devote themselves to art. This view from the other
side of the icon tends to leave sex out altogether or else invert the servility element,
transforming the woman into dominatrix mode. Madonna exemplifies the "power
geisha," but she is hardly unique.

Geisha in Woodblock Prints

The portrait of the geisha as an ornately groomed sex toy was not wholly
made up by Westerners, of course. Plenty of Japanese material was stitched into its
fabric as well.

From the 1860s through 1900, Europeans and Americans discovered Japan
largely through the medium of woodblock prints.[2] In 1863, Massachusetts-born artist
James McNeill Whistler was smitten by Japanese prints in London. He painted several
portraits of his red-haired mistress swathed in kimono surrounded by *japonaiserie*.
The same year, in Paris, Edmond and Louis Goncourt were fascinated by their
acquisition of an album of *shunga*, Japanese erotic prints. Throughout artsy

international circles, *les choses japonaises* (things Japanese) were the hot new thing. Japanese prints circulating abroad included landscapes, birds and flowers, and historical themes, but by far the most influential on contemporary western culture were the *bijin-ga*, pictures of beautiful women. It is true that some of the beautiful women were in fact geisha. But many others were *tayū* and *oiran*, the authentic courtesan queens among the licensed prostitutes. Still others were merchants' wives, and even servants. All were wearing kimono and sporting elaborate hairdos. To western eyes, they all appeared equally exotic, and they all came to be referred to as geisha. Among nineteenth-and twentieth-century collectibles is a category of painted porcelain that includes sugar bowls and cream pitchers, salt and pepper shakers and vases, as a genre defined by pictures of ladies wearing kimono. No matter what sort of lady she might be, this kind of porcelain is generically called "geisha-ware."

Cream Pitcher
Following the long-held idea that products from Asia must look somehow "oriental," porcelain from Japan was often decorated with Asian motifs, especially women in native dress.

Porcelain Figure of A Japanese Woman, c. 1876
This figure made for export actually depicts a woman of the samurai class, but within a few decades of its manufacture, many Westerners had come to assume that representations of Japanese women in traditional dress must be geisha. This figure was purchased at the 1876 Philadelphia World's Fair.

A small group of Westerners took up residence in Japan soon after its opening to the West. In 1859 the Japanese government provided them with their own special licensed brothel quarter, called Miyozaki in Yokohama. Located in a swamp behind the foreigners' dwellings, surrounded by a moat, this miniature Yoshiwara gave western men their first experience of both geisha and genuine prostitutes.[3] But what exactly did these western pioneers experience? Starved for female company, they undoubtedly enjoyed the sex (if not the music)[4] that was available, but whether they were able to discriminate among the various sorts of kimono-clad women who attended the parties at the Gankirō teahouse is another question.

During the century and a half since Westerners first discovered the Japanese Floating World and its pictures, the images in *ukiyo-e* have become familiar to the point of parody. Yet we still should ask what the artists themselves were seeking to depict. In fact, many woodblock artists intended to render the exquisite diversity of the Japanese demimonde of the seventeenth through the nineteenth centuries. This was the world that

The Elite Courtesan Hanaōgi of the Ōgiya, from the series *A Comparison of Elegant Beauties,* Keisai Eisen, 1820s

The subject of this print, one of the last of the several generations of *oiran* bearing the title Hanaōgi, displays an unusual hairstyle that falls over the shoulders of her kimono. Japanese hair was usually moistened with scented camellia nut oil, and was rarely allowed to contact and stain beautiful silk garments.

hatched the profession of the geisha to be sure, but within it geisha themselves were but one type of inhabitant. The way to recognize a geisha in many prints is to look for the more plainly attired figure next to a fabulously decorated courtesan who wears layer upon layer of gold-embroidered collars and forests of tortoiseshell combs in her hair.

The classic icon of the geisha—the trailing black kimono, whitened face, and oiled *Shimada* hairstyle, an image that appears ornate and mysterious next to modern styles of kimono and makeup—is actually the vestige of a style that was meant to be plain. In contrast to the finery of the professional courtesan in whose world geisha worked as entertainers, indeed their appearance was relatively simple. This was in part because under the law, geisha were not supposed to compete with the courtesans in looks or in enticing customers.

All this in turn took its place inside a larger cultural context. The Edo-period world of licensed prostitution was composed of an elaborate hierarchy of women whose sex was for sale. Those at the top were as celebrated as movie stars are today, while those at the bottom were simply streetwalkers. Geisha were registered separately from all of the above, on the theory that their job was different. When this system of regulated (and legal) prostitution was finally dismantled in 1958, geisha were technically not affected because, in the entire history of the profession, geisha were never licensed as prostitutes per se.

But that does not mean that all geisha were innocent lambs. Under the table, geisha did compete with courtesans and licensed prostitutes, which is why the feudal government had to issue edicts continually demanding that geisha keep their proper place. Their job as *geisha,* literally "arts person," artistes, was to entertain the courtesans and their clients as singers, dancers, and providers of sociable banter. Geisha were not supposed to make arrangements to meet clients for sex on their own, although clearly many of them did—otherwise there would have been no need for the barrage of edicts. However, sex with a geisha has seldom been a straightforward, purely economic exchange, and I would venture to guess that this was part of its appeal. Under historical conditions in which marriages were arranged totally for family considerations, while prostitutes (ranging up to the rank of courtesan) were available for purchase, geisha offered the possibility of that rarest of commodities, romance.

Japanese Women in Western Eyes

The widespread misapprehension that women dressed in fancy kimono must be geisha may simply be a matter of unfamiliarity with a particular historical setting. Meanwhile, another potent yet less palpable element involved in the creation of the geisha myth has to do with how Westerners perceive Japanese women in general. Anyone who claims to know the first thing about Japan will tell you that Japanese girls are discouraged from an early age from being assertive around men. Even allowing that such a cultural tendency has weakened in recent years, surveys of western beliefs about Japan invariably include the idea that Japanese women defer

Brothel in the Yoshiwara, Felice Beato, 1860s
The concept of legalized prostitution was new to most Westerners who visited Japan, so brothels such as this one were the subject of intense interest. The posing courtesans in the first-floor windows and the balcony are readily identified by the pastel-colored sashes that are tied at their waists in front.

Long-handled Fans, c. 1880
These fans reflect the growing use of geisha images as decorative motifs during the Meiji period. The fan on the left shows a geisha boarding a pleasure boat, while that on the right shows a geisha tying a paper charm to a blossoming cherry tree.

to men. The international context of the comparison itself reinforces this. Compared to American or European women, Japanese women probably *are* more deferential in general.

The fallacy that follows from this belief is that in Japan, where even ordinary women are supposed to put men first, the geisha must necessarily be ultra accommodating experts in the art of subservience. In other words, Westerners infer that the art of pleasing men would require a geisha to be even more servile than "normal"—a conclusion that is far from true.

It is important not to confuse the general cultural norms of Japanese politeness with subservience. Geisha are among the most outspoken Japanese women I know. Of course they are politic—like a good hostess in America they don't say things that would embarrass a guest. They are also very good at making small talk. But Japanese men do not consort with geisha because they crave more subservience. They crave interesting conversation and lively personalities. Looking back on my own preconceived notions about geisha, I probably expected geisha to be submissive as well—before I learned better from my experience as "Ichigiku." To my surprise, I found that the social give-and-take between geisha and customers in the teahouses of Kyoto was quite comfortable for an American-bred geisha.

Sex and Geisha Today

Now, at the beginning of the twenty-first century, the Allied Occupation of Japan is two generations behind us. We can see how it played a part in shaping the myth of geisha as sex toy. What about postwar Japan, land of the economic miracle, and now—with the current economic doldrums—post-economic miracle? Just how "available" is a geisha today? Could it be that despite all the talk of art, a geisha really is the world's most expensive prostitute, going so far as to auction her virginity to the highest bidder (as portrayed in Arthur Golden's novel, *Memoirs of a Geisha,* and vehemently denied by Mineko Iwasaki, author of the autobiographical *Geisha, A Life*)?[5]

A simple answer to the question of geisha and sex is just not possible. One reason is that we do not have an institution comparable to geisha in modern western societies. We can list characteristics of their profession that have similarities in the West, but they do not add up to something that looks familiar. Geisha do not marry,

Three Types of Beauties in Concert,
Utagawa Kunisada, 1820s–30s
Courtesans and geisha worked together to entertain clients in the pleasure quarters. Geisha (right) were the primary musicians, but some elite courtesans played the zither-like *koto* (center). In most popular trios of beauties, an unmarried young woman (*musume*) often completed the set, but here a lower-class prostitute fills the role instead, playing a violin-like *kokyu*.

Kyoto Geisha Playing A Hand Drum,
Tsukioka Settei, late 18th century
Settei was a Kyoto artist who specialized in depictions of beautiful women. He shows a *geiko* (the Kyoto/Osaka term for geisha) standing in a coy pose as she strikes the *tsuzumi* with her hand. Geisha dancers often learn *tsuzumi* as a second artistic specialty.

but they often have children. (Should we think of them, then, as unwed mothers?) They live in organized professional communities of women—complete with a vocabulary of "sisters" (*onēsan*) and "mother superiors" (*okamisan*). In this way, a geisha community is, in fact, rather similar to a religious order. But in other ways, it is hardly comparable because geisha regularly have affairs with married men, but can form other sexual liaisons at their own discretion. At the end of the day, they derive their actual livelihood from singing, dancing, and chatting with men at banquets. They devote much of their private time to learning and performing traditional forms of music and dance, and they always dress in kimono for work, although not always in the full formal geisha costume. And in the latter case, most Westerners would have trouble even recognizing them as geisha.

There is no doubt that coerced sex and bidding on a new geisha's virginity occurred in the period before World War II, the setting of Golden's novel. After Japan lost the war, geisha had largely dispersed and the profession was in shambles. When they regrouped during the Occupation and began to flourish in the 1960s during Japan's postwar economic boom, the nature of being a geisha had changed. In modern Japan, girls are not sold into indentured service, nor are they coerced into sexual relations. A geisha's sex life is her private affair.

From Japanese Eyes

As Japanese women, the most important social fact about geisha is that they are not wives. Geisha and wives are mutually exclusive categories because of the way women's roles have traditionally been defined in Japan. Wives have always controlled the private sphere of the home and children, while the profession of geisha, for all its exclusivity, came into existence in a space separate both from the private world of the home and the public one of business. Geisha inhabit a space where men get together on neutral territory to socialize. Although geisha are by no means the only women who serve this function—they are outnumbered a-thousand-to-one by bar hostesses in Japan today—this is still one of the two reasons the profession continues to exist.

Geisha dwell in the most exclusive reaches of Japan's *mizu shōbai*, the "water business" of bars, clubs, and entertainment. What differentiates a geisha from a bar hostess, waitress, dancer, call girl, escort, and other women of the *mizu shōbai* is her *gei*, or art. *Gei* is the other reason geisha continue to exist today.

As early as the beginning of the twentieth century geisha began to see that their profession had to change and adapt to new circumstances. The feudal regime under which they had come into being two hundred years earlier was gone. Individually, geisha could no longer count on the largesse of a single wealthy patron to finance their arts. So instead, they gradually went public in a conscious attempt to interest the larger society in their artistic activities. Eventually, the different geisha communities came to present lavish public performances of traditional music, dance, and theater several times a year. Like the dynasties of contemporary Kabuki actors, geisha have come to be recognized in Japan as an expertly trained cadre devoted to the traditional performing arts. Their *gei* has been transformed into their professional salvation. Since in general the Japanese are extremely proud of their artistic heritage, geisha have found their niche as curators of highly esteemed genres of music and dance.

As culture workers, geisha are certain to be affected by Japan's various economic downturns. In the mid-1970s, when I was transformed into my geisha persona of Ichigiku, we were busy every night of the week in the teahouses of Pontochō in Kyoto. Now I am told that Friday and Saturday nights are still booked, but weeknights are very slow. The business executives who party with geisha and once bought up hundreds of tickets to their dance performances have had to cut back. Naturally, when companies are pinched, entertainment expenses are the first perks to be trimmed. And when business is slow, the older geisha retire and the community's population shrinks.

None of this is new. The *mizu shōbai* is called the "water trade" precisely because its fortunes ebb and flow depending on larger economic tides. There is a direct connection between today's *mizu shōbai* and the *ukiyo*, or "floating world" depicted in woodblock prints of the past. Geisha are used to this and pay little attention to alarmed reports of their imminent demise.

Japanese are still fascinated by geisha, and I would be surprised if they would let them disappear—certainly not for reasons of mere economics. When Japan first opened to the west in the middle of the nineteenth century, the three outstanding symbols of the country to Westerners were cherry blossoms, Fujiyama, and geisha. I saw a recent article that recast the trio as "sushi, Fujiyama, and geisha." Mt. Fuji is not likely to go away. Neither are geisha.

Exotic in Japan

Take a shy Japanese high school girl in white blouse and dark, pleated skirt. Paint her face alabaster white. Pull her hair into side wings and rolls, smoothing it shiny with camellia nut oil. Brush safflower-red stain in the shape of a delicate rosebud mouth over her blotted-out lips—art now refashioning the very shape of her mouth. Dress her in kimono with long swinging sleeves as brightly patterned as a tropical bird, and a collar pulled down to her shoulder blades, her soft nape accentuated by the pronged pattern of the white makeup where it meets her hairline. Encase her torso in a swath of brocade so heavy it requires two people to tie it. This special kind of obi is tied in a pair of long tails that hang at her back, reaching from shoulder to ankle. Send her out on the street wearing six-inch platform clogs. In the neighborhoods of Gion, Pontochō, and Kamishichiken in Kyoto, the *maiko* may not cause local heads to swivel, but a prowling tourist, whether foreign or Japanese, will swoon.

A quite ordinary-looking Kyoto teenager becomes iconic when dressed as a *maiko*. Indeed, a *maiko*, the Kyoto term for an apprentice *geiko* (Kyoto dialect for geisha), is a poster girl for this city, renowned as the old capital of Japan. Although Tokyo geisha have apprentices too, no one pays special attention to the *hangyoku* (literally, "half-fee") or *akaeri* (red collars). Not many Japanese even know that is what they are called. In any case, women who become geisha in Tokyo are usually in their twenties, already a bit old to be donning the trappings of an authentic young apprentice. The elements of a *maiko*'s costume are based on traditional kimono

Caught Seducing an Apprentice,
Utagawa Toyoharu, c. 1794
In the unlicensed seaside pleasure district of Shinagawa, a man trying to seduce a virgin apprentice (identified as such by her long sleeves) is surprised by an older geisha. The geisha's cold expression and ready roll of paper makes it clear that she was expecting to spend the night with him instead.

Two Geisha "Sisters," 1930s

Traditionally, geisha lived in communities comprised almost entirely of women, in lodgings called *okiya* that were usually owned by retired geisha. These lodgings were completely separate from the venues in which geisha entertained. Geisha still refer to each other in familial terms: "mother," "elder sister," etc.

markers of childhood: the long sleeves, the obi tied high on the chest, in bright colors with the wide obi-scarf prominently displayed, and the hair done in the distinctive "split-peach" style, once common for unmarried girls.[6]

Maiko always go out in full dress. They are unmistakable. If they graduate to become adult geisha (not all of them do), they will acquire a wider, more varied kimono wardrobe. A newly designated full geisha may still wear the white makeup, the nape-revealing kimono, and an oiled traditional hairstyle that accords with the classic geisha image, but that would be her most formal outfit, worn only on special occasions, and her hair would be a wig. Most of the time, an adult geisha's hair is smooth and plainly upswept, and she will wear a modern kimono—elegantly subdued, never gaudy. Looking at her, a Westerner would probably not guess her to be a geisha. Some Japanese, ignorant of the finer points of the kimono aesthetic, might not know either. But to connoisseurs she is clearly a geisha, and this is where her mystique to Japanese begins.

The Japanese men who actually engage the services of geisha, whether as patron or occasional customer, do not dream of an abstract, grape-peeling, submissive sexual slave. Geisha connoisseurs look forward to an evening of drinking with congenial companions whom they know will be good company. Because of the expense, there is also great prestige attached to the ability to associate with geisha. Men are allowed to behave with geisha and other women in "the water business" in a loose and familiar way that seems a little shocking to Westerners. A geisha is at home with this kind of behavior. Japanese wives would not be, and neither would most western women. I have seen western men somewhat lost as guests at geisha parties. Because they cannot appreciate the banter and the jokes, their experience is little more than exotic and slightly disappointing. The truth of the matter is that most of a geisha's special skill is verbal.

At the same time, geisha take great pains to conform to a traditional notion of feminine allure (known as *iroke*) in their manner, looks, and dress. No matter her age, a geisha will never allow herself to look frumpy. I was impressed listening to a 65-year-old geisha talking about a modern plastic-impregnated collar for a kimono underrobe, the advantage of which is that it could be easily cleaned instead of being snipped off, dry-cleaned, and re-sewn like the traditional silk collar. "Ohh, I could never wear such a thing," she commented. "Absolutely no *iroke*." It would be difficult to imagine a Japanese wife of her age being concerned with *iroke*. Once married, Japanese women tend to adopt a mode of genteel domesticity deemed appropriate to the cultural notion of wife, in which *iroke* plays little, if any, role.

An Exotic in Retrospective

During a recent stay in Kyoto, I had an interesting experience that revealed another aspect of the image of geisha. My reason for being in Kyoto was to finish some research for my historical novel about the eleventh-century court lady Murasaki Shikibu. I had been invited to a shell-matching party, a reenactment of a pastime popular in Murasaki's day. All the ladies participating in this elegant parlor game were supposed to wear kimono to the event. Since I had not even thought to bring a kimono with me from the USA on this trip, I asked an old geisha friend if I might borrow one of hers. This was not a full-dress geisha costume, of course, but merely an informal, mauvish-brown kimono with hand-painted, thin stripes of blue, olive,

and dark orange at one-inch intervals. The obi she lent me was black with an open patch of white decorated in a slightly French-looking pattern of gold roses. The effect was modish rather than traditional, and subdued rather than showy. I thought

it perfect. Everyone at this event—leisured, cultured, upper-middle-class ladies all—wore expensive kimono and had their hair done up, as one must in order to accommodate the line of the kimono collar.

Running a little late, I was the last to arrive. I quickly slipped out of my sandals at the entrance to the restaurant. While hurrying down the corridor, I overheard one of the maids say to another as I rushed past, "I didn't know they were calling geisha to this party. . ."

It did not even register until I sat down, and then I suddenly understood that before even noticing I was a foreigner, they had responded to my borrowed kimono and the fact that my hair was up, smooth and plain, rather than short, permed, or gussied up with lacquer hair ornaments. To the fleeting glance, the message was "geisha."

I have always been fascinated

Apprentice Geisha Distributing Talismans at Shrine, Tom Haar, 1993
Maiko have become one of the symbols of Kyoto. They give away sweets for company promotions, do television commercials, and images of them appear in nearly every Japanese tourist brochure. This new *maiko* spends part of her New Year handing out sacred *sakaki* branches at the Yasaka Shrine.

Apprentice Geisha of the Pontochō District by the Kamo River, c. 1925
Maiko had already come to symbolize the romance of Kyoto by the early twentieth century. Today's *maiko* still dress every night in a style of costume that has been worn for at least 150 years. The outdoor balconies overlooking the Kamo River remain popular sites for geisha entertainment during the summer months.

Kimono with Hemp Leaf Pattern, c. 1930

GEISHA: BEYOND THE PAINTED SMILE

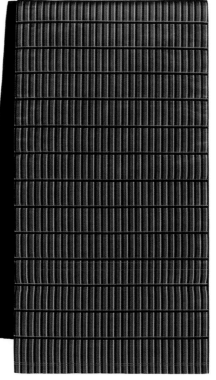

by the power of clothing to communicate subtle messages, but this occasion was extraordinary. I can only think that the fact that I originally learned to wear kimono from geisha, not bourgeois ladies, made a difference to those who recognized the cues.

In discussing the exoticism of the geisha, perhaps it is unfair to draw an absolute line between Westerners and Japanese. Few Westerners will ever be in a position to appreciate the real mystique of a geisha, but neither will most Japanese. Nevertheless, the geisha aesthetic will resonate among the Japanese simply because it so thoroughly reflects Japanese aesthetic values in general, while Westerners, on the whole, will remain fixated on the myth. As far as the geisha themselves are concerned, it's all fine—in the *mizu shōbai*, any publicity is always good.

NOTES:

1. To my chagrin and utterly outside of my control, the Dutch, Spanish, Italian, and Portuguese translations of my book *Geisha* use a variation of this image on their book jackets.

2. See Colta Feller Ives, *The Great Wave: The Influence of Japanese Woodcuts on French Prints* (New York: The Metropolitan Museum of Art, 1974).

3. See a picture and description of the Gankirō teahouse in Julia Meech-Pekarik, *The World of the Meiji Print* (Tokyo and New York: Weatherhill, 1986), pp. 33–35.

4. Rudolph Lindau, *Un voyage autour du Japon* (Paris: Hachette and Cie, 1864). Quoted in ibid., p. 32. Lindau calls the entertainers "geiko."

5. Golden's novel is, of course, fictional, and the story of his fictional heroine Sayuri is dramatic, but by no means impossible. In my view, the accusation brought by ex-geisha Mineko Iwasaki that he based his story on her experience is not plausible.

6. See "Geisha and Kimono" in Liza Dalby, *Kimono Fashioning Culture* (1993 and 2001) for a more detailed discussion.

Liza Dalby, PhD. in anthropology from Stanford University, specializes in Japanese culture and has conducted groundbreaking fieldwork among geisha. Her publications on women and entertainment in Japanese culture include *Ko-uta, "Little Songs" of the Geisha World* (1979), *Geisha* (1983), *Kimono, Fashioning Culture* (1993), and *The Tale of Murasaki* (2000).

Obi with Embroidered Plum Blossom and Chrysanthemum on Chiyogami Paper, c. 1930

Obi with Black, Brown and White Stripe Pattern, c. 1930

Obi with Gold and Silver Plum Blossoms on Black Ground, c. 1930

The four garments featured above and opposite were all owned and worn by the geisha Tsunaji, active in Kanazawa in the 1920s and 1930s. Her kimono and obi demonstrate the variety in fashion of a geisha's wardrobe, displaying classical motifs of a millennium ago; the chic *iki* look of narrow stripes popular in the eighteenth and nineteenth centuries, and innovative adaptations of traditional patterns. Surprisingly few geisha kimono survive. Because they are "work wear," they typically see long use, or are passed down to younger geisha. Because geisha like to stay current with changes in kimono fashion, older kimono that have survived, no matter how expensive they were when new, have often been discarded for ones more in keeping with contemporary fashion.

The Floating World Today

Photographs by Yoko Yamamoto

text by ANDREW L. MASKE

YOKO YAMAMOTO has spent the last twenty years living and working in Kagurazaka, one of the last remaining geisha districts in Tokyo. During that time, she has developed strong bonds of trust with geisha throughout Tokyo, giving her rare, intimate access to many aspects of the life and art of geisha. Moreover, she has been able to experience the unique geisha culture from the inside rather than as an outsider. Her strong empathy with her subjects is readily apparent in her photographic works, a result she attributes to the personal connections she maintains with many of the geisha she photographs. Because of her tremendous respect for their art, she assiduously observes much the same protocol that characterizes relationships within the geisha world. As a result, she herself is held in universal high regard among Tokyo geisha.

After graduating with a degree in archaeology, Yamamoto indulged her long desire to experience world travel in the most rational way possible: she joined an international flight crew for Japan Airlines. In her visits to diverse locales, she found herself framing visual snapshots of scenes that were particularly moving, especially those that involved a human element. This led her to enroll in a night class in modern photography to put her eye for beauty to practical use.

On many of her trips, people asked Yamamoto about her own country and culture. Uncertain of how to answer and embarrassed by her lack of knowledge, she began to ask herself, "What is my identity as a Japanese? What is the base of Japanese culture from which my aesthetic sense has grown?" In her mind she compared the elegant but restrained, plain wooden structure of the Kiyomizu Temple in Kyoto with the elaborately decorated gold and marble of St. Peter's in the Vatican, and concluded that, even if human beings were essentially all the same, their aesthetics differed greatly. She found that she somehow preferred the subtle and less ornate in art, the refined and chic over the rich and gorgeous. Intrigued that she felt that way, she began to look more closely at Japanese tradition.

For the exhibition held at the completion of her photography class, she decided to take some shots in one of Tokyo's geisha districts. Her teacher recommended Kagurazaka because of its proximity to her apartment, and thus began a connection to that area that has lasted more than twenty years. It took more than three years of taking pictures of the area's scenery and environment to earn the trust of the geisha and be allowed in to photograph private settings. As she became personally acquainted with many geisha and observed them up close in a variety of situations, Yamamoto was highly impressed not only by their skill in dance and musical performance, but

First Step Into Kagurazaka, March 1983, Kagurazaka, Yoko Yamamoto, from the series *Diaries of a Kagurazaka Woman*, 1983-2003
In 1983, photographer Yoko Yamamoto entered the geisha area of Kagurazaka for the first time. This image reflects the beauty and transience of the geisha life.

I. Geisha Today

also their etiquette, deportment, and customs. She came to see it as her role to record aspects of the geisha life and convey them to others.

Yamamoto refuses to "set up" or pose her photographs. She follows the rhythm of life of her subjects and takes only those images that present themselves in the course of their activities. At most, she will ask them to stop for a moment while she clicks the shutter. Sometimes she has stood for hours in the cold waiting for a geisha to emerge from a *ryōtei* (formal Japanese restaurant) where she has been entertaining, then dashed full speed to catch another geisha leaving a different party.

By depicting older members of the geisha community as well as those who are young and attractive, Yamamoto hopes to emphasize that the geisha profession is centered not on sex, but on art. How else could a 94-year old woman continue to participate as an active and valued Kagurazaka geisha? Yamamoto finds the idea intriguing that being a geisha is a lifelong commitment to artistic excellence. In some ways it echoes her own unending search for beauty and perfection as she explores the fascinating world of one of Japan's dying traditions.

© yoko yamamoto

A Geisha at Home, December 29, 2000, Yoko Yamamoto

Geisha in the New Millennium, January 11, 2001, Kagurazaka, Yoko Yamamoto

Two faces of Chika, a young geisha of the Kagurazaka area. Despite their mysterious reputation and the fact that they follow a tradition of artistic discipline that has evolved over centuries, geisha today relax in many of the same ways as other Japanese women.

GEISHA: BEYOND THE PAINTED SMILE

© yoko yamamoto

© yoko yamamoto

© yoko yamamoto

Shamisen Teaching, Shamisen Training, July 15, 2001, Kagurazaka, Yoko Yamamoto
An institution among Tokyo geisha, Kagurazaka's oldest member, ninety-one year old
Owaka, drills a younger member of her community (opposite) in singing and *shamisen*
accompaniment during a morning practice session.

© yoko yamamoto

Proper Form, May 1997, Shinbashi, Yoko Yamamoto
Mr. Hanayagi Jūsuke, head of the nation-wide
Hanayagi school of traditional dance, demonstrates
proper form for Shinbashi dancers preparing for an
upcoming stage performance.

Dance Training, May 24, 2000, Kagurazaka, Yoko Yamamoto
Geisha often practice their disciplines on the second floor of the
area's geisha registration office (*kenban*). About half of all top dance
teachers are men. Kabuki actors and geisha are the only performers
for whom dance school heads will lead practice themselves.

YAMAMOTO: THE FLOATING WORLD TODAY

III. Final Touches

Selfless Star, Marichiyo, September 24, 1994, Shinbashi, Yoko Yamamoto
The legendary Marichiyo of Shinbashi checks the coiffure of a fellow geisha prior to the start of her appearance on stage.

Curtain Time, September 10, 1993, Asakusa, Yoko Yamamoto
A geisha's long preparation of makeup, costume, and wig are completed minutes before a performance begins. This geisha from the Asakusa district readies herself for her entrance at Tokyo's National Theater.

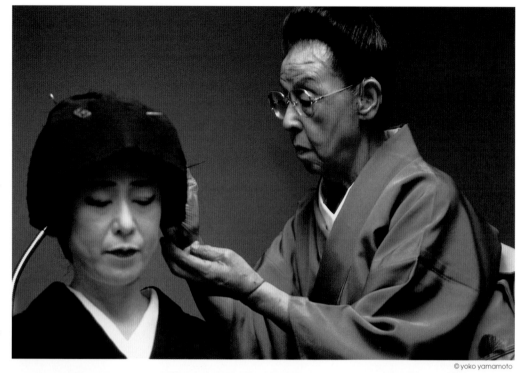

© yoko yamamoto

© yoko yamamoto

Iki **(Chic) Marichiyo, 86, May 31, 1994, Shinbashi,**
Yoko Yamamoto, from the series *Diaries of a Kagurazaka Woman, 1983–2003*
The Shinbashi geisha Marichiyo, arguably the most highly admired geisha dancer of the twentieth century, prepares for her final public performance of the *Azuma odori* performances at age 86. She reflects on a life that saw her rise to become one of the most highly respected Japanese performing artists of all time.

© yoko yamamoto

© yoko yamamoto

Formal Tea, May 31, 2000, Shinbashi, Yoko Yamamoto
Study and practice of the ancient tea ritual known as
chanoyu helps geisha improve concentration, dexterity,
and attention to detail.

© yoko yamamoto

© yoko yamamoto

Dancing Hand #1, December 27, 1997, Kagurazaka, Yoko Yamamoto, from the series *Diaries of a Kagurazaka Woman, 1983–2003*
The large, specially designed dance fan (*maiōgi*) adds color and scale to a geisha's performance. Sometimes closed, sometimes opened, it can be used to represent a wide variety of objects in the course of a dance.

Shamisen (Kanjinchō) **#5, January 14, 1998, Kagurazaka**, Yoko Yamamoto, from the series *Diaries of a Kagurazaka Woman, 1983–2003*
The strings of wound silk sing under the touch of a masterful geisha.

"Little Song" Dance, November 6, 2000, Akasaka, Yoko Yamamoto
Dance moves are sometimes created even for the short, informal ditties
called *kouta* (little songs). This Akasaka geisha demonstrates recherché
dance movements in a *kouta* known as "Hiyoshi."

Egret Maiden, 1992, Kagurazaka, Yoko Yamamoto
The pure femininity of a bride, tinged with the subtle
sensuality of a geisha, is exuded by a Kagurazaka dancer
performing the role *Sagimusume* (The Egret Maiden).

© yoko yamamoto

Geisha *Shōjō*, 1992, Akasaka, Yoko Yamamoto
Georgeous costumes form an important part of the spectacle in geisha stage performances and may even be paid for by the geisha themselves. Four Akasaka geisha are transformed into alluring *shōjō*—red-haired, sake-drinking monsters—in the Tokiwazu piece of the same name.

Amidst the Shadows, February 22,1993, Kagurazaka, Yoko Yamamoto, from the series *Diary of a Kagurazaka Woman, 1983–2003*. A geisha's daily work is entertaining at traditional restaurants. Here, the face of a geisha is subtly outlined through a paper umbrella. Yamamoto intends to express the beauty of the women's world of *In Praise of Shadows* by Junichirō Tanizaki.

© yoko yamamoto

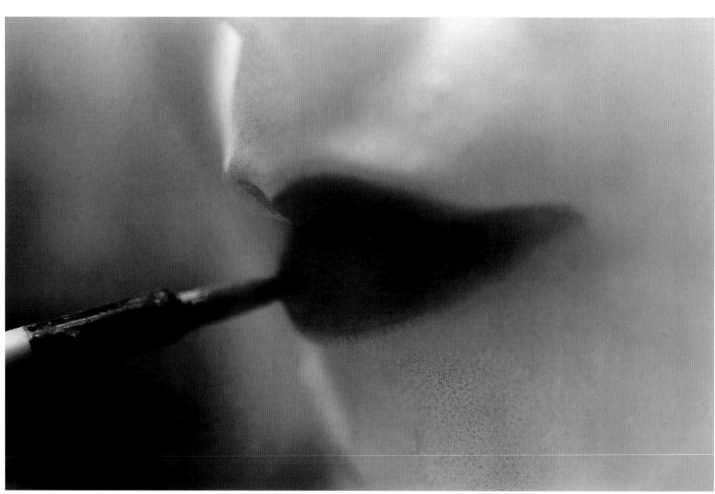

© yoko yamamoto

Rouge, January 8, 1998, Kagurazaka, Yoko Yamamoto, from the series *Diaries of a Kagurazaka Woman, 1983-2003*
The stark white face with blood red lips is an often-used image of sensuality inextricably linked with geisha in foreign countries. By creating her depiction in sepia, Yamamoto has attained a deep level of subtle beauty.

New Year's Gift, January 10, 1996, Kagurazaka, Yoko Yamamoto, from the series *Diaries of a Kagurazaka Woman, 1983–2003*
At the start of each year, Japanese children receive special presents of money from their parents. In the New Year's parties (*ozashiki*), geisha receive similar presents from regular supporters (*hiiki*). The givers of these "tips" are entitled to place them inside the back neck of the recipient's kimono collar. For Japanese, the nape of the neck has long been considered one of the most charming parts of a woman's body.

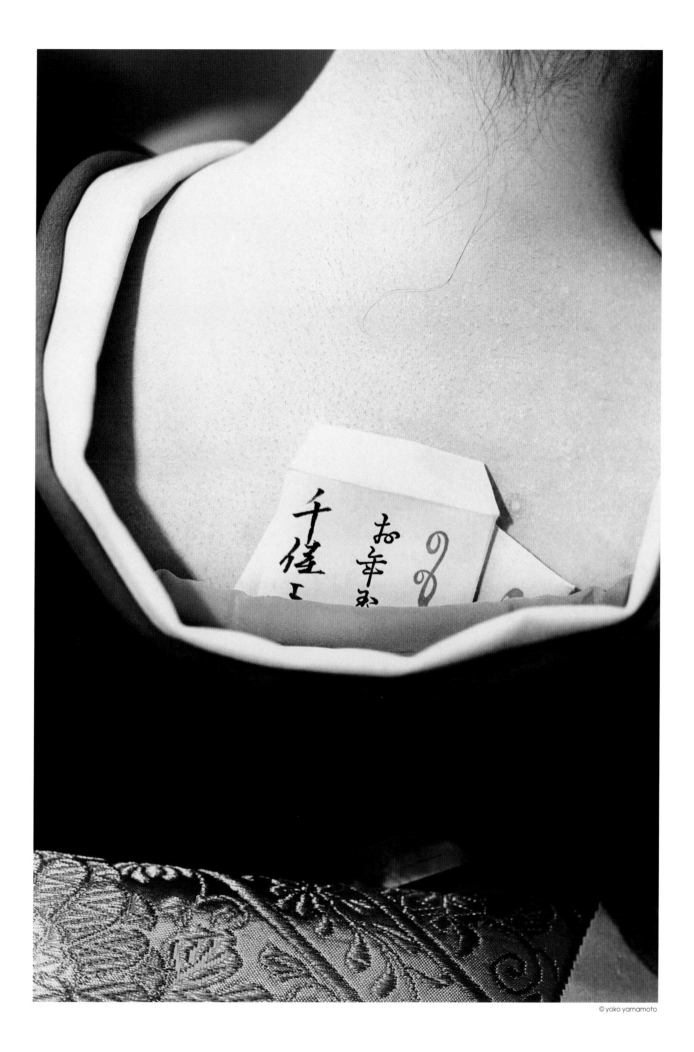

© yoko yamamoto

VI. The Perfect Moment

© yoko yamamoto

New Year's Party at Kanetanaka, January 18, 1997, Shinbashi, Yoko Yamamoto
Each New Year, geisha don their most formal kimono, called *denoishō* (going-out
costume), and perform for their most important supporters. The Kanetanaka *ryōtei*
(traditional restaurant) in Shinbashi features a stage on which geisha regularly
perform. The *fusuma* (sliding panels) surrounding the stage bear a depiction of
Mount Fuji by Yokoyama Taikan (1868–1958), the twentieth century's most highly
regarded artist of *Nihonga* (Japanese-style) painting.

© yoko yamamoto

Tossing Fans, April 12, 2003, Asakusa, Yoko Yamamoto

The game called *Tosenkyō* (tossing fans) developed more than 150 years ago in central Japan and quickly became a popular amusement at drinking parties attended by geisha, gaining particular prominence in the Asakusa area of Tokyo. The basic objective is to throw a fan so that it knocks over a "butterfly" perched on a wooden stand. Additional points are awarded based on the manner in which the fan falls. Great emphasis is placed upon fine form and adherence to protocol. This Asakusa geisha displays her skill during a tournament at the temple Denpō-in in April 2003.

© yoko yamamoto

Praying to *Bishamon* God, November 7, 1990, Kagurazaka, Yoko Yamamoto, from the
series *Diaries of a Kagurazaka Woman, 1983-2003*
All the active Kagurazaka geisha pray in a symbolic scene described in the *nagauta* song
"Kagurazaka odori," written by the famous writer Izumi Kyōka in the early twentieth century.
Kyōka married the Kagurazaka geisha Momotarō. Geisha are very devoted to their local
deities, whom they acknowledge as both protectors and bringers of good fortune.

© yoko yamamoto

At Sunset, 1987, Kagurazaka, Yoko Yamamoto
With fewer than one thousand still active, geisha are increasingly an anomaly in Japanese society, even as they continue to
symbolize Japan for much of the rest of the world.

Performance and Play

The Art and Accomplishments of Geisha

A<small>NDREW</small> L. M<small>ASKE</small>

OPPOSITE

New Year's Dancer, Mihata Jōryū, calligraphy by Sōkyū Dōjin, c. 1830-50 The dance fan, the girlish hairstyle, and the long, flowing kimono sleeves with an obi elaborately tied in back identify this figure as a *maiko*, an apprentice geisha dancer of Kyoto. Traditionally, dancers began training as early as age six. Today, they rarely start before their teens.

S<small>ITTING CROSS-LEGGED ON RED SILK-COVERED CUSHIONS,</small> two men wait expectantly. They are dressed in expensive European suits, but their attire cannot compare with the mellow elegance of the teahouse in which they have been drinking and conversing for the past hour. Suddenly, the sliding *fusuma* doors to the right whisk open, and two young women in kimono swiftly enter. They take their position and bow in front of a pair of glowing gold screens about fifteen feet away. One of the geisha is dressed in a striking kimono of sky blue decorated with a design of Japanese iris and flowing water. The other, slightly older, wears a sea-green robe displaying a mountain landscape in early summer. The hair of both women is jet black and pulled up, sleek and smooth.

Shan! A quick flick of the wrist and the tip of the ivory plectrum strikes the yellow silk strings of the *shamisen*, held by a small woman in her late sixties seated inconspicuously at the left. Her kimono is conservatively patterned in ash and brown and her hair is graying, but her back is straight, her mouth firm. Under her touch, the three strings of her instrument reverberate with the strains of a melody created before she was born, and her singing gives voice to melancholy lyrics in language long since out of common use. She is a master performer.

The two dancers stir, compelled by the music. Their movements flow from one position to another, always in perfect harmony, as they execute each gesture with effortless style and grace. Their faces are such masks of concentration, it is difficult to believe that a mere minute ago they were joking and sharing drinks with the men. But now they are one with the ancient song and with each other, dancing in the rhythm of their elder geisha sisters.

In a moment the music will end and all will return to the table for more drinking and laughter. That, too, is part of a geisha's work. The guests, shaken from their reverie by the necessity for applause at the end of the performance, will once more become the focus of attention. The conversation will move to the amusing, if somewhat mundane anecdotes of contemporary life. After all, these are people of the twenty-first century. For a few moments, though, the scene here echoes others played out in this same teahouse room one hundred years ago or more.

Three Young Geisha with Musical Instruments, 1880s These three teenage apprentices, called *akaeri* or "red collars" in the Tokyo area, pose with the three instruments most commonly played by geisha: (left to right) the *taiko* drum, the *tsuzumi* hand drum, and the *shamisen*.

Strolling Along the Riverbank,
Katsukawa Shunchō, calligraphy by
Rankō, early 1780s
This painting of a geisha and her *hakoya*
attendant reveals the artist's skill in
depicting the elegant dress of the geisha
as blown by the riverbank breeze.
Because the attendant carries a bundle
rather than a *shamisen* box, the geisha
depicted is likely a dancer.

The people gathered here, geisha as well as guests, are in pursuit of an ideal—Japan's romantic past, its beauty, and its art. The capture of that ideal is, for the guests, worth any amount of money to experience and, for the geisha, worth a lifetime's effort to achieve.

Art and Nothing but Art

It is ironic that two centuries ago, long before geisha became cultural icons and guardians of traditional performing arts, they were only supporting players in Japan's entertainment areas. In the licensed brothel district known as Yoshiwara in Edo (Tokyo), the *oiran* (elite courtesans) were the stars of the show, with a cast of younger courtesans to back them. Geisha served simply to contribute musical diversion and variety for an evening spent admiring the charms of the gorgeously dressed *oiran*. Originally, younger courtesans and even old men played the music to which customers danced in drunken revelry or sang in rousing choruses. Around 1750, however, a new group of women appeared who possessed much greater mastery of the three-stringed instrument of choice, the *shamisen*, and were often proficient in dance as well. Brought to the brothel areas for the express purpose of providing musical performance and accompaniment, these *gei-sha* (art-persons) dressed simply, if not plainly. Eventually stringent restrictions were instituted to forestall the possibility of overly intimate contact with customers. In other words, the first geisha played a role that was somewhere between a jukebox and a karaoke set, and were supposed to be no sexier than either.[1]

In short, geisha were not supposed to compete with or distract from the elite courtesans. These much sought-after women vied with each other not only in physical beauty and gorgeous apparel, but in such accomplishments as refined speech, regal bearing, a fine calligraphic hand and poetry.[2] Whereas geisha honed their musical skills to raise the level of their performance, the elite courtesans developed their artistic accomplishments for the sake of their personae. This difference may have been what led to the decline of the *oiran* and to the rise of the geisha in the late eighteenth century. Geisha projected an image of being practical and in touch with popular culture, while the top courtesans increasingly found themselves treated as old-fashioned. The behavior of an elite courtesan sometimes resembled that of a queen: haughty and aloof, she required suitors to follow elaborate ceremony and court her with expensive presents. In contrast, geisha were much more convivial and forthright with their guests.

It was not only their abilities as professional musicians and dancers that made geisha sought-after participants in pleasure-quarter parties. Because only courtesans were allowed to provide sexual services, geisha developed other ways to attract the patronage of potential customers by providing services that courtesans did not. They made it their role to fill customers' sake cups if a serving girl was inattentive and to stave off a customer's boredom while waiting for a tardy courtesan to arrive. The simple, restrained dress of geisha became fashionably chic, and from the 1780s on, depictions of geisha multiplied in such artworks as woodblock prints and paintings. During this time geisha unified their dress, makeup and hairstyle, creating by 1800 the classic look that continues to be associated with geisha today.

Geisha Go Solo

Geisha began to be distanced from the activities of the courtesans in the second half of the nineteenth century. At that time, Japanese authorities, intent on modernizing their country and concerned that legalized prostitution made Japan look immoral to western powers, encouraged the growth of establishments in which drinking and entertainment could be enjoyed separately from prostitution. The two primary types of such establishments to survive into the twenty-first century are *o-chaya* (literally, "teahouses") and *ryōtei* (elite restaurants). The main difference between the two is that while *ryōtei* maintain a fully staffed kitchen on the premises,

Entertainments at Shinagawa, late 1740s

This unsigned print is among the earliest known depictions of a geisha. With her rather dowdy hairstyle and outfit, the youngish woman at the right has just arrived, bearing her *shamisen* and ready to accompany a dancing girl, who looks back at her. One male client stands, while another sits with a courtesan, left.

o-chaya do not. (Despite the name, the *o-chaya* teahouse serves alcohol rather than tea; the term seems to have derived from the Edo-period *machiai chaya* [waiting-teahouses] of pleasure districts such as Yoshiwara, where small, impromptu meetings or gatherings could be arranged.) As the premier entertainment at such venues, geisha soon rose to the most prominent position in the pleasure quarters, while the *oiran* and *tayū* increasingly came to be seen as tawdry relics of the Old Japan. The brothels continued to operate until their abolition in 1958, but their connection to the activities of geisha became more tenuous as the years passed.

That geisha are expected to be beautiful and chic goes without saying, but there are other attributes for which they are even more highly admired. These include sophistication, wit, humor, dedication, faithfulness, sincerity, and attention to etiquette. Some of these qualities are shared by ordinary Japanese women; others are traits associated with respected Japanese men. The ideal geisha character exhibits a unique combination of resilience and softness, strength and vulnerability. These attributes are expressed through the highly developed skills that are central to their work as performers and entertainers—the arts of the geisha.

Artistic Accomplishments

Past and Present

In general, geisha have always specialized in one of two formal artistic disciplines: dance and musical performance. Dancers were first called *odoriko* or "dancing girls," but today are known as *tachikata*, or "standing ones." Those who kneel on the floor while performing, players of the *shamisen* (a three-stringed, banjo-like instrument) and singers are known as *jikata* or "ones on the ground." Geisha derive their identity as artists from the extent to which they have successfully developed their talents as either *tachikata* or *jikata*. In some communities, younger geisha tend

ABOVE LEFT

The Kanazawa Geisha Tsunaji and Her Teacher, Kineya Gosō, c. 1928

Older geisha often teach the formal arts to younger members of their district, but professional teachers also provide specialized instruction in their respective disciplines. The Kineya school is a major source of instruction in the singing and playing of *nagauta*, one of the primary music genres of the Kabuki stage.

ABOVE RIGHT

A Kanazawa Geisha Performing at a Teahouse, 1930s

Geisha sometimes dance excerpts from Kabuki plays that require minimal props, even when not danced in full costume. The simple straw hat held by the geisha indicates she is likely dancing the role of the Wisteria Maiden (*Fujimusume*), not on stage, but for a party held in a teahouse.

Child in Dance Performance, Kanazawa, 1920s

Girls born out of wedlock to geisha often started training in the geisha arts, so they would be able to support themselves when they reached maturity. Formal training commonly began on the sixth day of the sixth month of a child's sixth year, considered an auspicious day for such an undertaking.

to be dancers, and train to be *jikata* later in their careers, when their beauty has begun to fade. Long training is especially necessary for *shamisen* players and singers, since they must master a wide repertory of songs to provide music for dancers and to accompany guests who want to sing. As the number of customers who can sing traditional songs decreases in the contemporary geisha world, however, the demand for older *jikata* who have a large repertoire is rapidly declining.

During the eighteenth and nineteenth centuries, a variety of styles and schools of both dance and music developed. At the same time, oversight of geisha was instituted with the creation of *kenban*, registration offices controlled geisha who entertained within a particular district.[3] The office tracked the geisha's appointments and sought to uphold artistic and behavioral standards. Geisha areas quickly developed a strong sense of community, with the result that each embraced some styles of dance and music to the exclusion of others, distinctions that continue today in most traditional geisha areas. Differences in performance styles, customs, and even dialect are among the aspects that lend a unique character to each geisha group—distinctions that are relished by connoisseurs of geisha entertainment. For example, in Kyoto geisha are known as *"geiko"* and speak a dialect that is soft and feminine, an attribute that adds to their reputation for elegance and understatement. Tokyo geisha, on the other hand, are admired for their high-spirited, even saucy character, as well as their worldliness and sophistication. The Japanese author Akiyama Aisaburō, in his 1937 book *Geisha Girl*, contrasted at length the characteristics of geisha from Japan's three major cities, Tokyo, Kyoto, and Osaka. Although obviously blanket characterizations, his descriptions of geisha from each area reflect widely held opinions at that time: "Tokyo Geisha-girls are progressive and extravagant . . . [but] Kyoto Geisha-girls are very quiet and conservative." Furthermore, he described Osaka geisha as "clever and quick witted."[4]

Today, most Europeans and Americans recognize the legitimacy of diverse cultural

ABOVE LEFT

A Dancing Girl Performing "The Egret Maiden" for a Young Lord, Suzuki Harunobu, 1760s

Dancing girls (*odoriko*) were the predecessors of geisha. Early eighteenth-century documents record that these dancers were sometimes invited to perform for domain lords (daimyo). "The Egret Maiden" (*Sagimusume*) is a dance that is still performed (see photo p. 93).

ABOVE RIGHT

Dancer, late 17ᵗʰ century

Many depictions of dancing women survive from the late seventeenth century. These paintings, referred to as "Kanbun era beauties" (*Kanbun bijin*), often show women in colorful kimono dancing before a plain background. The women portrayed in this type of painting may be early examples of the entertainers known as *odoriko*.

manifestations and are generally willing to engage with new and unfamiliar forms of artistic performance from other cultures. However, many western visitors to Japan who encountered geisha in the late nineteenth and early twentieth centuries had a more difficult time comprehending the aesthetic qualities of traditional Japanese music and dance, even those initially favorably disposed to embrace them:

> After we had spilled a sufficiency of assorted food-stuffs over our clothes with the aid of the elusive chop-sticks, the fascinating Geisha, eight in number, began their world-renowned performance. Four unhappy, elderly spinsters twanged the more or less gay guitar of the country, with the same effect upon themselves, apparently, that such music might have produced upon a self-respecting dog, for it moved them to lift up their voices in the most melancholy dissonance.
>
> While these four distressful virgins shrilly moaned their woes, the other four, mere children, attired in bright dresses, postured and twisted with the haughty affectation of the British chorus girl.
>
> Alas, there perished my most cherished illusion![5]

While contemporary western neophytes of geisha entertainment are rarely as shocked and disappointed as their predecessors of a hundred years ago, challenges to true enjoyment of geisha performance remain. Perhaps for this reason, few of the several English-language documentary videos on geisha in recent years have dedicated any significant amount of screen time to the performing arts of geisha, focusing instead on the geisha's singular appearance and esoteric lifestyle.

The Drama of Dance

Although Kabuki theater is admired for its spectacle and Nō drama for its solemn mystery, pure dance derived from these forms, performed without special costume or scenery, requires a special sensitivity to appreciate it. The German doctor Siebold, physician to the Dutch trade mission at Nagasaki, saw such dance in the early nineteenth century and observed, "While the [Japanese] men look on in rapturous admiration . . . the utmost praise their Dutch visiters [*sic*] seem able to bestow . . . is that it is perfectly free from the licentious movements of the professional dancing girls of the East."[6]

The dances of geisha are derived from the major types of traditional *shamisen* music, the same types featured in Nō and Kabuki. The four or five main schools of

Three Geisha Dancers, Yokohama, c. 1885
The Boston doctor Charles G. Weld visited Japan in 1885,
and hired geisha to pose for many photographs. Unusual for
the time, Weld noted the names of the geisha he enlisted.
Those shown here are, left to right, Koto, Suzukichi, and Sada.

traditional dance have their own movements to the old songs that vary to a small degree in style and preference. Each geisha area in Japan follows the same one or two schools from generation to generation. Nearly all the songs and the dances based on them derive from literature and legend dating from the eighteenth century and earlier, though the dances themselves continue to evolve, sometimes with the incorporation of contemporary elements.

Japanese dance is confined by the strictures of the kimono itself. The robe, with its long, drape-like sleeves and thickly-layered obi sash, does not lend itself at all to acrobatic moves or extreme extension of the limbs. In this sense, it is the opposite of ballet. Japanese dance requires considerable strength of the thighs, buttocks and waist, since many of the maneuvers are executed with the knees slightly bent. Because it does not require extreme, awkward or sudden movements, nor places

intense or unnatural stress on muscles, tendons, and joints, the incidence of injury or chronic conditions related to its practice are extremely rare. On the contrary, Japanese dance seems to have a beneficial effect on the physical condition of its long-term practitioners, as demonstrated by a former head of the Inoue dance school, Yachiyo III, who was able to perform publicly on her 100th birthday. Her successor, Yachiyo IV, was still able to dance at age 95.[7] Geisha and *maiko* of Kyoto's Gion district all train in dance under the tutelage of the Inoue school.

Works of traditional Japanese dance commonly exhibit a succession of tiny vignettes that amplify the lyrics of the accompanying song. Fluid and expressive in nature, the beauty of its lyricism compensates for the lack of rhythmical movement to a steady beat that is so common in the dance music of other cultures. In the course of a performance a dancer may utilize a folding fan to represent waves, a falling leaf, and a sake cup, all

Dance Fan

Fans for Japanese dance typically have ten ribs joining thick, brightly painted or printed paper. This twentieth-century example incorporates gold leaf as well. Because they are sometimes thrown and caught in performance, many dance fans have a lead weight added for stability at the point where the ribs intersect.

Shamisen for *Nagauta* Performance, c. 1900–1950

Shamisen vary according to the type of music for which they are made. This example was used by a geisha from the Kazuemachi district of Kanazawa.

Obi of Nagoya Type Embroidered with Cherry Blossoms, Drums and Cock, c. 1930

Geisha played an important role in the development of the Nagoya-type obi in the early twentieth century. It is narrower on one end, making it easier to put on and less bulky to wear. Originally designed for informal dress, by the 1930s the style was sometimes used for formal sashes as well.

© yoko yamamoto

**Shadow *Shamisen*, September 22, 1992
(Kagurazaka)**
© Yoko Yamamoto

so subtle and fleeting that they are more impressionistic than explicit. She also uses only her body to express a sense of deep emotional involvement. Dance may also be a pantomime of a story, particularly when two dancers perform together. Geisha, like Kabuki actors, dance roles of either sex, and when such dances are presented in formal stage performances, they often appear in full costume. While strong facial expressions such as smiles are considered out of place, especially in the highly formal Inoue school tradition followed by the geisha of Gion in Kyoto, disposition of the head and movement of the eyes are used to convey both a sense of narrative action and emotion.

The dance styles followed by geisha differ considerably in approach from those of western or other forms of dance, and exist in a cultural context that is unfamiliar even to many Japanese today. Nevertheless, the beauty of the movements, matched admirably to the characteristics of the dramatically evocative kimono, make the dances of geisha easily appreciated by people of virtually any culture. A deeper understanding of the background of the dances, the meanings of the movements and their broader cultural milieu, however, can only increase a contemporary viewer's appreciation.

Living on Three Strings and a Song

The *shamisen* has been intimately associated with geisha since the beginnings of the profession and has been a symbol of geisha for centuries.[8] The relationship of geisha with their instruments is such that they frequently refer to them by the honorific, yet affectionate nickname "*o-shami.*" The *shamisen* arrived in Japan from China, via Okinawa, at the end of the sixteenth century. Originally covered in snake skin, in the seventeenth century the drum of the instrument began to be covered in cat skin, a material that continues to be used for all performance *shamisen* today. The wood may be ebony, rosewood, or Chinese quince. *Shamisen* types commonly used by geisha include those for the music style known as *nagauta* (long song) that feature ivory tuning pegs (p. 109), while those used for the rather similar Kiyomoto style have pegs of hardwood. The three strings are of wound silk, and are raised from the neck of the instrument by a removable bridge usually made of horn, ivory or whalebone. In playing, the strings are plucked with a large, handheld plectrum called a *bachi*, made of ivory, horn, or wood, and sometimes incorporating tortoiseshell at the tips that strike the strings.

The scale used in traditional *shamisen* music contains only minor thirds and sixths, giving the music its particular "melancholy" flavor. The only chords are created by occasional intervals of a fourth or fifth between two strings plucked together. Techniques such as slides and finger plucks add variety to a musical presentation that may feature dramatic changes in tempo, and, more rarely, in volume. The muted, poignant sounds a single *shamisen* produces are the result of the combination of silk strings and the removable bridge that is in direct contact with the skin covering the body of the instrument.

When presented on stage with multiple instruments, *shamisen* music usually involves one or two lines of melody. Lyrical sections are often played by a single instrument, while grandiose or narrative portions may feature a number of *shamisen* playing in unison. To build excitement, the players split into two parts, one playing the primary melody line, the other a complementary melody. The two parts may interweave with or echo one another, at last merging into unison to create the climax of the song. The accompaniment is punctuated by complicated percussion rhythms on drums of varying pitches and timbres. At times during a piece, a high, piercing flute joins the ensemble, adding tension and drama.

Traditional Japanese singing is approached in a completely different way than singing in the West. Whereas classical European singers are encouraged to open their throats to create a full and round sound, Japanese singing requires a constricted throat. Men and women sing in essentially the same register, which makes sense considering there are no "parts" divided by high or low voices. However, they rarely perform together, since there are small differences in vocal quality and style that are considered incompatible. Moreover, in Kabuki, the musicians and singers, as well as the actors, have traditionally been all men, while in geisha stage performances all are women. These distinctions have been in place for hundreds of years, and the mixing of the sexes in performance, while not completely unknown, remains relatively rare.

Combined, traditional *shamisen* music and singing create a unique musical experience, one full of the flavor of the Edo-period entertainment quarters. Over time, listeners learn to distinguish differences in narrative, dramatic and lyrical passages, and to appreciate the variety of tension and repose created by volume, pace, and the number and type of instruments used in a particular section. Lyrical sections have almost no background beat, allowing a singer considerable freedom in interpretation, the accompaniment designed to intrude only at certain junctures in the sung passages. The singers, who at first sound all the same, become distinguishable by their vocal tone, flexibility, and a quality known as *aji* (character), a distinctive mellowness of the voice that generally develops only with age and experience. Whether as part of a group on stage at a public performance, or as a single accompanist at an *ozashiki* party, the skills of a *jikata* geisha reflect a tremendous amount of effort expended toward attaining complete mastery of

Geisha Musicians Performing on a River Pleasure Boat, Eishōsai Chōki, 1790s
This view, one panel of a wood-panel pentatych, offers a rare, early close-up of an ensemble of geisha musicians in performance. Pleasure boats on the Sumida River offered patrons an enjoyable escape from the summer heat.

one of the most important areas of traditional music.

Although geisha all have one primary area of artistic concentration, they also have training in the geisha arts in which they do not specialize. Thus, dancers also study *shamisen*, singing, and percussion, while instrumentalists also train in dance. In geisha areas such as those of Kanazawa, younger geisha concentrate on dance, gradually shifting to *shamisen* as they acquire a more complete knowledge of the wide musical repertoire. Some geisha become most skilled in such "minor" instruments as the shrill, flute-like *fue* or the *tsuzumi* or *ōkawa* hand drums.

Young Geisha Playing Hand Drum, attributed to Ogawa Kazumasa, c. 1895
In addition to the *tsuzumi* on the young geisha's shoulder, this photograph shows two other types of drums played by geisha. Under her sleeve is an *ōkawa*, struck with an implement worn on the right hand to make a sharp click. The *taiko* on its stand is played with two wooden sticks.

ABOVE LEFT
Geisha and Child Dancer Entertaining the Daughter of a Lord, from the album *Twenty-four Scenes of Women*, Utagawa Toyokuni, 1816

The daughter of a daimyo has summoned a child dancer and her geisha accompanist to perform at her mansion. Surrounded by fine lacquerwares and other artworks, she comments on the dance to her lady-in-waiting, who wears a light blue kimono with fine stripes.

ABOVE RIGHT
Early Morning Lesson, from the album *Twenty-four Scenes of Women*, Utagawa Toyokuni, 1816

A stylishly dressed geisha has her hair done by a maid as she teaches *shamisen* fingerings to a shy, chubby trainee in a pink kimono. As in geisha districts today, trainees took their lessons first each morning.

Kanazawa Geisha Drums: *Taiko* and *Zashikidaiko*, 20th century

A special feature of geisha entertainment in the city of Kanazawa is the lively *zashikidaiko* performance, in which one or two geisha play two types of drums together. The rhythmical rumbling of the drums creates an exciting experience for guests, who are often invited to join in the drumming.

Taking the Stage

Although a geisha's artistic accomplishments are sometimes featured at the evening engagements during which they entertain a small group of customers, they are more prominently showcased at periodic stage performances and other public events. The performances are important to geisha because they provide opportunities to present polished, large-scale presentations in which their special skills can be highlighted, not only for the wider public but for other geisha and for performers such as the actors and musicians of the Kabuki theater who share their artistic repertoire. These public performances, Gion's "Dances of the Old Capital" (*Miyako odori*) in Kyoto, Shinbashi's "Dances of the East (*Azuma odori*) in Tokyo, and others, began in the 1870s and continue the tradition of the *niwaka* street festivals of the pleasure quarters during the eighteenth and nineteenth centuries in which geisha played a prominent part (see Hickman essay).[9]

Entertaining As an Art

Personal Preparations

For any particular engagement, a geisha's preparation for the evening begins at home. Whether she lives in an old-style geisha area where the houses of geisha are clustered together, or by herself in a metropolitan apartment, a geisha begins to assume her work persona before she exits her front door. The white face, elaborate hairstyle, beautiful trailing kimono and gorgeous sash are part and parcel of the geisha image (see Maske, pp. 37–42), but the care with which a geisha treats her appearance goes far beyond the details of that formal outfit. As a professional entertainer, a geisha realizes that the visual impression she makes, whether dressed in the full traditional costume or not, is almost as important to her success as her abilities as a formally trained performer. Geisha often refer to

those of their number who are endowed with physical beauty as being "one step ahead," but they also acknowledge that attractiveness goes far beyond physical attributes. Although not every geisha is beautiful, every geisha worth the name will devote the utmost attention to her makeup, hair, kimono, and accessories. To fail to do so would be an affront to her clients and a shame to herself.

Since she will always practice and work in some form of traditional robe, a geisha must be able to dress herself in kimono quickly and tastefully, something to which Japanese young women today are generally unaccustomed. Putting on a kimono by oneself is a skill; putting it on and wearing it in a manner that exudes a combination of sensuality and high taste is an art. As their experience grows, most geisha acquire a passion for fine kimono and accessories.[10] Although the white makeup known as *oshiroi*, literally "honorable white," the elaborate traditional hairstyle, and the long, trailing kimono are no longer worn by most geisha on a regular basis, the same attention goes into their less elaborate daily toilette. Like fashion models and actresses, geisha are careful that their western-style makeup is flawlessly elegant and that their hair, worn in a simple but chic rolled style, is perfect. Geisha may be taught special beauty or fashion "tricks" by their elders, but learn mostly through careful observation and imitation of more experienced geisha. Examples of the more surprising beauty secrets include the use of a facial whitening cream that incorporates elements derived from the droppings of the bush warbler (*uguisu*),[11] and the regular shaving of the entire face.[12] Whatever the particular techniques used, each geisha pays special attention to the most minute details of her dress, makeup and hair each time she appears or entertains; her professional reputation and that of her district are at stake.

The *Ozashiki*

Geisha take great pride in their artistic accomplishments, but the heart of their day-to-day professional work is the evening entertainment they perform at engagements that they call *ozashiki*.[13] An *ozashiki* usually takes place in a teahouse or a formal restaurant, but may be held at other venues as well. It differs from a cocktail party or other gatherings in the west, because the focus tends to be on the group as a whole, rather than on conversations between individuals. For this reason, the guests usually sit on cushions around a large, low, rectangular or round table, and avoid wandering around or engaging in private conversations that exclude others in the group. A typical geisha spends the vast majority of her work hours attending

ABOVE LEFT
Examining New Hair Ornaments, from the album *Twenty-four Scenes of Women*, Utagawa Toyokuni, 1816
The enthusiasm of the women for tortoise-shell hair ornaments is reflected in the increased numbers of such ornaments used in coiffures during the first half of the nineteenth century. All of the women shown here have shaved eyebrows, indicating they are married women with children, not geisha.

ABOVE RIGHT
Choosing Kimono Cloth, from the album *Twenty-four Scenes of Women*, Utagawa Toyokuni, 1816
The women in this prosperous brothel are selecting bolts of kimono cloth for the coming spring. The young woman in the striped kimono beckons the courtesan in the red and white robe to look at one sample as the manager, herself a courtesan, cleans her long pipe.

Parody of Ōishi Kuranosuke Feigning Debauchery at the Ichiriki, Hosoda Eishi, late 1790s

A drunken samurai with a fan tied to his head attempts to retrieve his medicine case through the game "Konkonchiki." This print triptych has been interpreted as a parody of the drama *Chūshingura*, in which the leader of forty-seven masterless samurai feigns debauchery while plotting to avenge his lord.

ozashiki, so she does well to hone a variety of less formal but important skills that enhance her ability to entertain. These skills are mostly attained through observation and participation in entertaining guests. In fact, like acolytes in other traditional Japanese professions, geisha trainees go through a period of preparation called *minarai,* literally "learning through observation." Nonetheless, it takes years before a geisha can approach each *ozashiki* with full confidence.

Cutting a Fine Figure

Incorporating posture, behavior, and body language, the deportment (*taido*) of geisha is inextricably linked to both costume and custom. Adjusting their body movements to move smoothly and elegantly in kimono is one of the first challenges for young women entering geisha training.[14] Wearing a kimono requires a different way of walking, sitting, and reaching. Dependent on the familiarity of the wearer, movement in a kimono can look breathtakingly refined or laughably awkward. Study of Japanese dance develops muscular control and elegance of gesture, while practice of tea ceremony (*chanoyu*) teaches economy of movement and concentration. Through such discipline, geisha develop a way of moving in kimono that sets them apart from others, even those who wear kimono every day.

People within the geisha world are especially sensitive to formality and protocol, and this is reflected in the body language exhibited by geisha. Their attitude in a formal setting differs markedly from that at an *ozashiki.* Geisha are required to take part in numerous formal events throughout the year, and must be aware of how to conduct themselves on such occasions. They also must be unfailingly polite to their elders in the profession, and to greet those elders whenever the opportunity presents itself. On the other hand, a party setting gives geisha the opportunity to relax, especially if they are with guests they know well. Nevertheless, geisha inwardly remain very alert on all occasions when they are in geisha "mode," whether performing, entertaining, or appearing in public.

Geisha pay the highest level of attention to the needs of their guests. If a sake bottle is emptied, a geisha must not be too engrossed in conversation to notice it and to see that it is refilled immediately. A match is usually lit for a customer before the cigarette is even out of the pack. Geisha must also be prepared for the unpleasant or unexpected. If a customer becomes drunk and passes out, as sometimes happens, geisha see the man awakened, helped into his shoes and a taxi, even accompanying him to his waiting wife, if necessary. An English visitor at the end of the nineteenth century experienced the dedication, concern, and resourcefulness typical of experienced geisha. He was preparing to photograph a group of geisha for a book he was writing when his flash exploded unexpectedly, burning most of the skin off his hand:

> Immediately there was a most perfect geisha performance. They flew to hold me up; to restore me, to heal my hand—anything to show their sympathy.... The geisha covered up the hand with a paste of flour and oil, and tied it up with portions of their attire.[15]

Geisha today are expected to have the same attitude of concern and selfless devotion to the well-being of the clients under their care as did the Kyoto geisha of the mid-nineteenth century who harbored advocates of the imperial cause at the risk of their lives. Although they rarely need to tear up their kimono to bandage an injured customer, the ability to react creatively to situations that present themselves is one of the ways in which geisha distinguish themselves in the eyes of those whom they entertain.

The Art of Banter

The most basic and useful skill a geisha has in her repertoire is the art of conversation. Indeed, many contemporary *ozashiki* consist of talk and nothing else. Since she is paid to entertain, a geisha needs to be sure that whatever she says will help her customers to have a good time. At the same time, her banter must have spontaneity and interest, so that it does not appear to be mere sycophancy. In general, conversation at *ozashiki* seems to be an act of balancing the mood of the occasion, the needs of the guests, and the personalities of the geisha who are attending. Some guests are known as great jokesters, as are some geisha. Others may be exceedingly sober or quiet. Because all customers gain entry to private geisha entertainment through direct introduction, a geisha usually can count on knowing at least one customer at every *ozashiki* she attends. First-time customers always have someone knowledgeable there to guide them, and so a basic level of social comfort at every gathering is assured. In a society that is founded in large part on interpersonal relations and hierarchy based on age and position, Japanese have an aversion to placing themselves in situations of close contact in which they know nothing about the background of others involved. This is increasingly true at higher social levels. Among the clients of geisha are elite members of Japanese society, who require special assurance that there will be no gaps in discretion when they attend *ozashiki*. Geisha are very sensitive to this and adjust their conversation and behavior appropriately. In fact, to prevent undue familiarity between individual guests and geisha, the several geisha will usually change places over the course of a two-hour gathering. In larger *ozashiki*, five, six, or even more geisha may make this change on a pre-arranged signal, creating an effect of beautifully kimono-clad women rising at once and shifting one position to the right or left that can look something like a dance in itself.

Of course consumption of alcohol is part of virtually every *ozashiki*, and it

Summer Entertainments at the Shikian Restaurant, Kubo Shunman, early 1790s
The Shikian was a well-known Edo restaurant that offered music and the company of geisha as well as food and drink. Here, a party is winding down as a customer plays a pantomime game with one geisha while two other geisha put away their musical instruments in preparation to leave.

adds considerably to the ease with which the occasion proceeds. A major role of geisha is to pour sake or beer for customers. This act, which in the west is left to bartenders and waitresses, is in Japan an intimate ritual of interaction between the pourer and the recipient. The geisha proffers the sake flask or beer bottle toward the guest, who usually drains the remaining contents of his small beer glass or tiny sake cup and holds it out as a courtesy. These actions are typically accompanied by appropriate expressions of welcome from the geisha and appreciation from the guest. As elsewhere in East Asia, the offering of alcohol is inextricably linked with hospitality, relaxation, and celebration, all of which may be part of an *ozashiki*. As a measure of respect and reciprocity, a guest also pours for a geisha who has poured for him. Because geisha are not guests, but are providing entertainment, cups are not provided for them, so a guest offers his own cup. Although sometimes rinsing bowls (*haisen*) are provided at the table, a geisha may accept the cup without allowing the customer to rinse or wipe it, thereby adding a further level of familiarity. As with all interaction at *ozashiki*, the objective is to make the guest feel special, and it may be that rinsing bowls are in place to give geisha the opportunity *not* to use them. That could explain why rinsing bowls continue to appear at geisha entertainment when their use has long since ceased elsewhere.

Cooling Off At Nakasu, from the series *Selection of Current-Day Beauties from the Pleasure Quarters*, Torii Kiyonaga, 1780s

Following large fires in the Yoshiwara pleasure quarters, the brothels were temporarily relocated to the area of Nakasu, near the Sumida River. Here, two geisha chat as one restrings her *shamisen*, while a customer with a pipe listens in on their conversation.

Work As Play

To further enliven a party's proceedings, one or more games may be proposed in the course of an evening. Such diversions can be as simple as the hand signal game Paper, Rock, Scissors, in which the loser must down a cup of sake or glass of beer, or as complex as a choreographed musical pantomime in which the participants (usually a geisha and a customer) end up in a farcical embrace. As with drinking games around the world, the hilarity and silliness increase with the amount of alcohol consumed, and geisha are responsible for maintaining sufficient control to keep the situation from getting truly out of hand. For this reason, many geisha only touch the cup to their lips when offered a drink, and are well aware of ways to avoid losing at drinking games.

The Englishman Richard Gordon Smith noted in 1903 that variations on the Paper, Rock, Scissors game were known generically as *ken*. Geisha were, then as today, experts in such games, displaying a level of skill that quickly put a supercilious western man in his place:

> Geishas play *ken* with great rapidity and scarcely ever lose a point, while the European idiot, who fancies himself proficient, loses not only every time, but also half-a-dozen points in each game which generally leads to his hopeless intoxication. It is part of the geisha's business to see to this.[16]

An extended variation of *ken* is known as "Watōnai."[17] Rather than using merely hand signals, the opponents stand and, placing a high folding screen between them, pantomime a short tune, cheered on by the other guests and geisha. At the climax of the song, each steps forward in one of three characters: a tiger, a hunter, or a little old lady. The winner is determined by a formula which dictates that the hunter can kill (spear) the tiger, the tiger can eat the old lady, but the little old lady can beat the hunter, for he is her grandson.

Another *ozashiki* game popular in the eighteenth and nineteenth centuries was called "Konkonchiki." A player was required to thrust one hand through a loop in a cord held by a different player on each end, grab a precious item such as a lacquered *inrō* medicine box and bring the hand back out of the loop without getting caught (see fig. p. 114). As in "Watōnai," the point at which the object had to be grabbed was determined by the lyrics of the accompanying song.

Flirtation: Guest and Geisha

The flirtatious behavior of geisha at *ozashiki* parties contrasts sharply with the usual behavior of Japanese women in mixed company. Flirting serves a very specific purpose, helping to break down barriers of formality between geisha and their guests. It also also serves to reinforce the customer's sense that the flower-and-willow world he has entered operates by different rules than the outside world. In general, geisha will flirt more with a new customer than with one they have known for many years. Part of this is intended to draw out a guest who may be reticent or slightly nervous, and to encourage him to enter into the spirit of the evening. Such flirting may include teasing or mildly shocking discussion of risqué topics, leading to titillation, but nothing more.

Geisha themselves sometimes speak in place of a regular customer and by so doing intimate to the others that they know him well: "Oh, Tanaka-san really can't stand women dyeing their hair. He thinks natural is best. Isn't that right, Tanaka-san?" The other customers are impressed, making the regular feel gratified. Both the obvious and more subtle types of flirtation or implied intimacy are intended to polish a customer's ego, and to help him have a good time. In the geisha world, both customer and geisha understand that flirting is not a prelude to a sexual encounter, but an end in itself. Men pay well to patronize geisha entertainment because it makes them feel special, both because the geisha are so adept at cultivating a customer's sense of importance, and, increasingly, because it offers the opportunity to bask in the allure and exclusivity of geisha entertainment itself. What could inflate a man's ego more than flirtation with an exceptionally accomplished woman of exquisite taste?

Two Young Women Playing a Gesture Game, Suzuki Harunobu, 1760s
Two young women of the pleasure quarters are engaged in a heated game of "Kitsune-ken" (fox-fighting) with the loser apparently downing cups of sake. The girl on the right signs "Hunter," defeating the one on the left who has signed "Fox." An older *shamisen* player behind them looks on in astonishment.

Art and Relationships

The *Danna*: A One-and-Only Patron

As beautiful single women with a taste for an elegant lifestyle and various professional expenses, geisha have for centuries commonly attached themselves to patrons known generically as *danna*. The word can mean either "patron" or "husband"; some geisha areas have used the term for all customers as a kind of flattery.[18] The *danna*–geisha relationship is a formal one, involving the blessing of a third party, usually the house with which a geisha is registered.[19] If a man who falls in love with a geisha is unmarried, he generally will ask the geisha to marry him; therefore, a *danna* is almost always a man who is already married. A *danna* will usually allow his geisha partner to continue in her profession if she wishes, though sometimes he will encourage her to quit. In either case, he pays off any debts she might have with her sponsoring house and makes a commitment to support her financially, including provision for an apartment or house. In exchange for this

Party for a Military Man, Kanazawa, 1930s
Along with politicians and wealthy businessmen, members of the military elite were among the most prominent supporters of geisha prior to World War II. The participants in this party are gathered in front of the formal display alcove (*tokonoma*), the place reserved for seating honored guests.

support, a geisha becomes essentially a mistress, staying with her *danna* when he wishes, accompanying him on trips, and perhaps even bearing his children. If she continues to work, a geisha will have the benefit of vastly expanded resources with which to pursue and polish her art; if she retires, she can continue her training as an avocation. In general, geisha who do not marry their *danna* remain active in their vocation if given the choice.

Hiiki: Supporters of Artistic Accomplishment

Discussion of geisha in the contemporary world brings up the topic of the geisha supporters called *hiiki*. Falling somewhere between a patron and a fan, a *hiiki* is a customer of the geisha world who has selected one or more geisha on whom to bestow particular financial and moral support. A popular geisha may have several, or even many *hiiki*, all of whom will make a point to call for her when they go for geisha entertainment. In addition, the *hiiki* of a particular geisha will be generous in their tips to her, and will buy multiple seats, or even blocks of seats, for performances in which she appears. In essence, *hiiki* do their best to help a geisha succeed in her profession and especially in her art. There are *hiiki* in the world of sumo as well, who may pick out a promising wrestler in the lower divisions and support him in hopes that he might make it to the highest division.

A *hiiki* differs from a *danna*, in that there is no exclusivity in the relationship. A man may be a *hiiki* for as many geisha as he chooses, and a geisha may have any number of *hiiki*. Often, in fact, a geisha's *hiiki* may know each other. One reason geisha generally avoid sex with those who enlist their services is fear that it will create jealousy and enmity among their supporters. While a *danna* has a formalized relationship that gives him certain rights in return for taking full responsibility for a geisha's well-being, a *hiiki* has no such rights. For a *hiiki* of a geisha to enter into a sexual relationship with her is bound to be considered by her other supporters to be both presumptuous and offensive because it debases the intention behind their support, which is to encourage and sustain a geisha in the pursuit of her art.

Upholding an Aesthetic Tradition

From the eighteenth century to the present, the single most important defining characteristic of geisha has been artistic accomplishment. To be a geisha, a woman need not be young or beautiful, she need not wear an old-style kimono and traditional hairstyle, but she must be trained in the arts of that profession or she is a fraud. A geisha is at once both a highly expert stage performer and an intimate drinking companion. She must have the versatility to accommodate an individual customer's preferences, but do so in a way that maintains the harmony of the gathering. Ideally, she should be able to hold her own in conversation with world-class politicians and business leaders, and on the stage with top professional performers.

Customers who engage geisha today seek a sophisticated aesthetic experience. Spending an evening being entertained in an exquisitely constructed and maintained teahouse or traditional restaurant by beautifully dressed, accomplished, and worldly women is an experience with which a visit to a cramped, noisy hostess bar simply cannot compare. Men (and, increasingly, women) of means are willing to pay a premium price for the chance to relax in spacious rooms where the rich and powerful of past generations passed their time. They can do so while enjoying highly accomplished traditional performances presented especially for them by geisha, the heirs of a two-hundred-and-fifty-year-old tradition renowned around the world. In light of this, the outlay of perhaps $1000 or more for an evening is not unreasonable. In some sense, then, geisha themselves are only one component of an elite, if shrinking, world of entertainment.

Some older geisha complain that young geisha today in no way compare to the great performers of the past. If artistic standards for geisha have slipped in recent decades, it is partly because compulsory education has made it impossible for girls to begin training full time before their seventeenth birthday. Moreover, Japanese women now who need to work can pursue a wide array of job opportunities, unlike the past, when becoming a geisha was one of only a few employment options. As a result, today only those young women who really want to become geisha do so. Despite the much greater competition for suitable candidates, the geisha profession hopes to overcome the challenge of recruiting young women to join the ranks. Whereas in the past girls frequently entered training as geisha out of family necessity, today's new geisha are attracted by the profession's romantic appeal and the possibility to learn from masters of the top schools of dance and music. Older geisha, for their part, appear determined to uphold the strictest possible standards of artistry and behavior, many asserting that they would rather see the profession disappear completely than allow it to dissolve into mere dress-up and role play.

As geisha numbers decline and as politicians and businessmen increasingly are called upon to exercise restraint in their entertainment expenses, the geisha districts are decreasing rapidly, and moving further and further away from the mainstream of Japanese society. To counteract this trend, efforts are being made to make geisha entertainment accessible to a wider audience. Geisha are presenting more performances at public events to familiarize ordinary citizens with the traditional arts. Meanwhile, organizations are springing up in Kyoto and elsewhere to provide information and contacts to geisha districts for those who would like to experience geisha entertainment, but have no one to introduce them. The recent surge of international interest in geisha has affected Japan as well, resulting in the production

Mutamagawa (Six Jeweled Rivers),
Keisai Eisen, c.1825
A geisha changing a *shamisen* string is distracted by the silhouette of a striking man who appears to be staring at her through the translucent paper screen. The subtle hint of mutual attraction reflects the allure that geisha hold for their customers.

Three Apprentice Geisha, attributed to Raimund or Franz von Stillfried, 1879–1882 Like film and sports stars, geisha and apprentice geisha often attract stares when they go out in full dress. Because full-fledged geisha now wear wigs when appearing in formal dress, only *maiko*, the contemporary sisters of those shown here, have to wear their hair in the traditional style twenty-four hours a day.

of numerous magazine articles and television documentaries on geisha, and even some bestselling books. Moreover, local governments and tourist organizations have begun taking steps to preserve their geisha districts from both re-development and neglect, and are exploring ways to support and promote geisha and their traditional arts.

Despite these efforts, debate continues about whether geisha will survive as part of an ongoing cultural tradition. The author has little doubt that the number of geisha will continue to decline, but that the tradition will survive in some form for years to come. What will not remain for long, however, are the highly skilled older women who as children began their training in *shamisen* and dance and continue to perform and entertain. In addition to their invaluable artistic abilities, these older women hold a wealth of knowledge about the geisha world of the past, including the activities of geisha in the old pleasure quarters that were abolished in 1958. For now, geisha continue to play an important role in the performing arts of Japan and remain a vibrant part of the world of traditional entertainment. From their beginnings as simple accompanists in the eighteenth century, to trendsetters in fashion and entertainment in the nineteenth century, geisha today exemplify and preserve some of Japan's most significant artistic and cultural traditions.

NOTES:

1. Beginning in 1779, restrictions were enforced on the type of kimono and number of hair ornaments that Yoshiwara geisha could wear, an implication that in the 1770s, geisha had begun dressing in ways that were considered too eye-catching for the subsidiary role they were supposed to play. Moreover, in 1899, J.E. De Becker wrote that eighteenth-century geisha were "recruited from among comparatively plain women so as not to set up a counter-attraction to the *oiran*." (*The Nightless City: Or the 'History of the Yoshiwara Yukwaku.' By an English Student of Sociology* [Yokohama: Z. P. Maruya, 1899], p. 482).

2. An examination of the artistic accomplishments and sensibilities of a high-ranking courtesan named Takahashi featured in Ihara Saikaku's novel *Life of An Amourous Man* (Kōshoku ichidai otoko, 1682) is found in Kazue Edamatsu Campbell's essay "A Portrait of a New Woman–in a Cage," in Elizabeth de Sabato Swinton, ed., *Women of the Pleasure Quarter* (Worcester, MA: Worcester Art Museum, 1996), pp. 135–138. The character, though fictional, was likely based upon a *tayū* named Takahashi from the Shinmachi pleasure quarter, Osaka's counterpart to the Yoshiwara in Edo.

3. Cecelia Segawa Seigle, *Yoshiwara: The Glittering World of the Japanese Courtesan* (Honolulu: University of Hawaii Press, 1993), p. 174, relates how Daikokuya Shōroku became the first *kenban* of the Yoshiwara. At first, the *kenban* was a person; however, today it refers to an office, or even the building housing not only the office but also the practice studio for the quarter's geisha.

4. Akiyama Aisaburō, *Geisha Girl* (Yokohama: Yoshikawa Book Store, 1937), pp. 20–24.

5. A.M. Thompson, 1911, in Andrew Watt, ed., *The Truth About Japan* (Tokyo: Yen Books, 1988), pp. 32–33.

6. Philipp Franz von Siebold, *Manners and Customs of the Japanese in the Nineteenth Century* (Rutland, VT: Charles E. Tuttle Co., Inc., 1973), p. 135.

Whispered Secret at a Wayside Teahouse, from an album of *Twenty-four Scenes of women*, Utagawa Toyokuni, 1816

A waitress approaches a geisha wearing an informal cotton kimono, slipping a letter inside her kimono. She leans over to whisper the sender's name within earshot of the well-dressed religious pilgrim seated on the bench. As unattached women, geisha frequently have been the subjects of rumor and intrigue among wider society.

7. A film clip of Yachiyo III's final dance performance, circa 1930, as well as footage of Yachiyo IV dancing at age 95 were featured in the NHK television special "Gion: Kyoto Dances in Spring, with Inoue Yachiyo and Inoue Michiko" (*Gion kyōmai no haru, Inoue Yachiyo, Michiko*), aired 8 April 2000.

8. A.C. Scott, *The Flower and Willow World: The Story of the Geisha* (New York: Orion Press, 1960), p. 65.

9. Ibid., p. 125.

10. Liza Dalby, *Geisha* (Berkeley, CA: University of California Press, 1983), pp. 292–293.

11. Ibid., *Geisha*, p. 279. The bush warbler is sometimes referred to as the "Japanese nightingale."

12. Mineko Iwasaki, *Geisha, A Life* (New York: Atria Books, 2002), p. 140.

13. Liza Dalby, who appeared at Kyoto engagements as a geisha in the 1970s, defines and describes some examples of *ozashiki* she experienced in her book *Geisha*, pp. 139–161. That book omits the honorific "o," referring to the gatherings as simply "*zashiki*," meaning a room for welcoming guests, the word from which *ozashiki* is derived.

14. Dalby, *Geisha*, p. 282.

15. Douglas Sladen, *Queer Things About Japan*, 3rd ed. (London: Anthony Treherne and Co., 1904), p. 159.

16. Victoria Manthorpe, ed. *Travels in the Land of the Gods [1893-1907]: The Japan Diaries of Richard Gordon Smith* (New York: Prentice Hall, 1986) p. 154. The "Paper, rock, scissors" version of *ken* is the most common form and goes by the name *Jan-ken*, short for *Jan, ken, pon*, the calls used in that game.

17. Watōnai is a character in Kabuki, son of a Chinese father and Japanese mother, who fought to restore the Ming dynasty in China.

18. Geisha of Hakata (Fukuoka) have long called their customers "Dan-san," a colloquial form of *danna*.

19. The details of a formal agreement establishing a *danna* - geisha relationship are related in Iwasaki, *Geisha, A Life*, pp. 243–245.

Geisha to the Fore

Niwaka *Festivals and the New Luminaries of Edo*

MONEY L. HICKMAN

I
N HIS ENGAGING NOVEL *Ukiyo monogatari* (Tales of the Floating World), the popular writer Asai Ryōi (d.1691) captured a new preoccupation that had come into vogue among the common populace in the great cities of Kyoto, Osaka, and Edo. The essence of this attitude—one might even call it an ideal—was unabashedly hedonistic; it celebrated the seductive notion of enjoying oneself to the fullest, of living for the pleasure of the moment, unencumbered by the tedious concerns of duty or daily toil. Two irresistible lodestones attracted people to this infectious new spirit: the glamorous realms of the stage and the demimonde. The captivating performances of the Kabuki and *jōruri* puppet theatres operated from dawn to sunset; while in the heady, sybaritic locales of the pleasure quarters, the serious working day began at sundown.

It is in Asai's book, published around 1661, that the term for this fashionable new milieu, composed of two characters, *uki* (floating) and *yo* (world or realm) makes its first appearance. "The Floating World," he observes, consists of "living for the moment, savoring the moon, the snow, the cherry blossoms, and the maple leaves, singing songs, drinking sake, and diverting oneself in floating, unconcerned by the prospect of imminent poverty, buoyant and carefree, like a gourd carried along with the river current."

Another word, identical in pronunciation but with a different initial character, signifying "this world of sorrow and grief," had been used since ancient times in literature influenced by Buddhist thought. While the contrasting connotations of the new and the old *ukiyo* are obvious—the one ebullient and pleasure-seeking, the other imbued with gentle stoicism and poignancy—a common meaning pervades both. This is the realization that life is transitory and that human endeavor is therefore ephemeral in nature. While the earlier term *ukiyo* reflected the Buddhist concept of the impermanence and fragility of existence, the later one inspired the individual to appreciate life as he found it, to pursue pleasure and enjoy oneself whenever the chance arose.

In the following decades, "Floating World" gained ever greater currency in popular speech and literature, where its connotations ranged from "erotic" and "risqué" to "stylish" and "up-to-date." Moreover, it was regularly prefixed to a growing array of other words to associate them with the new milieu, such as the popular new literary genre known as *ukiyo-zōshi* (Floating World booklets). As a visual equivalent, *ukiyo-e* (pictures of the Floating World) and lively schools of popular illustration and woodblock printing developed to portray the plebian culture and popular interests of the bustling cities.[1]

OPPOSITE:
The Kashima Dance, Torii Kiyonaga, 1783
The image conveys a spirit of festive celebration, and the impressive float and its ornate decor attest to the considerable labor already devoted to staging *niwaka* in Yoshiwara less than a decade after its introduction.

青樓仁和嘉女藝者部

大万度

萩江
おいよ
竹次

哥麿画

Ômando performace: Oiyo and Takeji from the Ogie school, from the series *Female Geisha Section of the (Yoshiwara)* Niwaka *Festival,* Kitagawa Utamaro, 1783

The geisha Oiyo and Takeji are depicted here with stylized masculine hairdos and in richly decorated brocades embellished with twisted gold and silver pendant cords, Hanging from the hems of their aprons are miniature *suzu* bells, that resonated as they moved.

Niwaka enter the scene

As Japan slowly evolved from an agrarian to a mercantile economy, during the late seventeenth and eighteenth centuries the enterprise and financial power of the *chōnin* (the non-samurai merchant and artisan classes) in the great cities grew stronger. This phenomenon, with its attendant affluence, generated a spectrum of vibrant creative developments in the arts, drama, and literature. The seductive meccas of the Floating World, the gaudy licensed quarters and the popular theatres, patronized primarily by townsmen, not only inspired new tastes, aesthetics, and fashions but also gave rise to innovative developments in the broader realms of entertainment and recreation. It is against this backdrop that geisha come to the fore as performers in the later decades of the eighteenth century, establishing their own groups not only in the prestigious confines of the officially sanctioned pleasure quarters—Shimabara in Kyoto, Shinmachi in Osaka, and Yoshiwara, the "Nightless City," in Edo—but also in promising brothel and entertainment districts, where they diligently worked to develop the artistic disciplines and distinctive traditions that distinguish their activities even today.

Festivals and other public spectacles have always been part of Japanese tradition, and in the eighteenth century special festivities, known as *niwaka*, began to be staged as regular events of the Yoshiwara pleasure quarter. These *niwaka* extravaganzas consisted of colorful processions, floats, and spirited dancing, as well as engaging skits that drew enthusiastic crowds to the streets and establishments of the quarter. The performers consisted of various entertainers, geisha (both men and women) representing different segments of the quarter, and various ancillary artists, such as chanters, musicians, and organizers. Some lower-ranking members of the Yoshiwara brothel hierarchy, child and adolescent attendants of the great courtesans known as *kamuro* and *shinzō*, also participated. Illustrations of *niwaka* festivals in the Yoshiwara evolved as a new subject genre in *ukiyo-e* during the Temmei and Kansei periods (1781–1801). That geisha had assumed an essential role in the activities of the great Edo pleasure quarter during the late eighteenth century is evident from these depictions.

The evocative term *niwaka* (sudden, spontaneous) denotes an activity that is unpremeditated, improvised, or extemporaneous, prompted by an occasion or inspired by circumstance, like an impromptu speech, prayer, or song, or some form of ad-lib performance, such as a pantomime. Its connotations suggest actions that are informal and spontaneous, arising from the impulse of the moment, and free of any restraint or compulsion. [2] It is clear that these qualities also reflected the ideals of the Floating World, the search for uninhibited diversion and pleasure, liberated from the tedium of prosaic daily concern.

The genesis of *niwaka* as a performance genre is unclear, but it is thought to have evolved from the ceremonial rituals and religious processions held at the

Sumiyoshi Shrine in Osaka every summer. According to one traditional account, in the early eighteenth century, a group of merchants from Osaka and Kyoto was enjoying these ceremonies at the shrine, and began performing spontaneous skits and comical masquerades while dancing rhythmically in procession. Performances by such amateurs, dressed in fashionable disguises and motley costumes, soon became popular throughout the region, and animated groups of *niwaka* (or *niwaka-kyōgen*) mummers appeared in Shinto festival observances at other locations, such as the Imamiya, Gion, and Goryō Shrines in Kyoto, as well as other traditional celebrations held in local neighborhoods. In the following years *niwaka* groups also appeared in Edo, adding their colorful activities to long-established festivals, such as the annual events held at the Sannō and Kanda Shrines.[3]

The zeal for *niwaka* among Edo amateur groups and its potential for attracting customers eventually led *niwaka* to the Yoshiwara, perhaps during the late 1760s, but certainly by the 1770s. One account relates that a teahouse operator, Kiriya Ihei, who enjoyed mimicking the dramatic deliveries of noted Kabuki actors, and several fellow enthusiasts, gathered at a brothel in the quarter, the Manjiya. Motivated by the prospect of creating a droll *niwaka*, they concocted a farce of some sort. As they were performing outside one of the prestigious teahouses in the Nakanochō section, some visitors admired their animated gestures and syncopated movements and were inspired to join them. These congenial revelers made the rounds of the elite teahouses, where they were enthusiastically received.

Dragon King Procession, from the series *Compendium of the (Yoshiwara)* Niwaka *Festival*, Torii Kiyonaga, 1783 Formally attired like young men, a pair of *kamuro* carry lanterns and escort a second pair of *kamuro* costumed as attendants of the Dragon King, the mythical monarch of the sea. A man carrying a parasol with miniature *suzu* bells impersonates the sea bream represented on his head.

Geisha and *Niwaka*

From these impromptu amateur efforts *niwaka-kyōgen* developed into established professional attractions organized and staged by geisha of the quarter. These performances were held in Yoshiwara for about fifteen days during the eighth lunar month, when geisha of both sexes, accompanied by *shamisen* ensembles, presented a variety of group performances, processional and other dances, engaging skits, and masquerades.[4] On the first evening of the festivities, geisha made the rounds of the teahouses playing drums to draw attention to the coming events. In the following days elaborate decorative floats were paraded through the quarter. Some of these were carried, while others of substantial size were moved about on wheels escorted by promenading geisha, who proudly displayed their festival finery while dancing to the strains of *shamisen* in front of the individual teahouses. By the early 1780s *niwaka* were among the best attended festivities in the quarter. Geisha groups were the principal performers in the autumn *niwaka* extravaganzas, in contrast to the other

Performers in Korean Costume, as a Lion Dancer, and as a Sumo Wrestler, from the series F*emale Geisha Section of the (Yoshiwara)* Niwaka *Festival,* Kitagawa Utamaro, 1793

A Korean musician wears a distinctive gauze hat topped by a peony and holds a small flute. A Lion Dance participant with folding fan displays firmly bound hair in preparation for a spirited performance; the character "Kiyo" inscribed on her fan may be a part of her name. Another geisha appears in the guise of a casually dressed sumo wrestler equipped with a stage-prop sword. The character "Toku" on her sleeve is probably part of her name as well.

splendid annual events, the Cherry Blossom Festival in the spring and the Lantern Festival in the summer, in which the courtesans and their retinues assumed a primary role.

During the Kansei Period (1789–1801), specialists in staging *niwaka* events appeared, evidence of the broad interest in presenting these events not only in Yoshiwara but also in other pleasure and amusement districts in Edo. Stage performances were held at small *yose* (neighborhood theatres), and *niwaka* events remained popular in other urban settings until the end of the nineteenth century, when the genre finally declined. But the historical influence of the *niwaka* tradition can still be seen in the annual pageants put on by geisha organizations today, particularly in Kyoto, where geisha in elaborate costumes appear in traditional dance programs, with their own chanters and musical accompaniment.

Although some information on late eighteenth-century *niwaka* appears in the annual guides to the Yoshiwara, *ukiyo-e* of the period provide the most instructive picture of the dramatic circumstances and animated details of these events. Geisha in *niwaka* performances appear in the prints of many of the artists active in the last two decades of the century, among them Eishi, Eishō, Shunzan, Sozan, Chōki, Shun'ei, Shuntei, and Toyohisa. However, the most insightful and accurate depictions of *niwaka* and their participants are from the hands of Torii Kiyonaga (1752–1815) and his contemporary Kitagawa Utamaro (1754–1806), the greatest *ukiyo-e* talent of the age.[5]

A print designed by Kiyonaga in 1783 features an elaborate wheeled float that simulates a covered recreation boat, with a majestic prow in the form of an elegant peacock (see p. 122). Festive lanterns are hung above, and the floral decorations—bright maple and red ivy leaves, and chrysanthemums—are the emblems of autumn, the season when the *niwaka* festival was held. The smaller inscriptions above indicate that the float was of large size, and accompanied by a substantial number of musicians, several of whom are identified: "*Shamisen*: the geisha Tome and Ben of the (teahouse) Tobaya, and Kayo and Tayo from the Kineya." Two male musicians, probably also geisha, perform on the flute and drum. The larger inscription at the upper right notes that the performance is a "Kashima Dance" presented by the Kyōmachi Nichōme sector of the quarter.

Two Yoshiwara geisha appear in elaborate *niwaka* costumes in Utamaro's early composition, "Ōmando: Ogie Oiyo and Takeji," from his 1783 series *Seirō niwaka onna geisha bu* (Female Geisha Section of the [Yoshiwara] *Niwaka* Festival; see p. 124). Of the series' six known designs, three are identified as *ōmando* events. This term is said to have originated in simple, comic shrine-festival dances (*teko-mai*). In Yoshiwara, *niwaka ōmando* performers typically appeared in male attire with their hair arranged in fashionably casual masculine style. The appelation Ogie in the inscription indicates that Oiyo and Takeji were geisha of the Ogie family or

GEISHA: BEYOND THE PAINTED SMILE

school of musicians. Other examples of geisha with the name Ogie appear in a number of *niwaka* representations, and this professional (or familial) lineage seems to have specialized in both chanting and instrumental music for some years toward the end of the eighteenth century.

Another Kiyonaga print from 1783 features a group of figures at the head of a "Dragon King" procession, representing the Kyōmachi Itchōme sector of the quarter (see p. 125). At the front is a young boy in an octopus costume, simulations of its globular eyes affixed prominently to his forehead. Following him are two pairs of *kamuro* (young girl attendants of a courtesan). *Kamuro* appear together with geisha in many *niwaka* prints, but this example is unusual, for the inscription above indicates that they seem to dominate the procession. Unlike the more animated demeanor of adult geisha, the sedate manner and serious expressions of these diminutive troupers reveal their awareness of the gravity of their roles and the admiring scrutiny of spectators. Although *kamuro* served as apprentices and attendants to the prestigious courtesans in the licensed quarters, and aspired to move up in the brothel hierarchy as they grew older, the fact that they occasionally appear in *niwaka* processional dances under geisha supervision suggests that their participation and experience in these performances led some of them to subsequent careers as geisha.

Utamaro's elegant series *Seirō niwaka onna geisha no bu* (Female Geisha Section of the [Yoshiwara] *Niwaka* Festival) was produced a decade later, in 1793. Set off against a mica background, each design shows three geisha dressed for different roles (at right and opposite). Each consists of three half-length figures in a triangular arrangement, a compositional format perfected by Utamaro. He also used this triangular design to great effect in a rare untitled print of three performers beneath an ornate float embellished with felicitous butterfly and peony decorations (see p. 128). Below the float to the left is a geisha holding a collapsible vertical paper lantern with her name, Ito. The man with a small processional lantern in the lower right is Ogie Matsuzō. His name appears in a list of performers associated with a *niwaka* event depicted on a medium-sized (*chūban*) triptych by Kiyonaga ten years earlier. There, he is listed as one of four *shamisen* players who all have the surname (or performer's group name) of Ogie. Although these men may have been independent musicians, hired to help out in *niwaka* events, it seems more likely that they were members of the Yoshiwara geisha establishment, and regular participants in the annual activities. The appearance of Matsuzō here, in a *niwaka* performed a decade later, reveals that he began his career as a musician at an early age and was an experienced performer by the autumn of 1793.

Five vivacious geisha, members of a group of twenty identified as a "Lion Dance Troupe," appear in an Utamaro print of about 1795 (see p. 129). Leaders in the sinuous processional dance, they hold its emblematic symbol, an impressive red

Tea Whisk Seller, Firewood Seller, and Shrine-Festival Performer, from the series *Female Geisha Section of the (Yoshiwara)* Niwaka *Festival,* Kitagawa Utamaro, 1793

Above, a geisha in the guise of a peddler of tea whisks holds a *hyōtan* (bottle gourd) that she strikes rhythmically as she dances; a traveling firewood peddler appears at the right; and to the left an itinerant reciter of ballads (*saimon*) raises a miniature priest's staff with rings shaken as she narrates her tales of love, passion, and tragedy.

The Geisha Mine and Ito, with Ogie Matsuzō, Kitagawa Utamaro, 1793
This rare print appears to be one of a limited edition produced by Utamaro's famous publisher Tsutaya Jūsaburō. It may have been specially commissioned by the three individuals pictured: Ogie Matsuzō (lower right); the geisha Mine, whose name is written on her sleeve; and the geisha Ito, whose name is inscribed on a collapsible paper lantern. They may well have had an established, congenial working relationship by the autumn of 1793.

lion mask, above them. Originally inspired by Chinese tradition, the Lion Dance became a familiar ceremonial offering at festival events during the Edo period, and was admired for its dynamic rhythms and theatrical display. *Niwaka* group performances such as the Lion Dance drew inspiration from shrine, temple, and folk traditions, where the coordinated efforts of dancers were motivated by a shared religious devotion, and this spirited sense of common purpose was carried over into the world of popular entertainment in Yoshiwara. The Lion Dances there are said to have been made up of older, accomplished geisha, an apparent indication of the event's prestige as well as a reflection of the workings of the geisha hierarchy in the quarter. Most of the *niwaka* prints were produced in small and medium formats, and apparently served as inexpensive souvenirs of the events. Today, the fact that many are rare and others only preserved in small numbers indicates that they were less valued than the larger prints, and probably soon discarded or recycled.

Niwaka's Many Forms

Among the most impressive spectacles of the annual *niwaka* programs were the large simulations of real or legendary vessels as floats that were moved about on wheels and crewed by animated geisha. Various types of vessels served as prototypes for the floats. Some, like the "Treasure Ship" of the Seven Gods of Good Fortune, were inspired by popular folk traditions; others were based on actual boats such as those used on the Sumida River in Edo, where geisha often served as entertainers. These roofed vessels were colorfully decorated in keeping with the lively diversions that took place on board. In contrast, a triptych by Utamaro of 1798 incorporates a boat inspired by a more utilitarian prototype, a commercial transport vessel (see p. 130). Geisha simulate the hard labor of poling such a vessel as they move in unison to the syncopated cadences of *shamisen* and drum, exhorted on by the actions of dancers with fans.

Profit, like all the activities in the Yoshiwara district, was the basic motivation in staging *niwaka*, and the wide variety of presentations that were held there over the years demonstrates the fundamental motive of the organizers to attract as many visitors from Edo as possible. Some processions took the form of parades, such as the one honoring the fabulous Dragon King of the Kasuga Shrine and his marvelous jewel, where *kamuro* (literally, "balds"), dressed in elegant costumes, were the main participants. The perennial favorite, the Lion Dance, with its distinctive serpentine movements, combined dramatic spectacle with processional dance. Ondo, processional pieces of a more energetic sort, reflected vocational and laboring activities, such as "Ise Fishermen Hauling in their Nets," or the visceral actions of laborers moving lumber in unison. The "Harvest Shrine Dance" celebrated autumn's abundance, while re-creations of the felicitous tradition of making *mochi* (pounding a special glutinous rice compound with mallets in a wooden mortar, and subsequently

GEISHA: BEYOND THE PAINTED SMILE

fashioning round, flat cakes), a chore that requires close cooperative timing, lent itself to *niwaka* with musical accompaniment.

Much of the Edo populace had come from other regions, and the fact that many topographical references are incorporated into *niwaka*, either as themes for performances or in the chanter's librettos, indicates the effort made to stage events that would appeal to people nostalgic for their home regions. "Rewards of the Spring and Fall: Famous Products of the Yamato Region," and "Famous Crops: the Glow of Sunset at Uji" are among the numerous references of this sort.

Niwaka events were filled with elaborate floral imagery and distinctive seasonal motifs, such as autumn maple leaves, lush peonies, bright morning glories, and glorious clusters of plum and cherry blossoms. The ebullient atmosphere and colorful display not only drew visitors to the quarter, but also filled them with something of the light-hearted, hedonistic mood of the Floating World. The numerous decorative lanterns that dramatically illuminated the *niwaka* as they continued into the night heightened the ephemeral atmosphere.

The fact that many *niwaka*, especially those made up of companies of dancers performing in processional events, were derived from time-honored religious observances reflects the perennial influence of the past in the evolution of Japanese performing arts, and also reveals how spectators must have been drawn to these events because of their familiarity with and nostalgia for vibrant local spectacles of this sort. Other *niwaka* had their genesis in Japanese folklore and traditional custom: *Takasago* (long a part of the Nō repertory) and celebrating the felicitous theme of conjugal longevity; the captivating legend of the Wedding Procession of the Foxes; or the Therapeutic Waterfall of Long Life. Commonplace activities and familiar characters were also represented in *niwaka*: geisha masquerading as boatmen, vendors, artisans, dancing girls, prostitutes, and comely peasant girls, as well as the everyday itinerant peddlers who solicited the neighborhood residents of Edo. Finally, there are subjects depicted in *niwaka* prints that reveal the diversions and pleasures of the Floating World: incidents such as "Sleeping in a Boat with One's Clothes on" (perhaps as a consequence of an intoxicated tryst with a "boat girl"), or "Returning from a Brothel in the Morning," or "(Listening to) *Nagauta* Chanting with Music in the Pleasure Quarter."

Lion Dance, Kitagawa Utamaro, 1795
The geisha are attired in the *ōmando* fashion, with their hair tied up in rough masculine manner, and their outer garments thrown back so as not to inhibit their energetic movements.

Niwaka and Kabuki

Dramatic offerings, in the form of skits, farces, mimes, and melodramatic pieces, were staged at locations where the entertainers could set up simple portable stage props and lanterns that served as overhead illumination and footlights. *Niwaka* of this sort were acted by small groups of geisha who drew on the traditional repertoire of familiar dramatic themes, and occasionally on stage presentations at the Kabuki theatres.

The Flourishing Harbor of Takase,
Kitagawa Utamaro, 1798, from the series,
Yoshiwara *Niwaka* Festival, Second Part
Passing in front of the float are a stately
courtesan and her entourage of lantern
bearer, *kamuro* and adolescent *shinzō*.
Proud of her high status in the quarter and
preoccupied with her own affairs, the
dignified beauty cooly ignores the geisha
and their boisterous performance.

The influence of Kabuki is apparent in a print by Utamaro of 1795, *Yoshiwara niwaka ni no kawari* (*Niwaka* Performances in Yoshiwara, Second Part; see p. 131). The subtitle is *Shitennō ōeyama iri* (The Four Heavenly Kings Enter Mount Ōe), an offering based on an act in the *kaomise*, the annual beginning-of-season program staged at the Kiriza Theatre in the eleventh month of 1785, where the roles of Yamauba and Kintarō (called "Kaidomaru" in the play) were played by the celebrated actors Segawa Kikunojō III and Ichikawa Monnosuke II to enthusiastic acclaim. Although Yamauba and Kintarō were already familiar figures in Japanese folklore and drama—according to legend, Kintarō was raised in the remote vastness of the Ashigara mountains by Yamauba (literally "Old Woman of the Mountains")—the Kabuki performances stimulated new interest in these rustic figures among the residents of Edo, as evidenced by the many illustrations of them by Kiyonaga and Utamaro. A mysterious reclusive figure, said to have been originally demonic in nature, she served as Kintarō's stepmother when he was a boy. In the print, patterns of leaves are worked into her kimono; her hair is unkempt; and she carries bundles of firewood—all indications of her rustic origins. Below, Kintarō poses in a courageous manner with his prodigious axe. Their elegant robes reveal the influence of the colorful costumes of the Kabuki stage, while the stylized postures of the two figures clearly simulate a Kabuki *mie* (a momentary or "arrested" pose), a kind of dramatic tableau. Six geisha are listed above, suggesting that other roles from the Kabuki play may also have been portrayed. On the Kabuki stage, the actors were accompanied by chanters of the Tokiwazu school; in the print, two male geisha holding fans are also members of this school.

The direct influence of *jōruri* (puppet theater music) modes adapted from the *ningyō-shibai* (puppet dramas) and Kabuki theatres is evident in the chanting and *shamisen* accompaniment of Tokiwazu, Tomimoto, and Ogie performers supporting smaller geisha groups in these theatrical skits and mimes. Moreover, the growing prestige and important role of geisha in the Floating World of the late eighteenth century is reflected in certain Kabuki dramas of the period. In *Katakiuchi adana kashiku* (Vendetta; the Geisha known as Kashiku), staged at the Nakamuraza Theatre in the autumn of 1779, Iwai Hanshirō V appeared in the role of the geisha Kashiku. Another example is the *jōruri shosa* dance, *Fūkyoku Edo geisha* (Fashionable Music, Edo Geisha), a segment of the signature *kaomise* (face-showing) program at the same theatre in 1785, in which two members of the Tomimoto school, Tomimoto Buzennojō II, and Tomimoto Itsuki-dayū, served as chanters.

Geisha as *Ukiyo-e* Luminaries

Yoshiwara *niwaka* were an essential ingredient in the rise and development of geisha in the late eighteenth century. Organized and staged by enterprising geisha groups, *niwaka* provided these entertainers with the opportunity to display their skills and accomplishments to the public as well as to habitual patrons. The continuity of the event and its status as one of the prestigious annual events in the great pleasure quarter was impetus for geisha to elevate the standards of their arts in coordinated ensembles as well as in individual acts. Success brought stability and assurance to geisha groups, and this, in turn, contributed to the innate sense of self-esteem, decorum, and hierarchical structure that remain defining characteristics of geisha organizations today.

A number of names of geisha active in Yoshiwara during the later decades of the eighteenth century appear in the semi-annual *saiken* guides to the quarter and on *ukiyo-e* prints. Occasionally of four syllables but more frequently two, these brief monikers were probably conferred on geisha by their mentors, although it is possible that some are abbreviated given names. Beyond their evocative names, however, we know nothing more about the identities of these early geisha who entertained customers in the Yoshiwara.[6]

The Four Heavenly Kings reach Mount Ōe, Kitagawa Utamaro, 1795, from the series, *Niwaka* Performances in Yoshiwara, Second Part
A small backdrop of mountainous terrain and a waterfall simulates props used on the Kabuki stage. The backdrop and the curtain stretched horizontally indicate that these mime-skits were moved from one temporary location to another in the Yoshiwara district, and were probably performed indoors as well as outside.

By the 1790s, however, a few geisha had finally joined the Floating World elite, and emerged as recognizable celebrities. This occurred, in large part, because of the debut of a new popular feminine ideal in the 1760s, epitomized by the charming young women who worked in *mizujaya*.[7] *Mizujaya* (literally "water teahouses") were small handy shops and simple stalls that catered to the public by providing a variety of inexpensive refreshments and commodities, such as steeped tea, sweetmeats, fans, cosmetics, and medicinal preparations, and also, in certain locations, sexual services. Some of these *mizujaya* employees were highly successful in attracting customers, and, because of their engaging demeanor and beauty, became great favorites among the Edo townspeople. In the late 1760s, the most admired of these popular paragons were Osen, a waitress who served tea and cakes at the Kagiya, at the entrance to the Kasamori Shrine; and Ofuji of the Motoyanagiya, in the temple grounds of the Sensōji in Asakusa. Osen and Ofuji are the subjects of more than twenty of the prints of Suzuki Harunobu (1724–1770), whose renditions undoubtedly contributed to the acclaim of these young women (see p. 132).

Harunobu's innovative vision marks a watershed in the history of *ukiyo-e*.

The Beauties Ofuji and Osen, and the Actor Segawa Kikunojō II, Suzuki Harunobu, c. 1769
Harunobu presents the willowy beauties in front of their shops, flanking the noted Kabuki *onnagata* actor Segawa Kikunojō II, who was also an exemplar of femininity, celebrated for his convincing stage portrayals of fetching maidens.

During the 1760s he had introduced a broader and more diverse range of human activities into his works. Inspired in part by book illustrations of the Kyoto artist Nishikawa Sukenobu (1671–1751), he moved away from the traditional Floating World themes, which had focused for a century on the glamorous courtesans of the pleasure quarters and the actors of the Kabuki stages. Harunobu turned to the larger world, delineating the varied people, events, and livelihoods that reflected the habitual activities and interests of the inhabitants of Edo. Prints and paintings of popular beauties, such as Osen and Ofuji, exemplify this new orientation. The artist's broader view of human activities, in turn, reflected the enlarged parameters of the Floating World, where geisha, *mizujaya* grisettes (teahouse waitresses), and popular personalities like Osen and Ofuji now joined the hierarchy of the fashionable demimonde.

Osen (pictured on the right) appears to have been the more admired of the two willowy beauties, for she was mentioned in contemporary literature, and represented on hand towels and broadsheets, as well as in *ukiyo-e*. But the ultimate manifestation of her acclaim occurred in the summer of 1768, when the Kabuki actor Nakamura Matsue portrayed her on the stage of the Kiriza, when she was seventeen. Ofuji also served as the model for a stage performance, in the third month of 1769, by the celebrated specialist of female roles, or *onnagata*, Segawa Kikunojō II. Nothing of a reliable nature is known about the lives of Osen and Ofuji in the following years, although both seem to have disappeared at the height of their popular esteem, some months after the death of their pictorial promoter, Harunobu.

By the Kansei period (1789–1801) substantial geisha groups were active not only in the Yoshiwara, but also at lively sporting and entertainment centers throughout Edo, in districts such as Fukagawa (Tatsumi), Nakasu, Shinagawa, and Shinjuku. Individual geisha became chic local celebrities of the fashionable Floating

World in these years, as we know from the prints of Utamaro, whose intimate acquaintance with the members of the demimonde is superbly revealed in his inspired depictions. One of these local luminaries was the geisha Kamekichi, who worked in a teahouse at Sodegaura, a location close to Shinagawa, which looked out on Edo Bay. Utamaro's bust-portrait of 1794–95 captures her in a coquettish pose, hands clasped, head turned, and lips slightly parted (above, left). A cartouche provides a miniature view of Edo Bay. Many of the teahouses where geisha entertained were situated so that they looked out over the Sumida River or portions of Edo Bay, locations where scenic vistas stimulated high spirits and took advantage of cooling breezes in the humid summer.

Toyohina, A Geisha Star

The most famous and frequently depicted geisha of the 1790s is Tomimoto Toyohina, who was admired not only for her beauty but also for her exceptional talents for chanting and playing the *shamisen*. She was a member of the revered Tomimoto line of musicians, a school of *jōruri* narrative music that was at the height of its popularity in the late eighteenth century, not only on the Kabuki stage but also in the more intimate circumstances of teahouse entertainment.[8] One of Utamaro's most admired prints (above right), done in 1793, shows Toyohina at the top, flanked below by her most famous demimonde contemporaries, the teahouse waitress Takashima(ya) Ohisa on the left and Naniwaya Okita to the right. Utamaro's particular admiration for these celebrities bordered on obsession, for he depicted them repeatedly, either singly, as a trio, or in combination with other popular paragons of the pleasure quarters, such as Yoshiwara courtesans, sumo wrestlers, geisha, and Kabuki actors, over a period of roughly four years, beginning about 1792. Although Ohisa and Okita were associated with *mizujaya*, their establishments were more

ABOVE LEFT
The Geisha Kamekichi of Sodegaura,
Kitagawa Utamaro, 1794–95
The adulatory poem to the right notes:
"Not even Urashima's beloved Otohime
could equal her, Kamekichi of the Sode-
ga-ura shore in her cool summer
garment."

ABOVE RIGHT
**Three Beauties of the Present Day:
Tomimoto Toyohina, Takashimaya
Ohisa, and Naniwaya Okita**, Kitagawa
Utamaro, 1793

Neck Tug-of-war between the Wrestler Tanikaze and Strong-Boy Kintarō,
Kitagawa Utamaro, c. 1793
While Ohisa and Okita encourage their favorites in this tug-of-war, Toyohina, the referee, holds a fan to confirm the eventual winner.

impressive structures than the simple stalls where people had come to admire Osen and Ofuji more than two decades earlier. Ohisa performed as the chief drawing card and animated advertisement for her father's shop and teahouse at Yagenbori (Ryōgoku), the Takashimaya, where visitors admired Ohisa's scintillating movements and decorous behavior as they drank steeped tea and ate the special *senbei* crackers made on the premises. The Naniwaya, where fortunate patrons could exchange pleasantries with Okita, was a fine structure situated just outside the Zuishin gate, the eastern entrance to the Sensōji in Asakusa.

In another woodcut Utamaro shows the beautiful trio together with two stalwart opponents, the formidable sumo wrestler Tanikaze and the rustic strong-boy Kintarō (a familiar role in Kabuki and *niwaka*) who resolutely face each other in a "neck tug-of-war." Although Toyohina appears in several of Utamaro's compositions in which female celebrities compete in symbolic rivalry, she is never a competitor, but invariably an arbitrator or judge, placed in a central, or high position, reflective of her prestige and high status as a geisha.

Utamaro's 1793–94 composition "Seven Lucky Beauties: Their Appearances Compared" (opposite) shows Okita, Toyohina and Ohisa above, with four winsome rivals below. These are, from the left: Fujita Otao, Tachibana Otatsu, Hiranoya Oseyo, and Kikumoto Ohan, all of whom were employed in *mizujaya* in different sections of Edo. Toyohina was somewhat older and already an established geisha, while her companions were hardly more than adolescents. Ohisa and Okita acted as alluring attractions for their establishments, and it is likely that the others pictured here functioned in the same manner, although it is possible that one or another was also an aspiring performer or geisha.

Tomimoto Toyohina was a noted performer by the early 1790s, when Utamaro depicted her in her early twenties as one of the "Three Beauties of the Present Day." Ohisa was probably sixteen at the time, and Okita a year younger. Although *ukiyo-e* provide some sense of their beauty and the milieu in which they flourished, details of their personal lives and relationships remain little more than conjecture. Toyohina's prominence, however, suggests that she may have been related to the head of her school, Tomimoto Buzennojō II (1754–1822), perhaps even his daughter.

There is, however, an intriguing handwritten note on a second-state version of "Three Beauties of the Present Day," in an unidentified Japanese collection, that

Seven Lucky Beauties: Their Appearances Compared, Kitagawa Utamaro, 1793–94
The celebrated trio of Okita, Toyohina, and Ohisa are depicted above four beautiful rivals, Otaye, Otatsu, Oseyo and Ohan.

seems to shed light on the later lives of the celebrated trio. It reads: "Naniwaya Okita went off to Osaka, Takashima Ohisa married into a family that made *senbei*, and Tomimoto Toyohina became the concubine of a daimyo."

A rare triptych by Utamaro, published by Iseya Kimbei about 1795–96, seems to commemorate the last occasion when the trio appears in a composition together (see p. 136). The title, "Eminent Young Women of the Present Day," attests to their popular acclaim. Once again Toyohina appears in the center, clothed in an elegant white kimono beside a vase of blossoming plum. This is an auspicious occasion, more than likely held in honor of prospective nuptials. She sits sedately under a ceremonial canopy on three futons, traditional components of a bride's trousseau. She wears the formal head covering known as *agebōshi* then fashionable among cultivated women, who wore these caps of pale pink or white silk when traveling to protect their oiled coiffures from wind and dust. The *tsunokakushi* (horn concealer) worn by brides at traditional marriages derives from this headdress. Toyohina holds a folding fan, which because it can be opened wide, is emblematic of success or auspicious fortune. Okita bows formally to her and Ohisa pauses in arranging the congratulatory presents secured with festive *noshi* ties to acknowledge them.

Other elements of the triptych also point to the anonymous note: "Naniwaya Okita went off to Osaka . . ." Naniwa is both an ancient name for Osaka and the name of the teahouse where Okita worked in Edo. The votive painting of flower sprays in a tea bowl is a nod to her success in attracting customers to the Naniwaya; metal mounts of the frame are embellished with her paulownia crest. A noted *ryōtei* (restaurant teahouse) named Naniwaya, famous for its ancient umbrella pine, was in the province adjoining Osaka; the allusion suggests an affiliation with the Osaka area, and the likelihood that she had come from there. The inclusion of Jō and Uba, symbols of conjugal fidelity, in a roundel above Ohisa implies the prospect of matrimony: ". . . Ohisa married into a family that made *senbei*." *Senbei* rice crackers were the specialty of her family's establishment so it is not surprising that Ohisa may have married into another family that produced them.[9]

About 1796 Utamaro produced a set of large prints with bust portraits of women from the pleasure quarters. Only four designs are known, but it may have been that this untitled series originally included at least one more design. Topographical locations appear on three of them, together with a single syllable or abbreviation for

Eminent Young Women of the Present Day: Okita, Toyohina, and Ohisa,
Kitagawa Utamaro, c. 1795–96
This rare triptych may be the final commemoration of the three beauties of Edo and a celebration of the impending nuptials of Toyohina, in the center panel.

the name of the subject, none of whom has been identified. The three pleasure quarters represented are: Shinagawa (south), Fukagawa (Tatsumi, east), and Shinjuku (west), and it is likely that there was another one for Yoshiwara (north), completing the four directional quadrants. The last of the known designs has no topographical reference, and is titled simply *Geikoku*, the "Realm of Geisha," accompanied by the single syllable *to*, which identifies the subject as Toyohina (see p. 137).[10] It appears that Utamaro's intention here was to celebrate Toyohina's personal fame as well as to represent her in a larger sense as a living symbol of the geisha of Edo. That Utamaro should have commemorated Toyohina in this manner attests to his personal admiration for her and also affirms her influential role as a performer. Toyohina's historical importance lies in the fact that she was the first geisha celebrity to rise to the highest level and to achieve an equal footing with the glamorous courtesans of the pleasure quarters and the idolized actors of the Kabuki stage. Moreover, her inclusion in this select company also reflects a more fundamental development—geisha had come to the fore and were now a vital, dynamic component in the world of the performing arts, an achievement brought about through their industry and devotion to their disciplines, and realized within the brief span of three decades. The foundations for their unique tradition in Japanese culture were now firmly in place, and they must have faced the future with optimistic expectations, despite the ephemeral nature of the Floating World.

NOTES:

1. The vocabulary that evolved with the prefix *ukiyo* is extensive. Among these terms are *ukiyo-kasa* (Floating World umbrella), *ukiyo-motoyui* (Floating World hairstyle), and *ukiyo-bōshi* (Floating World hat). For others, see *Nihon Kokugo Daijiten*, vol. 2 (Tokyo: Shōgakukan Press, 1973), pp. 526–30.

2. Examples of the use of the word *niwaka* include: *niwaka bugen* (a mushroom, or overnight millionaire); *niwaka keiki* (a sudden, temporary economic or business boom); *niwaka benkyō* (in contemporary use and familiar to all Japanese students, "cramming" in preparation for an imminent examination); *niwaka odori* (a humorous dance performed extemporaneously).

3. *Niwaka* became widespread among local amateurs and professional geisha as a distinctive performance genre with various local and regional variations such as Osaka *niwaka*, Yoshiwara *niwaka*, and Hakata *niwaka* (reportedly still performed occasionally).

4. The schedules may have varied at times, for the annual festivities occasionally started in the middle

of the month and extended over into the ninth lunar month. In addition, as the *niwaka* vogue grew, these performances were also staged at other times, such as New Year's, and in local teahouses.

5. It appears that the earliest *ukiyo-e* depictions of *niwaka* in Yoshiwara (at least those that are so identified in a series title) are the six prints designed by Kiyonaga in the 1781 series *Seirō niwaka kyōgen zukushi* (A Selection of *Niwaka* Performances in Yoshiwara), published by Nishimura Eijudō. Produced only a few years after the *niwaka* was first introduced into the quarter, the variety of performances depicted here, and sponsored by five different sections of the Yoshiwara, demonstrate that it was an established, popular annual event in the quarter. Kiyonaga continued to design *niwaka* prints in the following years, producing a substantial number in 1783, and several others in 1787 and 1794–95. But *niwaka* subjects make up only a small number of his large and diverse oeuvre. By contrast, his great contemporary, Utamaro, was preoccupied by this subject, producing numerous *niwaka* prints between 1783 and 1803.

6. Many represent natural phenomena, such as *Fuji* (Wisteria), *Ume* (Plum Blossom), *Nami* (Wave), *Kiku* (Chrysanthemum), *Yama* (Mountain), *Taki* (Waterfall), *Shio* (Tide), and *Ishi* (Pebble). Others come from seasons, *Haru* (Spring), and *Aki* (Autumn), or animals, birds, or insects, *Tora* (Tiger), *Shika* (Deer), *Tsuru* (Crane), *Tonbo* (Dragon Fly), or precious metals, *Kin* (Gold), and *Gin* (Silver).

7. The earliest *mizujaya* are said to have been erected in Edo in the Sensōji precincts in the seventeenth century. By the 1740s *mizujaya* complexes had appeared in Shinto and Buddhist precincts at the Kanda and Shiba Myōjin, at Atago, Ryōgoku, and Honjō. As they flourished they grew in variety: there were also *chahan-jaya* (fried-rice teahouses); *chazuke-jaya* (stalls where simple meals of rice and tea were served); and *deai-jaya* (meeting or assignation teahouses). At the Shijō-kawara entertainment district in Kyoto, *mizujaya* were operated by actors and theater managers, and customers could meet these celebrities and make reservations for the performances. *Mizujaya-share*, a special genre of vulgar colloquial language also evolved, designed to tease and entertain the women who worked in *mizujaya*.

The Realm of Geisha, Kitagawa Utamaro, c. 1796
The subject of this print is believed to be Tomimoto Toyohina.

8. The school of *jōruri* musical chanting and accompaniment known as *Tomimoto-bushi* was founded by Fukuda Danji (1716–1764), who in 1748 established his own separate line, which came to be known as *Tomimoto-bushi*. Under the name *Tomimoto Buzennojō* he performed in Kabuki dramas together with Tokiwazu musicians for some years. Under the leadership of his son Umanosuke ("Umazura," Horseface) the Tomimoto school flourished during the An'ei and Temmei (1772–1789) periods, surpassing even the Tokiwazu school, and the ubiquitious imagery of the Tomimoto *sakurasō* (primrose) crest demonstrates the popularity of the school's accompaniment in narrative theatrical music to love scenes, travel vignettes, suicide and elopement interludes, and *shosa* dance segments. Tomimoto music is considered more refined and subtle than its older contemporary, *Tokiwazu-bushi*, and is admired for its intricate *shamisen* accompaniment. These characteristics made it appropriate not only for dramatic stage performances, but also for the more intimate circumstances of teahouse entertainment.

9. According to tradition, Ohisa married into a respected samurai family. She is depicted in Utamaro's 1795–96 series *Kōmei bijin rokkasen* with her eyebrows shaved, an indication that she was married. She would have been about seventeen or eighteen at the time. Another story suggests that she married a man from Kameido who had been adopted into her family.

10. During the Kansei period, the new administration of Matsudaira Sadanobu enacted a series of prohibitions intended to discourage the excesses of the previous Temmei period, and in *ukiyo-e*, only the names of Yoshiwara courtesans were allowed on prints from 1793 on. The use of various abbreviations, and rebus devices, some easily comprehended, others of considerable complexity, were utilized by print designers to avoid this regulation.

Money L. Hickman, PhD. in Fine Arts from Harvard University, was a Research Fellow in Japanese art at the Museum of Fine Arts, Boston, from 1968 to 1995. Among his more than fifty publications and exhibitions—many of which deal with *ukiyo-e* prints and paintings and traditional Japanese entertainment—are *Japan Day by Day* for the Peabody Essex Museum in 1977, *The Paintings of Jakuchu* (1989), and *Japan's Golden Age: Momoyama* (1996).

Geisha on Stage and Screen

PETER M. GRILLI

MONG THE VARIED ROLES geisha play in Japanese society, they figure prominently in the cinema and performance arts of Japan. Inherently more glamorous in appearance and lifestyle than conventional housewives or other working women of modern Japan, geisha seem to have a natural relationship with the dramatic arts. Performance—with a capital "P"—is the essence both of the geisha's art and the dramatic arts, and there is a close affinity between the songs, dances, and conversations performed by geisha for the benefit of a few lucky clients in the intimate *tatami*-floored rooms of an elegant Japanese restaurant or teahouse, and the audience-pleasing entertainments writ far larger on the cinema screen or the theatrical stage. Highly trained in the arts of entertainment, geisha themselves form the most discerning audience for traditional Japanese performing arts and are avid and knowledgeable members of the audiences attending Kabuki plays, films, and other popular entertainments.

In this essay, geisha will be described both as performing artists and subjects (or "characters") for cinema and stage. Historically and culturally, much about the characteristics of geisha may seem unique to Japan, but important aspects may be clarified by comparison to western counterparts. To illustrate my comments, I will elaborate on specific depictions of geisha in Japanese films or plays, but will speculate as well on how such particular portrayals may be emblematic of broader themes. And, finally, I hope to explore aspects of the intimate personal and professional relationship of geisha in the contemporary Japanese *geinōkai* or "world of the performing arts." Though the "exotic" image of the geisha in non-Japanese eyes is of less interest to me here, I may touch on it obliquely in noting how native authors have sometimes cast geisha as a foil for more conventional Japanese womanhood in order to highlight or dramatize fundamental cultural issues of society or history.

Eroticism in the Arts of Performance

The great Japanese Kabuki actor Bandō Tamasaburō, who is an *onnagata*, or specialist in female roles, once explained the essence of his acting style as follows: "All performance is essentially erotic. To really capture the attention of the audience— *to fully ensnare the yearnings of each member of that audience*—a performance must be based in eroticism." Apart from all matters of training and intellect, apart from art and technical skill, the performer must establish a deep and powerful bond with each member of his audience or the performance will seem flat.

According to this most successful actor in comprehending and representing

OPPOSITE

Kabuki Actor Bando Tamasaburō in the Play *Kanda Matsuri.*

Bandō Tamasaburō as the Geisha Okō in the play *Nihonbashi* by Izumi Kyōka.

virtually every nuance of female personality, the bond between actor and audience is in its essence erotic. If it is no more than that, the performance may be merely pornographic: it will be overly obvious, self-revealing, and quickly tiresome. But if the essential eroticism is polished (some might say "disguised") by artistry and technique, the performance becomes fascinating, captivating, eternally fresh—and the ineffable bond between performer and observer becomes compelling. A performance based exclusively on the beauty or seductiveness of an actor's face or body, unsupported by artistry, soon palls or sinks into burlesque. But one that grows authentically from the erotic messages emitted from the depths of an actor's soul (even if his face and body are less than ideal) becomes continuously more fascinating.

It is beyond the limits of this essay to argue whether Tamasaburō's "truth" in fact imbues the work of any fine actor or whether an erotic bond renders any theatrical work distinctive and memorable to any audience. But it does suggest a key to understanding the artistry of the Japanese geisha. Only when it is understood that a geisha is essentially a performer—nothing more, nothing less—and that every aspect of her performance is, on some level, erotic, can the nature of her art be fully appreciated. No moral judgment is implied in this perception: I am neither suggesting that geisha are bad because of their eroticism or necessarily good because of their artistry. All the debates about geisha and sexuality should be set aside, for the moment at least, and recast in the question of whether each geisha's performance is effective or not. Does it work or not? Here, the test should not be whether she lands her customer in bed, but whether he is captivated enough by her performance to return for more. Is the customer fascinated and intrigued? And, more generally, does the society find enough value in the geisha performance to retain the institution and allow it to continue? The answer to all such questions is, apparently, "yes" because geisha remain an integral part of Japanese culture. Though their numbers may decline or swell with the economic health of the society, geisha endure.

Geisha performance has been described as "the art of titillation," and that is perhaps true, to an extent. But only a very limited extent, and one that is far too shallow to define the enduring appeal of the geisha as a cultural institution. Though a geisha may be comely of face and beautiful in body, the success of her performance depends ultimately on totally integrated artistry. The elegance of her appearance, the merit of her musical or dance performance, the intelligence of her witty conversation, the intuitive instinct to gauge the atmosphere of an intimate gathering and respond appropriately to the particular interests and needs of the guests: the geisha brings all of these skills to her performance. To be genuinely titillating, one standardized performance will not fit all situations and all occasions. Although her witty repartee, tinged with innuendo and erotic puns or double entendres, may seem similar from party to party, a geisha's intelligence, intuition, and artistry differentiate the needs of each party and make each guest seem uniquely important.

Geisha Onstage

As long as geisha have existed, the boundaries between geisha-as-subject and geisha-as-interpreter of traditional forms of Japanese performance arts have been fluid. Because the many artifices of geisha activity are essentially theatrical, it has been easy to transfer these "actresses" of the teahouse or the elegant restaurant to

The Kamo River Dances, Pontochō District, Kyoto, c. 1880-1900
Geisha have been featured in public stage performances since the 1870s. This view of the Kamo River Dances (*Kamogawa odori*) shows *maiko* apprentices kneeling on the stage and the geisha playing *shamisen* on the riser behind them. The plover (*chidori*) insignia on the lanterns above signify the Pontochō district.

the stage or, more recently, the silver screen. The geisha's work in the teahouse or at a special banquet is in essence a kind of performance: while entertaining their clients they are "onstage"—even though the "stage" in this case may be hardly more than a corner of the room where a meal is being served.

In their dual roles as both performing artists and subjects (or "characters") for the arts of screen and stage, geisha appear in regularly scheduled pageants or dance performances in large theaters in Kyoto and Tokyo. On such occasions as the *Kamogawa Odori* (Kamo River Dances), performed each spring at the *kaburenjō* theater in the Pontochō geisha district of Kyoto or the *Azuma Odori* (Dances from the East), performed by the Tokyo geisha of the Shinbashi district, they display their skills as classical dancers in colorful programs comprised of many scenes. These seasonal spectacles hark back to eighteenth-century pageants when geisha or courtesans paraded through the streets of Kyoto or presented dance performances in various outdoor settings (see Hickman essay).

As characters, geisha and their historical predecessors often have appeared as protagonists of classic Kabuki plays as well as modern novels or dramas. Their lives have been depicted as colorful and glamorous, but the glamour usually masks tragedy or moments of pain and unhappiness. Since Japanese literature has traditionally taken special pleasure in portraying the subtle nuances of loneliness and melancholy, it is not at all difficult to understand why novelists and playwrights might find rich material for melodrama and tragedy in true stories about geisha. Traditionally separated from their families as children in order to be trained as professional entertainers, young women who become geisha form alternative familial ties among their geisha colleagues, and such relationships are often transient and short-lived. Required to entertain or cheer up paying guests under any circumstances, geisha also must disguise their true feelings and pretend to be gay and carefree even when their hearts are torn by other emotions. Every performance culture in the world features scenes in which a leading character must conceal heartbreak in order to entertain or inspire others, and the audience is invited to perceive the true tragedy lurking behind the surface gaiety. This theme underlies virtually every depiction of geisha in popular Japanese fiction, dramas, and films. Readers and audiences delight in the empathetic tears they shed on behalf of the distraught geisha heroines.

A sharp distinction must be drawn between the colorful annual dance performances, in which geisha in Kyoto or Tokyo herald the arrival of spring or autumn, and plays depicting the inner lives of geisha themselves. The dance-pageants tend to be bright and colorful, uncomplicated in plot and lacking profound emotional content. They might be compared to performances by the Rockettes of New York's Radio City Music Hall or the "Can-can" dancers of nineteenth-century Parisian revues. Their intent is to dazzle the audience with colorful costumes and superbly choreographed dance movment, but not to plumb the emotional depths of a dramatic situation. On the other hand, the melodramas with geisha heroines are more somber examinations of the psyches of women forced to entertain or manipulate men when their true emotions lie elsewhere.

The performance career of the great Kabuki actor Bandō Tamasaburō as an *onnagata* serves to highlight most clearly these distinctions between the cheerful dance performances and the dramatic depictions of geisha in literature and drama. In the dance-play *Kanda-Matsuri* (Festival at Kanda), he enacts the role of an innocent young geisha performing the traditional dances of this popular Edo festival. The dramatic content of the play is minimal, and all emotion is expressed through dance movement rather than dialogue. It is a cheerful, colorful performance, but Tamasaburō's rendition of this role is somewhat vapid: beautiful and willowy in appearance, but as shallow as the personality of a doll in a glass case. His performance captures perfectly the quality of many geisha dances that depend for their effect on the perfect execution of elegant movement and gentle erotic innuendo, rather than the communication of any emotional depth.

In contrast, a role like the geisha Okō in Izumi Kyōka's 1915 play *Nihon-bashi* demands far different skills from the same actor. She is a complex female character, combining icy vindictiveness and strength with an intense vulnerability as her reason is overcome by her romantic passions. As in many other depictions of geisha in modern plays and films, the role of Okō is full of challenging ambiguities. Kyōka's play is named for its setting, the section of Tokyo near the famous Nihonbashi Bridge that was the first station on the Tōkaidō highway linking the city to the ancient capital of Kyoto. The geisha Okō represents the tragic anachronisms inherent in the life of a modern woman unable to escape from a social role that many consider archaic and repressive. She is a beautiful, intelligent, highly trained woman of strong character and independent mind, forced to behave as a plaything of men, disguising her true passions as she teeters on the edge of madness while struggling to maintain a sense of reality in a situation that constantly demands unreal emotions of her. She hides her fierce love for a younger geisha sister by taking on the other woman's discarded lovers, and then she seems to fall genuinely in love with one of the hapless young men. Confused by the various roles that she is forced to play (an occupational hazard of all geisha), Okō deludes herself with successive fantasies and slips finally into insanity. Like a Japanese Hedda Gabler or Nora in *A Doll's House*, the geisha Okō can be viewed as an iconic figure representing the conflict of the modern personality in a world not yet ready to allow her to be fully herself.

Specific depictions of geisha in Japanese literature and drama are emblematic of broader social themes. It is the unique character of geisha in Japanese society—both traditional and modern—that qualifies them as effective symbols of social contradictions or conflicts. Their identity as entertainers and performers sets them apart from ordinary women and allows them to highlight issues that might appear less clear or less dramatic in conventional life. It is precisely because they are atypical that they prove so useful to writers and dramatists. The "exotic" image of the geisha is often used as a foil for more conventional Japanese womanhood in order to highlight or dramatize fundamental cultural issues. As already indicated above, some geisha characters are remarkably successful as compelling portraits of complicated—often tragic—Japanese women.

Geisha characters in the traditional Japanese performing arts represent a broad range of female stereotypes, encompassing women who are powerful and manipulative at one end of the spectrum and helpless victims at the other. That they are beautiful and stylish, superbly costumed and coiffed, almost goes without saying. Likewise it can be assumed that they are keenly intelligent and self-aware. Beneath the artifice of their magnificently created exteriors beat some hearts that are tough and bitter and others that are soft and pitiable. In every instance, however, the geisha characters are colorful, dramatic, and command attention.

The great parts on the Japanese stage—especially female roles—tend to the melancholic and tragic in character, more so than joyous or triumphant. Women who are victimized by men, or overwhelmed by social pressures, generally elude or overcome their oppressors through self-sacrifice or suicide. The role of Okaru in *Kanadehon Chūshingura* (The Treasury of Loyal Retainers), a perennial favorite of the Kabuki stage and Bunraku puppet theater, conforms to this type. Although it is set in the fourteenth century, the plot closely parallels a celebrated vendetta in eighteenth-century samurai society, describing an event that had occurred shortly before the play was written. In the single role of Okaru, the performer must first portray a well-trained subservient wife of a samurai and later—after her husband has been killed and her family destroyed—a gorgeous courtesan/prostitute who has been sold to the Ichiriki, the greatest teahouse in Kyoto. In her geisha-like role, Okaru participates with cunning guile in the grand conspiracy that will restore honor to her husband's overlord (Act VII of the eleven-act *Chūshingura*). Okaru is one of the archetypal examples of strong but self-sacrificing Japanese womanhood. Smiling through her tears, her inner emotions torn with despair, she must be duplicitous in fending off enemy spies and play the role of conspirator even when it requires her to disguise her true objectives from her own beloved brother. One can almost recognize in Okaru a premodern "sister" to the geisha Okō of *Nihonbashi*, who suffers a similar dilemma in a twentieth-century setting.

Ichikawa Yaozō III and His Geisha Mistress, Torii Kiyonaga, c. 1785
Similar training and interests have made both long-term relationiships and trysts common between geisha and Kabuki actors. Though not recognizable today, the crest on the geisha's kimono would have made her identity obvious to knowledge-able viewers at the time this print was made, just as that on the actor's kimono identifies him as Ichikawa Yaozō.

Geisha On the Silver Screen

Geisha have been at center screen, as many of the most memorable female characters in Japanese cinema, since the very beginning of its history. When moving pictures were still a kind of technical toy, viewed in peepshows and turn-of-the-century carnivals, recreations of geisha dances or postcard scenes of geisha at favorite travel sites were popular subjects for film. Later, as films developed true plots and other narrative devices, fashionable geisha and their eventful lives remained popular subjects for dramatic presentation on film.

Depicting the seasons of a woman's life is a favorite theme of Japanese writers and film directors. The last childlike moments of a girl on the threshold of womanhood, brilliantly captured in Higuchi Ichiyō's 1895 novel *Takekurabe* (translated as "Growing Up"), have provided rich plot material for a number of film adaptations. The 1955 film version of *Takekurabe*, directed by Goshō Heinosuke, stars the popular singer Misora Hibari as the heroine Midori, who grows from girlhood into geisha-hood in the story. Carefree, tomboyish Midori plays recklessly as a young girl with other children in the neighborhood and then develops a secret affection for the shy, reclusive son of the abbot of the local temple. The tone grows more somber as Midori—maturing faster than the uncomprehending boys around her—recognizes the changes in her body that signal what her parents have arranged for her: that she follow her elder sister into the geisha life. Her fate gives the story a deep poignancy. Midori will probably never marry, but must veil her innermost emotions and love for the priest's son by a superficial gaiety as she follows her professional destiny of entertaining male guests in the pleasure district of downtown Tokyo.

The public personality of a geisha is as much her creation as is her beauty and costume. While accepting the conventions that give this artifice its potency, the viewer (whether it be a client or dinner guest, a reader of a novel, or an audience member at a play or film) knows that he is witnessing a performance. When a geisha flirts with her guests at dinner, only a foolish neophyte would mistake it for genuine affection or love. But recognizing the artifice of her "performance" does not reduce

A scene from the 1957 film *Snow Country (Yukiguni)*, directed by Toyoda Shirō, with (left to right) Yachigusa Kaoru, Ikebe Ryō and Kishi Keiko as the hotspring geisha Komako. (Photograph courtesy of Toho Co. Ltd.)

affection or love. But recognizing the artifice of her "performance" does not reduce the pleasure in participating in it; in fact, it is precisely in going along with the game of their seductive performance that patrons of geisha find their greatest pleasure. An essential objective of the geisha's professional training is the ability to make ordinary events seem somehow special, to make small emotions larger, to make insignificant gestures dramatic, and to make dull guests seem uniquely interesting.

Part of the dramatic appeal of geisha in film lies in the blurred distinction between "real life" and "performed life," between reality and artifice, between the contemporary existence of these women and the anachronistic world to which they belong. When is a geisha "acting" and when is she revealing her "true" emotions? It is from this essential ambiguity that art develops. Actresses playing actresses offers a special challenge to a performer and an intriguing twist to delight the audience as well.

Komako, the geisha in a mountain hotspring resort who is the protagonist of Kawabata Yasunari's famous novel, *Yukiguni* (Snow Country), is one example of a character whose motives are ambiguous. Can the hero Shimamura (or the reader) ever be completely certain of what she really feels? Is she in love with him, or merely playing with him? When she bites his finger to give him a frisson of erotic pain, is she performing part of her repertory of geisha games or is she expressing genuine passion? Whom does she really love? Shimamura, or the young girl Yōko (whom she rescues from the fire at the novel's most dramatic moment), or some self-created image of herself? In his 1937 novel, which was one of the first modern Japanese works of fiction to win a broad international readership, Kawabata creates an extraordinary portrait of a woman struggling to free herself from her provincial environment (by trying to run off to Tokyo) as well as from her destiny as a plaything of men. The novel has been filmed several times, most successfully perhaps in the 1957 version, directed by Toyoda Shirō and starring Kishi Keiko as Komako and Ikebe Ryō as Shimamura. As a provincial hotspring geisha, Komako is different in many ways from her urban sisters in the geisha districts of Tokyo, Kyoto, and Osaka. It is interesting, however, that the international popularity of this novel, underscored by Kawabata's later celebrity as a Nobel prizewinner, may have instilled the rather atypical Komako of this book as the image of "geisha" in the western mind.

The master film director Mizoguchi Kenji, whose long career spanned the first six decades of the twentieth century, built a number of films around stories of

A scene from the 1956 film *Flowing (Nagareru)*, directed by Naruse Mikio, set in a geisha house in Tokyo.
Left to right: Kurishima Sumiko, Takamine Hideko, Yamada Isuzu and Tanaka Kinuyō.
(Photograph courtesy of Toho Co. Ltd.)

geisha and the traumatic events of their lives. A constant theme of Mizoguchi's films is the victimization of Japanese women. Among a vast repertory of female types, he created several notable portraits of geisha whose lives are beset by tragedy. In his 1936 film, *Gion no shimai* (Sisters of Gion), Mizoguchi cast the two great film actresses, Yamada Isuzu and Umemura Yōko, in geisha roles of distinctively different personality. Umemura plays the older woman, Umekichi, a weak, conservative, and self-sacrificing geisha, resigned to her lot and grateful for any hints of genuine affection from her clients. Her "sister" Omocha is willful and defiant, repelled by Umekichi's vulnerability and quick to manipulate her male clients for her personal enrichment. In the savagely explicit ending of the film, Omocha — her body broken and bandaged from having been thrown from a moving car by a rejected lover — gazes straight into the camera and cries defiantly: "Why are women treated this way? Why must life be so unfair? Why must there be such things as geisha!" Through Omocha's passionate outcry at the end of this film, Mizoguchi protests not only the specific plight of a geisha, but also the repression of all women everywhere.

Nearly a quarter century later, in 1953, Mizoguchi returned to similar themes in the film *Gionbayashi* (A Geisha). The film's central plot is the story of two geisha in the Gion district of Kyoto: Miyoharu, well established as one of the leading entertainers in the district, and Eiko, her young protégée, who is about to graduate from apprenticeship and make her debut as a full-fledged geisha. As Eiko struggles to maintain her independence, while becoming deeply entangled in the web of relationships of the geisha world, her elder "sister" Miyoharu is forced to sacrifice both her savings and her own personal integrity in attempting to protect Eiko. Although Japanese society had undergone revolutionary changes in the decades separating the two films, the mores of the tradition-bound world of Kyoto geisha remained much the same. Women were still dependent on men who patronized them lavishly before abruptly discarding them, and geisha remained tightly indentured to their houses by social relationships and by the financial debts they could almost never escape. Depicting in this film different aspects of geisha personality (from innocent vulnerability to self-protecting manipulativeness and shrewish or calculating avarice), Mizoguchi decries the victimization of women both by the confines of the narrow geisha world and by the pressures of the society beyond.

A somewhat more benevolent image of a geisha is to be seen in the 1947 film, *Anjōke no butōkai* (A Ball at the Anjō House), directed by Yoshimura Kōzaburō. At

Actress Yamada Isuzu as the Geisha Omocha in the 1936 film _Sisters of Gion_ _(Gion no Shimai)_, directed by Mizoguchi Kenji.

(Photograph courtesy of Shochiku Films.)

the climax of this film, a woman makes a dramatic entrance to a grand party where everyone is costumed in ball gowns and other finery. The camera shows only the back of her feet and the hem of her kimono as she enters the ballroom. Although the identity of this guest is a mystery, those few visible inches of feet and kimono leave no question but that she is a geisha. Her identity is indicated by the simplest visual shorthand: the elegance of her embroidered hem and the soft gracefulness of her walk reveal her character—but it is absolutely unmistakable. This brief glimpse convinces the viewer that the character's entire grooming is impeccable, and as the camera moves upward to reveal her full figure, she is seen to be dressed and coiffed with the sort of perfection that few but a geisha can command. Grooming reveals character, and this particular geisha's personality is soon shown to be as elegant and refined as her appearance.

The other guests fall away in hushed surprise as Chiyo, a geisha and the longtime mistress of the widowed Baron Anjō, host of the party, makes her way through the crowded room to his side. The party is the last that will take place in the aristocratic Anjō house, which will soon go on the auction block, symbolizing the collapse of an entire social class. Though she has long been hidden in the shadows of Baron Anjō's public life, Chiyo has come to stand by him at this moment of intense pain. Murmuring that she need never be made his wife, she quietly asserts her place at his side, supporting him as his world disintegrates. Accepting the reality of her situation, she is strong but not defiant, supportive without being subservient. Chiyo reveals the ideal personality of a geisha whose training and artistry have merged with personal strength in a character of thoroughgoing integrity.

Naruse Mikio's fine film _Nagareru_ (Flowing), made in 1956, depicts a downtown Tokyo geisha residence in the years following World War II. A variety of women occupy the house, including the stern madam who oversees this brood of "sisters." All are viewed through the eyes of a young maid, who is innocently unaware that she is witnessing the decline of an entire world. As Japan struggled in the mid-1950s to emerge from the social, economic, and psychological depression of the war, elegant female entertainers patronized by wealthy businessmen were not among its chief priorities. A world struggling to survive could hardly accommodate the luxury of geisha entertainment. The quiet desperation of the women who were trained for nothing but the geisha world is movingly captured in the novel by Kōda Aya on which this film is based. The underlying theme of films about geisha made during the 1950s is that the gradual erosion of the traditions and values of the geisha world is somehow emblematic of the transition of all Japanese society from the familiar mores of the prewar world into the unfamiliar, uncharted territory of the new postwar period.

Although the economic situation of geisha improved as Japanese affluence increased in the decades of the 1970s and 1980s, their numbers declined and the world of geisha never quite regained a position of central importance in postwar Japanese society. Geisha continue to exist in present-day Japanese society, of course, but their world is generally regarded as a rather archaic relic of earlier glory. Wealthy businessmen continue to patronize the geisha districts of Kyoto, Osaka, and Tokyo, but their expense accounts are not as permissive as they once were nor their wallets as fat. Even more importantly, there are fewer and fewer clients who appreciate the classical forms of music, dance, and poetry well enough to enjoy a traditional evening of geisha entertainment. Few younger businessmen today would leap at the opportunity to spend an evening dining and dallying in the company of geisha. If they must go out for a night on the town, it is more likely to be drinking and dancing at a disco, or going to a movie or concert or sports event. Even a quiet night at home with family seems more attractive to younger Japanese than the unfamiliar classical songs and rather artificial parlor games of geisha entertainment. Perhaps the decline of the geisha world is most manifest in the changes of the streets and alleyways of certain districts of Kyoto that had once been the unchallenged territory of geisha. Gion and Pontochō, which in earlier eras were a magical terrain at night, lit by candles and peopled by elaborately dressed women, are now bright with neon lights advertising bars, nightclubs, and discos, and crowded with wide-eyed tourists pushing their way through the alleys. Where once was heard only the clack-clack of geisha clogs, a hushed giggle, or the gentle refrain of a *shamisen*-accompanied traditional love song, there now prevails a raucous cacophony of rock music, loudspeakers calling out the starting times of the next show or the season's discount prices.

As geisha graciously withdraw from the center stage of the modern Japanese entertainment world, they also seem to have disappeared from fiction or popular entertainments like plays and movies. If they appear at all in contemporary fiction, it is usually in secondary roles and rarely as the principal protagonists. Japanese women of great talent or organizational skills no longer become the proprietors of geisha houses or singing/dancing entertainers specializing in traditional arts. Instead, they turn to politics or become corporate executives, museum directors, or painters and sculptors. They have left the *tatami*-matted rooms for energetic lives in executive offices, traveling the world, or enjoying games of golf and tennis. The women who inhabit the novels and plays and movies of the present day lead totally different lives from the geisha of the prewar period or the 1950s.

The inhabitants and employees in today's shrinking geisha districts travel very different career paths from those of their sisters of earlier eras. No longer indentured for decades or for life, a modern geisha may spend only a few years of training in the traditional arts or work part time as a geisha while completing a university education and preparing for a life in other fields. Many women who have learned to be accomplished entertainers in the old mode of geisha styles now go on to become successful wives of politicians, diplomats, artists, or famous actors, helping their husbands maneuver through the pressures and demands of life in the public eye. It seems ironic that geisha, who were once considered rivals to the wives of professional men, should now be considered exceptionally well qualified to serve as wives themselves.

Like the tea ceremony and many other vestiges of traditional Japanese arts, geisha will never vanish entirely from Japanese culture. Japan has a genius for preserving important elements of its cultural history, maintaining them in a museum-like atmosphere of veneration and respect. The world of the geisha will no doubt be preserved in similar fashion. But as living, breathing individuals, geisha will resist preservation as relics on the altar of the past, and instead will find a more vital role for themselves as performers of traditional music and dance, as teachers of poetry and calligraphy and other classic arts. Ultimately, they will survive as arbiters of an elegant lifestyle that—though no longer prevalent in the daily lives of modern Japanese people—will always be remembered nostalgically as glorifying an earlier era.

Peter M. Grilli, President of the Japan Society of Boston, was previously Director of the Donald Keene Center of Japanese Culture at Columbia University. He has devoted his career as a writer and filmmaker to cultural exchanges between the United States and Japan, where he was raised. He is the author of *Furo: The Japanese Bath* (1985), and his award-winning documentary films include *Dream Window: Reflections on a Japanese Garden* (1994) and *Kurosawa* (2003).

Bibliography

English Sources

Books

Aihara, Kyoko. *Geisha: A Living Tradition.* London: Carlton Books, 2000.

Akiyama, Aisaburo. *Geisha Girl.* Yokohama: Yoshikawa Book Store, 1937.

Allison, Anne. *Nightwork: Sexuality, Pleasure, and Corporation Masculinity in a Tokyo Hostess Club.* Chicago: University of Chicago, 1994.

Anderson, Isabel. *The Spell of Japan.* Boston: The Page Company, 1914.

Asahi Newspapers, Japan. *Japan: A Pictorial Interpretation.* Tokyo: Asahi Shinbun Publishing Co.,1932.

Bacon, Alice Mabel. *Japanese Girls and Women.* Boston and New York: Houghton, Mifflin and Co., 1891.

De Becker, J. E.. *Yoshiwara: The Nightless City.* New York: Frederick Publications, 1960, orig. 1899.

Benedict, Ruth. *The Chrysanthemum and the Sword: Patterns of Japanese Culture.* Boston: Houghton Mifflin Co., 1946.

Bisland, Elizabeth, ed. *The Japanese Letters of Lafcadio Hearn.* Boston and New York: Houghton Mifflin Co., 1910.

Bornoff, Nicholas. *Pink Samurai: Love, Marriage & Sex in Contemporary Japan.* New York: Simon & Schuster, 1991.

Browne, Waldo G. *Japan: The Place and the People.* Boston: Dana Estes & Co., 1901.

Chamberlain, Basil Hall. *Things Japanese: Being notes on various subjects connected with Japan for the use of travellers and others.* London: Kelly & Walsh, 1902.

Chamberlain, Basil Hall and W.B. Mason. *Handbook for Travellers in Japan including the whole empire from Saghalien to Formosa.* London: Kelly & Walsh, Ltd., 1907.

Clark, Timothy. *Ukiyo-e Paintings in the British Museum.* London: British Museum Publications Ltd., 1992.

Clarke, Joseph I.C. *Japan at First Hand.* New York: Dodd and Mead Co., 1918.

Cobb, Jodi. *Geisha: The Life, the Voices, the Art.* New York: Alfred A. Knopf, Inc., 1997.

Cook, Alice and Hiroko Hayashi. *Working Women in Japan.* Ithaca, NY: Cornell University Press, 1980.

Crihfield [Dalby], Liza. *Ko-uta: "Little Songs" of the Geisha World.* Rutland, VT: Charles E. Tuttle, 1979.

Dalby, Liza. *Geisha.* Berkeley and Los Angeles: University of California Press, 1983.

Fujiya Hotel, ed., *We Japanese.* Kanagawa: Fujiya Hotel, 1930.

Downer, Lesley. *Women of the Pleasure Quarters: The Secret History of the Geisha.* New York: Broadway Books, 2001.

_____. *Madame Sadayakko: The Geisha who Bewitched the West.* New York: Gotham Books, 2003.

Durston, Diane. *The Living Traditions of Old Kyoto.* Tokyo: Kodansha International, 1994.

La Farge, John. *An Artist's Letters from Japan.* New York: The Century, 1897.

Fraser, Mrs. Hugh. *The Heart of a Geisha.* New York and London: G.P. Putnam's Sons, 1908.

Fujimoto, T. *The Story of the Geisha Girl.* London: T. Werner Laurie, n.d. (ca. 1920).

Golden, Arthur. *Memoirs of a Geisha.* New York: Vintage Contemporaries, 1997.

Goodwin, Shauna J. *The Shape of Chic: Fashion and Hairstyles in the Floating World.* New Haven, CT: Yale University Art Gallery, 1986.

Hane, Mikiso. *Peasants Rebels and Outcastes: The Underside of Modern Japan.* New York: Pantheon Books, 1982.

Harris, Sara. *House of the 10,000 Pleasures.* New York: E.P. Dutton and Co., 1962.

Hearn, Lafcadio. *Exotics and Retrospectives.* Boston: Little Brown, 1898.

Hibbett, Howard. *The Floating World of Japanese Literature.* Tokyo: Charles E. Tuttle, 1959.

Hildreth, Richard. *Japan as It was and is.* Boston: Phillips, Sampson & Co., 1855.

Holme, C.G. *Glimpses of Old Japanese from Japanese Color Prints: The Geisha.* New York and London: The Studio Publications, n.d. (1923).

Inouye, Jukichi. *Sketches of Tokyo Style.* Yokohama: Torando, 1895.

Iwasaki, Mineko and Rande Brown. *Geisha—A Life.* New York: Atria Books, 2002.

Jackson, Laura. "Bar Hostesses." In *Women in Changing Japan,* edited by J. Lebra, J. Paulson and E. Power. Boulder: Westview Press, 1976.

Jenkins, Donald. *The Floating World Revisited.* Portland, OR: Portland Art Museum, 1993.

Jippensha Ikku. *Hizakurige.* n.p., c. 1800–20. Reprinted as *Shank's Mare.* Translated by Thomas Satchell. Tokyo: Charles E. Tuttle, 1960.

Kanzaki, Emigiku (Miss Kikuya). *I, A Geisha.* Tokyo: Tokyo News Service, 1969.

Kuki, Shōzō. *Reflection on Japanese Taste: The Structure of Iki.* Translated by John Clark. Sydney: Power Institute, 1997.

Laidlaw, Christine Wallace, ed. *Charles Appleton Longfellow: Twenty Months in Japan, 1871–1873.* Cambridge, MA: Friends of the Longfellow House, 1998.

Louis, Lisa. *Butterflies of the Night: Mama-sans, Geisha, Strippers, and the Japanese Men They Serve.* New York: Weatherhill, Inc., 1992.

De Mente, Boye. *Some Prefer Geisha: The Lively Art of Mistress-keeping in Japan.* Rutland, VT: Charles E. Tuttle, 1966.

Murphy, U.G. *The Social Evil in Japan and Allied Subjects with statistics, social evil test cases, and progress of the anti-brothel movement.* Methodist Publishing House, 1908.

Nagai, Kafu. *Geisha in Rivalry.* Kurt Meissner, transl. Rutland, VT: Charles E. Tuttle, 1963.

Nakano, Makiko. *Makiko's Diary: A Merchant Wife in 1910 Kyoto.* Translated by Kazuko Smith. Stanford: Stanford University Press, 1995.

Nishiyama, Matsunosuke. *Edo Culture: Daily Life and Diversions in Urban Japan, 1600–1868.* Honolulu: University of Hawai'i Press, 1997.

Okamoto, Kanako. *The Tale of an Old Geisha and Other Stories.* Santa Barbara: Capra Press, 1985.

Perkins, P.D., with photographs by Francis Haar. *Geisha of Pontocho.* Tokyo: Tokyo News Service, 1954.

Saga, Junichi. *Memories of Silk and Straw: A Self-Portrait of Small-Town Japan.* Translated by Garry O. Evans. Tokyo: Kodansha International, 1987.

Saito, R. *Japanese Coiffure.* Japan Tourist Library no. 28. Tokyo: Board of Tourist Industry, 1939.

Scott, A.C. *The Flower and Willow World: the Story of the Geisha.* New York: Orion Press, 1960.

Seigle, Cecilia Segawa. *Yoshiwara: The Glittering World of the Japanese Courtesan.* Honolulu: University of Hawaii Press, 1993.

Sitwell, Sacheverell. *The Bridge of the Brocade Sash: Travels and Observations in Japan.* Cleveland and New York: The World Publishing, 1959.

Sladen, Douglas. *Queer Things about Japan.* London: Anthony Treherne & Co., 1904.

Smith, Richard G. *Travels in the Land of the Gods.* Edited by Victoria Manthrope. New York: Prentice Hall Press, 1986.

Sneider, Vern. *The Teahouse of the August Moon.* New York: G.P. Putnam & Sons, 1951.

Statler, Oliver. *Shimoda Story.* Rutland, VT and Tokyo: Charles E. Tuttle, 1969.

Swinton, Elizabeth de Sabato. *The Women of the Pleasure Quarter: Japanese Paintings and Prints of the Floating World.* New York: Hudson Hills Press, 1995.

Taylor, Marion. *American Geisha.* London: Geoffrey Bles, 1956.

Underwood, Eleanor. *The Life of a Geisha.* New York: Smithmark, 1999.

Von Siebold, Philipp F. *Manners and Customs of the Japanese in the Nineteenth Century.* Tokyo: Charles E. Tuttle, 1985.

Waterhouse, David. *Images of Eighteenth-Century Japan.* Toronto: Royal Ontario Museum, 1975.

Watt, Andrew, ed. *The Truth About Japan!* Tokyo: Charles E. Tuttle, 1988.

Whitney, Clara. *Clara's Diary: An American Girl in Meiji Japan*. Edited by M. William Steele and Tamiko Ichimate. Tokyo, New York and San Francisco: Kodansha International, 1981.

Williams, Harold S. *Foreigners in Mikadoland*. Rutland, VT: Charles E. Tuttle, 1963.

Yabuta, Yutaka. *Rediscovering Women in Tokugawa Japan*. Edwin O. Reischauer Institute of Japanese Studies Occasional Papers, Harvard University, 2000.

Yamata, Kikuo. *Three Geishas*. New York: John Day Co., 1956.

Yoshikawa, Mako. *One Hundred and One Ways*. New York: Bantam Books, 1999.

PERIODICALS

Baker, Colgate. "The Heart of a Geisha." *The Metropolitan Magazine* 20 (July, 1904): 419–28.

Befu, Harumi. "Ritual Kinship in Japan: Its Variability and Resiliency." *Sociologus* 14 (1964): 150–69.

Fisher, Luchina. "Putting a Face On a Culture." *The New York Times* (August 29, 1999).

Goldscheider, Eric. "Studying Geisha Life from the Inside Out." *The Boston Sunday Globe* (November 7, 1999): 5, 7.

Morris, Narrelle. "Innocence to Deviance: The Fetishization of Japanese Women in Western Fiction, 1890s–1990s." *Intersections: Gender, History and Culture in the Asian Context* 7 (March 2002).

Nakagawa, Tokuemon. "Sumiya: Social, Banqueting and Cultural Salon for Celebrities of the Edo Period." *Daruma* 5, vol.2, no.1 (Winter 1995): 17–20.

Sellers-Young, Barbara. "'Nostalgia' or 'Newness': Nihon Buyō in the United States." *Women in Performance* 23 (Performing Japanese Women, 2002).

Strong, Sarah M. "Performing the Courtesan: In Search of Ghosts at Zuishin-in Letter Mound." *Women in Performance* 23 (Performing Japanese Women, 2002).

Unpublished Sources

Crihfield, Liza. "The Institution of the Geisha in Modern Japanese Society." Ph.D. diss., Stanford University, 1978.

Warner, Langdon. *Kobe to Luchu, Kagoshima, Japan* (A Diary of Langdon Warner), 1909. Manuscript in the collection of the Peabody Essex Museum, Salem, MA.

Japanese Sources

BOOKS

Aihara Kyōko. *Kyoto: Maiko to geiko no okuzashiki* (Kyoto: A Back Reception Room with Apprentice Geisha and Geisha). Tokyo: Bunshun Shinsho, 2001.

Adachi Naorō. *Geinin fūzoku sugata* (Silhouettes of Performing Artists in the Pleasure Districts).Tokyo: Gakufū Shoin, 1957.

[Anonymous]. *Geishagaku nyūmon* (An Introduction to Geisha Studies). Shizuoka: Kinjōkan, 1969.

Hashimoto Sumiko, ed. "Musubigami to kamikazari" (Hairdressing and Hair Ornaments) *Nihon no bijutsu*, no. 23 (March 1968).

Hayashida Kametarō. *Geisha no kenkyū* (Research on Geisha). Tokyo: Chōbunkaku, 1929.

Hida Chiho. *Shinbashi seikatsu yonjūyonen* (Forty-four Years of Living in Shinbashi). Tokyo: Gakufū Shoin, 1956.

Ida Yoshisato. *Maiko no shiki* (Four Seasons of Maiko). Kyoto: Shinshindō, 1975.

Inoue Seizō. *Hakata fūzokushi: yūrihen* (History of the Entertainment Business in Hakata: The Pleasure Quarters). Fukuoka: Sekibunkan, 1968.

Ishihara Tetsuo. *Nihongami no sekai: kamigata to kamikazari* (The World of Japanese Hair: Coiffure and Hair Ornaments). Kyoto: Media Sekkei, 2000.

Iwasaki Mineko. *Geiko Mineko no hanaikusa* (The *Geiko* [Geisha] Mineko's Forays in the Flower World). Tokyo: Kōdansha, 2001.

_____. *Gion no kyōkun: noboru hito, noborikirazu ni owaru hito* (Precepts of Gion: People Who Rose in the World And Those Who Could Not). Tokyo: Gentōsha, 2003.

Kikkawa Eishi. *Nihon ongaku no rekishi* (The History of Music in Japan). Osaka: Sōgensha, 1990.

Kishii Yoshie. *Onna geisha no jidai* (The Age of the Female Geisha). Tokyo: Seiabō, 1974.

Kuki Shūzō. *Iki no kōzō* (The Structure of *Iki*). Tokyo: Iwanami Shoten, 1930.

Kumagai Yasujirō. *Gion to maiko* (Gion and Maiko). Kyoto: Tankōsha, 1974.

Kurokawa Mamichi, ed. *Edo fūzoku zue* (Pictorial Record of Life in Edo). Tokyo: Kashiwa Bijutsu Shuppan, 1993.

Masuda Sayo. *Geisha kutō no hanshōgai* (A Geisha's Bitter Struggles over Half Her Life). Tokyo: Heibonsha, 1973.

Matsunoya Tokiwa. *Geisha tora no maki* (A Key to Geisha). Tokyo: Inoue Teikichi, 1894.

Minakami Tsutomu. *Onna no morite* (A Heaping Batch of Women). Tokyo: Iwanami Shoten, 1975.

Mitamura Engyō. *Edo geisha no kenkyū* (Research on Geisha in Edo) in *Mitamura Engyō Zenshū* (Complete Works of Mitamura Engyō) vol.10. Tokyo: Chūōkōronsha, 1975.

——— *Kyō no geiko no shinjō tate* (A Kyoto Geisha's Steps Toward Suicide) in *Mitamura Engyō Zenshū* (Complete Works of Mitamura Engyō), vol.10. Tokyo: Chūōkōronsha, 1975.

Mitani Kazuma. *Ukiyoe: Edo no ichinen* (Ukiyoe: The Year in Edo). Tokyo: Ukiyoe Ōta Kinen Bijutsukan, 1988.

Miyake Kōken, ed., *Geigi tokuhon* (The Geisha Reader). Tokyo: Zenkoku Dōmei Ryōriya Shinbunshahan, 1935.

Mizobuchi Hiroshi. *Gion Ichisuzu* (Ichisuzu of Gion). Tokyo: Shōgakkan, 2000.

Nakamura Kiharu. *Edokko geisha ichidaiki.* (Story of An Edokko Geisha) Vols. 1–3. Tokyo: Shisōsha, 1983, 1984, 1987.

Nakanishi Rei. *Nagasaki bura bura bushi* (The "Bura Bura" Song of Nagasaki). Tokyo: Bungei Shunjū, 1999.

Nakano Eizō. *Yūjo no seikatsu* (The Lives of Courtesans). Tokyo: Yūzankaku, 1966.

Nihon Fūzoku Shigakkai, ed., *Shiryō ga kataru Edo no kurashi hyaku nijū ni wa* (One Hundred Twenty-two Stories of Life in Edo from Historical Documents). Tokyo: Tsukubanesha, 1994.

Ōsawa Makoto, Kaneko Shigetaka, and Matsui Hideo. *Keisai Eisen ten: botsugo 150 nen kinen* (Exhibition of Keisai Eisen on the 150th Anniversary of His Death). Tokyo: Ukiyoe Ōta Kinen Bijutsukan, 1997.

Sasama Yoshihiko. *Edo seikatsu zukan* (Pictorial Compendium of Life in Edo). Tokyo: Hakushobō, 1995.

Satō Yōjin and Hanasaki Kazuo. *Edo shokoku yūri zue* (Pleasure Quarters in the Various Districts of Edo). Tokyo: Miki Shobō, 1994.

Satō Yōjin. *Seirō wadan shinzō zui* (Gentle Talks of the Green Houses: Some Examples of *Shinzō*). Tokyo: Miki Shobō, 1976.

Setouchi Harumi. *Kyō mandara* (Mandala of Kyoto). Tokyo: Kōdansha, 1972.

Shinohara Haru. *Kikugasane* (Overlaid Chrysanthemums). Tokyo: Tanshiki Insatsu, 1956.

Sumita Yoshihisa. *Aru bazoku geisha den* (Traditions of an Adventurous Geisha). Tokyo: Sōshisha, 1980.

Takahashi Hakushin. *Ukiyoe zanmai: Kunisada to Eisen* (Nothing But *Ukiyoe*: Kunisada and Eisen). Obihiro City: Arita Shobō, 1980.

Takashimaya Department Store. *Tsuruta Eitarō kinsaku ten: maiko to odoriko to rafu* (Recent Works by Tsuruta Eitarō: *Maiko*, Dancing Girls and Nudes). Tokyo: Takashimaya, 1982.

———. *Tsuruta Eitarō aburae ten: maiko to Kyōraku no shiki* (Oil Paintings by Tsuruta Eitarō: *Maiko* and the Four Seasons of Kyoto). Tokyo: Takashimaya, 1984.

Tobacco & Salt Museum. *Ukiyo-e*. Tokyo: Tabako to Shio Hakubutsukan, 1984.

Watari Keisuke. *Miyako no hanamachi* (The Pleasure Districts of the Old Capital). Tokyo: Sekkasha, 1961.

Yomiuri Shinbunsha, ed. *Baaton Hōmes shashinshū* (Collection of Photographs by Burton Holmes). Tokyo: Yomiuri Shinbun, 1974.

JAPANESE EARLY-MODERN SOURCES

[Anonymous]. *Kanten kenbunki* (during or after 1789–1801). In *Enseki jisshū*, vol. 5, edited by Iwamoto Kattōshi. Tokyo: Kokusho Kankōkai, 1979.

[Anonymous]. *Yoshiwara zatsuwa* (c. 1781–1889). In *Enseki jisshū*, vol. 5, edited by Iwamoto Kattōshi. Tokyo: Kokusho Kankōkai, 1979.

Baba Bunkō. *Tōsei takeno zokudan* (1752). In *Enseki jisshū*, vol. 2, edited by Iwamoto Kattōshi. Tokyo: Kokusho Kankōkai, 1907.

Ishihara Toryō. *Dōbō goen ihon kōi* (c. 1781–89). In *Nihon zuihitsu taisei*, vol. 3(2), edited by Nihon Zuihitsu Taisei Henshūbu. Tokyo: Yoshiwara Kōbunkan, 1976.

Keisai Eisen. *Ukiyo gafu* (Drawing Manual of the Floating World), vols. 1–3. Edo: no publ., n.d. (c. 1830).

Kitagawa Morisada. *Morisada Mankō* (1853). In *Morisada Mankō*. 5 vols. Tokyo: Tōkyōdō Shuppan, 1992.

Kitamura Nobuyo. *Kiyūshōran* (1830). In *Nihon zuihitsu taisei*, vol. 1(1), 1(2), edited by Nihon Zuihitsu Taisei Henshūbu. Tokyo: Yoshikawa Kōbunkan, 1996.

_____. *Kagai manroku seigo* (date unknown). In *Nihon zuihitsu taisei*, vol. 1(23), edited by Nihon Zuihitsu Taisei Henshūbu. Tokyo: Yoshikawa Kōbunkan, 1994.

Moriyama Takamori. *Ama no takumo no ki* (1798). In *Nihon zuihitsu taisei*, vol. 2 (22), edited by Nihon Zuihitsu Taisei Henshūbu. Tokyo: Yoshiwara Kōbunkan, 1974.

_____. *Shizu no odamaki* (1802). In *Nihon zuihitsu taisei*, vol. 3(4), edited by Nihon Zuihitsu Taisei Henshūbu. Tokyo: Yoshiwara Kōbunkan, 1977.

Ōta Nanpō. *Yakko dako* (1813). In *Nihon zuihitsu taisei*, vol. 2(14), edited by Nihon Zuihitsu Taisei Henshūbu. Tokyo: Yoshiwara Kōbunkan, 1994.

Oyamada Shōsō. *Sangenkō* (1847). In *Kinkō bungei onchi sōsho*, vol. 5, edited by Kishigami Shikken. Tokyo: Hakubunkan, 1891.

Ryūtei Tanehiko. *Geisha tora no maki*. Original woodblock edition, c. 1830.

Shōji Katsutomi. *Ihon Dōbō Goen* (1720). In *Nihon zuihitsu taisei*, vol. 3(1), edited by Nihon Zuihitsu Taisei Henshūbu. Tokyo: Nihon Zuihitsu Taisei Kankōkai, 1929.

Shūsanjin. *Ryūka tsūshi* (1844). In Kinsei bungei sōsho, vol. 10, edited by Kokusho Kankōkai. Tokyo: Kokusho Kankōkai, 1911.

Tegara Okamochi. *Nochi wa mukashi monogatari* (1803). In *Nihon zuihitsu taisei*, vol. 3(6), edited by Nihon Zuihitsu Taisei Henshūbu. Tokyo: Nihon Zuihitsu Taisei Kankōkai, 1930.

PERIODICALS

Asahara, Sumi. "Fūfu de iku hanamachi" (Visiting Geisha Districts as a Couple). *Sarai* 23 (1997): 12–31.

Bigi bishū, hitoya no yume: Gion (Beautiful Geisha, Delicious Sake—A Night of Dreams: Gion). *Taiyō* no 6, 1972.

Edo no iki (The Flair of Edo). *Bessatsu Taiyō* 35, Heibonsha, 1981.

Geisha-san ni aitai (I Want to Meet A Geisha). *Tōkyōjin* 154, June 2000.

Ichido wa shitai: ozashiki asobi (We All Want to Do It Just Once: Attend A Geisha Party) *Fukuoka 2001* 8, (November, 1999): 6–17.

Kanbayashi Toyoaki. "Kushi no hanashi." *Chawan* 85 (March, 1938): 41–56.

Nagasaki Iwao. *Onna no sōshi gu. Nihon no bijutsu*, no. 396 (May, 1999).

Niimoto, Ryōichi with Arthur Golden. "Geiko monogatari: Sayuri tanjō hiwa" (*Memoirs of a Geisha*: Secrets of the Birth) *Bungeishunjū* (December, 1999): 190–199.

Ryōtei saiken. Bessatsu Taiyō 255, Heibonsha, 1983.

VIDEOS AND FILMS AVAILABLE IN ENGLISH

Bangiku (Late Chrysanthemums), directed by Naruse Mikio (subtitled, 1954). Explores the plight of geisha as they age, and by extension, that of older, unmarried women everywhere.

The Barbarian and the Geisha, directed by John Huston (1958). Starring John Wayne, this action-packed film covers the fictionalized exploits of Townsend Harris, first U.S. consul to Japan, and his supposed geisha/concubine, Okichi.

Geisha, produced by Films for the Humanities (2000).

The Geisha Boy, directed by Frank Tashlin (1958). A Jerry Lewis comedy in which Lewis plays a USO magician who befriends a Japanese boy and falls in love with his geisha mother.

Gion-bayashi (English title *A Geisha*), directed by Mizoguchi Kenji (subtitled, 1953). The best-known Japanese geisha film in the West. Reflects the postwar environment of Japan, as well as the situation of geisha in the Gion district of Kyoto in the postwar period.

My Geisha, directed by Jack Cardiff, starring Shirley MacLaine (1961). Interesting for its exploration of attitudes about geisha in the U.S. in the aftermath of the Occupation, and for the real geisha it features.

The Secret Life of Geisha, A&E Television Networks documentary, narrated by Susan Sarandon (1999). Gives a broad and varied view of geisha, both historical and contemporary. Includes interviews with researchers, customers of geisha, and geisha themselves, active and retired, young and old.

The Secret World of Geishas, Discovery Channel, (2002). Looks at the various aspects of geisha life, from makeup and dress to practice and performance, by following geisha in the Gion district of Kyoto.

Yukiguni (Snow Country), directed by Toyoda, Shiro (subtitled, 1957). Based on the novel by Nobel Prize for Literature-winner Kawabata Yasunari, this film explores the respective feelings of isolation of a Tokyo artist and his rural geisha who lives in the snow country of northern Japan.

Women of the Pleasure Quarter: A Journey of the Imagination, Worcester Art Museum (1995). Looks at the Japanese pleasure quarters of the seventeenth through nineteenth centuries, emphasizing the women who populated these areas as they were depicted in woodblock prints and paintings.

List of Illustrations

p. 37
Unidentified artist
Apprentice Geisha, c. 1925
Printed postcard
5 1/2 x 3 1/2 in. (14 x 8.9 cm)
Peabody Essex Museum, Salem, Massachusetts
Gift of Kojiro Tomita
Photography by Jeffrey Dykes

p. 38
Tsukioka Yoshitoshi (1839–92)
Geisha Looking in a Mirror, 1860s
Ink and color on silk
45 3/8 x 15 in. (155 x 38 cm)
Private collection

p. 39
Unidentified artist
Kimono with Chinese Bellflower Design,
c. 1930
Silk
62 1/2 x 51 7/8 in. (159 x 131.6 cm)
Private collection
Photography by Noca Wakihiko

p. 40 right
Unidentified artist
Kimono with Decoration of Pinks, c. 1935
Silk
64 x 50 in. (162.8 x 126.5 cm)
Private collection
Photography by Noca Wakihiko

p. 40 left
Unidentified artist
The Former Kanazawa Geisha Tsunaji, c. 1940
Gelatin silver print
Private collection
Photography by Noca Wakihiko

p. 41 left
Felice Beato (1825–1903)
Dressing the Hair, 1860s
Albumen print
Peabody Essex Museum, Salem, Massachusetts
Photography by Jeffrey Dykes

p. 41
Unidentified artist
A Nagasaki Geisha, c. 1800
Ink and color on paper
38 x 19 in. (96.8 x 48.4 cm)
Peabody Essex Museum, Salem, Massachusetts
Gift of Captain Henry King; E6540
Photography by Jeffrey Dykes

p. 42 left
Unidentified artist
Hair Ornament (Kanzashi) with Design of
Bodhidharma, 19th century
Silver, gold
8 3/4 x 1 in. (22.1 x 1.9 cm)
Peabody Essex Museum, Salem, Massachusetts
Gift of Museum of Fine Arts, Boston; E20302
Photography by Jeffrey Dykes

p. 42 center
Unidentified artist
Hair Ornament (Kanzashi) with Compass,
1780–1820
Silver, gold, glass, magnet, lead
6 3/4 x 1 in. (17 x 2.5 cm)
Peabody Essex Museum, Salem, Massachusetts
Museum purchase, R. C. Billings Fund;
E14731
Photography by Jeffrey Dykes

p. 42 right
Unidentified artist
Hair Ornament (Kanzashi) with Mother-of-

Pearl Bead, mid-to-late 19th century
Silver, mother-of-pearl
7 1/2 x 3/4 in. (19.3 x 1.9 cm)
Peabody Essex Museum, Salem, Massachusetts
Museum purchase, R. C. Billings Fund;
E14720
Photography by Jeffrey Dykes

p. 43 top right
Unidentified artist
Hair Ornament (Kanzashi) of Tortoiseshell in
Cherry Branch Design, 19th century
Tortoiseshell, silver, coral
7 1/2 x 1 3/4 in. (18.8 x 4.3 cm)
Peabody Essex Museum, Salem, Massachusetts
Gift of Lassell Seminary; E14719
Photography by Jeffrey Dykes

p. 43 top left
Unidentified artist
Decorative Comb with Design of Sparrow and
Chrysanthemum, mid-to-late 19th century
Gold and colored lacquer on wood
1 1/2 x 4 x 3/8 in. (3.6 x 10.4 x 0.7 cm)
Peabody Essex Museum, Salem, Massachusetts
Gift of Dr. Charles Goddard Weld; E6163
Photography by Jeffrey Dykes

p. 43 center
Unidentified artist
Decorative Comb with Design of Crows, first
half 19th century
Colored lacquer on wood
2 3/4 x 4 1/8 x 1/4 in. (6.9 x 10.7 x 0.6 cm)
Peabody Essex Museum, Salem, Massachusetts
Gift of Edward S. Morse; E7246
Photography by Jeffrey Dykes

p. 43 bottom
Unidentified artist
Decorative Comb with Design of Azaleas, first
half 19th century
Colored lacquer on wood
2 3/4 x 4 3/8 x 1/4 in. (6.9 x 11.9 x 0.6 cm)
Peabody Essex Museum, Salem, Massachusetts
Gift of Dr. Helen Abbot Michael; E7992
Photography by Jeffrey Dykes

p. 44
Hosoda Eishi (1756–1829)
The Oiran Kasugano of the Sumidamaya and
Her Retinue (Sumidamaya nai Kasugano,
Tomichi, Urano), c. 1790
Woodblock print
17 x 12 7/8 in. (43.7 x 32.5 cm)
Peabody Essex Museum, Salem, Massachusetts,
Gift of Lee Higgenson, Jr.; E37895
Photography by Jeffrey Dykes

p. 45
Kitagawa Utamaro (1754–1806)
Geisha and Attendant in Snow, c. 1793
Woodblock print
14 1/8 x 9 1/4 in. (35.9 x 23.5 cm)
Honolulu Academy of Arts
Gift of James A. Michener, 1970
(15,579)

p. 46
Keisai Eisen (1790–1848)
The Oiran Michitose of the Miuraya with Her
Child Attendants (Miuraya nai Michitose,
Chiyono, Kakushi), c. 1825
Woodblock print
14 7/8 x 10 in. (37.8 x 25.4 cm)
Peabody Essex Museum, Salem, Massachusetts
E300132
Photography by Jeffrey Dykes

p. 47 left and right
Keisai Eisen (1790–1848)
Floating World Characters, from the woodblock
printed book, Drawing Manual of the Floating
World (Ukiyo gafu), c. 1830
Woodblock print
8 7/8 x 6 1/4 in. (22.7 x 15.7 cm) [each]
Peabody Essex Museum, Salem, Massachusetts
Photography by Jeffrey Dykes

p. 48
Katsushika Hokusai (1760–1849)
Reclining Courtesan, c. 1802
Ink and colors on silk
11 1/2 x 17 1/2 in. (29.2 x 44.5 cm) [image]
Collection of Peter Grilli and Diana Grilli
Photography by John Bigelow Taylor

p. 49
Unidentified artist
The Geisha Apprentice Tsunaji, c. 1926
Gelatin silver print
Courtesy Keiko Tanada, Kanazawa, Japan
Photography by Noca Wakihiko

p. 50
George Henry (1858–1943)
Geisha Girl, 1894
Oil on canvas
29 3/8 x 24 1/2 in. (74.6 x 62.2 cm)
National Gallery of Scotland

p. 51
Attributed to Raimund (1839–1911) or Franz
(act. Yokohama 1879–85) von Stillfried
Japanese Woman, c. 1879–82
Hand-colored albumen print
Peabody Essex Museum, Salem, Massachusetts
Gift of Mrs. Sumner Pingree
Photography by Jeffrey Dykes

p. 53
Yōshū Chikanobu (1838–1912)
Entertainments in the Tenth Month (Jūgatsu),
from the series Edo Customs of the Twelve
Months (Edo fūzoku jūnikagetsu no uchi), 1889
Woodblock print
14 1/8 x 27 1/2 in. (36.1 x 70.1 cm) [sheet]
Private collection
Photography by Jeffrey Dykes

p. 54 left
Unidentified artist
Teahouse at Oji, 1880s
Hand-colored albumen print
Peabody Essex Museum, Salem, Massachusetts
Photography by Jeffrey Dykes

p. 54 right
Attributed to Raimund (1839–1911) or Franz
(act. Yokohama 1879–85) von Stillfried
Young Woman at Home, c. 1879–82
hand-colored albumen print
Peabody Essex Museum, Salem, Massachusetts
Gift of Mrs. Sumner Pingree
Photography by Jeffrey Dykes

p. 55
Felice Beato (1825–1903)
Geisha on Charles' Veranda, 1872
Hand-colored albumen print
Peabody Essex Museum, Salem, Massachusetts
Gift of Mrs. Sumner Pingree
Photography by Jeffrey Dykes

p. 57
Unidentified artist
The Yoshiwara, Tokyo, 1880s–90s
Albumen print

p. 79 center
Unidentified artist
Obi with Black, Brown and White Stripe
Pattern, c. 1930
Silk
155 1/2 x 12 3/8 in. (395 cm x 31.5 cm)
Private collection
Photography by Noca Wakihiko

p. 79 right
Unidentified artist
Obi with Gold and Silver Plum Blossoms on
Black Ground, c. 1930
Silk, metallic thread
175 1/2 x 12 3/8 in. (446 x 31.5 cm)
Private collection
Photography by Noca Wakihiko

p. 80
Yoko Yamamoto
First Step Into Kagurazaka, March 1983
From the series *Diaries of a Kagurazaka
Woman, 1983–2003*, 1983
Gelatin silver print
© yoko yamamoto, all rights reserved

p. 82
Yoko Yamamoto
A Geisha at Home, December 29, 2000
(Kagurazaka), from the series *Tokyo Geisha
1985–2003*, 2000
C print
© yoko yamamoto, all rights reserved

p. 83
Yoko Yamamoto
Geisha in the New Millenium, January 11,
2001 (Kagurazaka), from the series *Tokyo
Geisha 1985–2003*, 2001
C print
© yoko yamamoto, all rights reserved

p. 84
Yoko Yamamoto
Shamisen Training, July 15, 2001 (Kagurazaka),
from the series *Tokyo Geisha 1985–2003*, 2001
C print
© yoko yamamoto, all rights reserved

p. 85
Yoko Yamamoto
Shamisen Teaching, July 15, 2001
(Kagurazaka), from the series *Tokyo Geisha
1985–2003*, 2001
C print
© yoko yamamoto, all rights reserved

p. 86
Yoko Yamamoto
Proper Form, May 1997 (Shinbashi), from the
series *Tokyo Geisha 1985–2003*, 1997
C print
© yoko yamamoto, all rights reserved

p. 87
Yoko Yamamoto
Dance Training, May 24, 2000 (Kagurazaka),
from the series *Tokyo Geisha 1985–2003*, 2000
C print
© yoko yamamoto, all rights reserved

p. 88 top
Yoko Yamamoto
Selfless Star, Marichiyo, September 24, 1994
(Shinbashi), from the series *Tokyo Geisha
1985–2003*, 1994
C print
© yoko yamamoto, all rights reserved

p. 88 bottom
Yoko Yamamoto
Curtain Time, September 22, 1993 (Asakusa),
from the series *Tokyo Geisha 1985–2003*, 1993
C print
© yoko yamamoto, all rights reserved

p. 89
Yoko Yamamoto
Iki (Chic) Marichiyo, 86, May 31, 1994
(Shinbashi), from the series *Diaries of a
Kagurazaka Woman, 1983–2003*, 1994
Gelatin silver print
© yoko yamamoto, all rights reserved

p. 90
Yoko Yamamoto
Formal Tea, May 31, 2000 (Shinbashi), from
the series *Tokyo Geisha 1985–2003*, 2000
C print
© yoko yamamoto, all rights reserved

p. 91 right
Yoko Yamamoto
Shamisen (Kanjinchō) #5, January 14, 1998 ,
from the series *Diaries of a Kagurazaka Woman,
1983–2003*, 1998
Olive black gelatin silver print
© yoko yamamoto, all rights reserved

p. 91 left
Yoko Yamamoto
Dancing Hand (#1), December 27, 1997
(Kagurazaka), from the series *Diaries of a
Kagurazaka Woman, 1983–2003*, 1997
Olive black gelatin silver print
© yoko yamamoto, all rights reserved

p. 92
Yoko Yamamoto
"Little Song" Dance, November 6, 2000
(Akasaka), from the series *Tokyo Geisha 1985–
2003*, 2000
C print
© yoko yamamoto, all rights reserved

p. 93
Yoko Yamamoto
Egret Maiden, 1992 (Kagurazaka), from the
series *Tokyo Geisha 1985–2003*, 1992
C print
© yoko yamamoto, all rights reserved

pp. 94
Yoko Yamamoto
Geisha *Shōjō*, 1992 (Akasaka), from the series
Tokyo Geisha 1985–2003, 1992
C print
© yoko yamamoto, all rights reserved

p. 95
Yoko Yamamoto
Amidst the Shadows, February 22, 1993
(Kagurazaka) from the series *Diaries of a
Kagurazaka Woman, 1983–2003*, 1998
C print
Peabody Essex Museum, Salem, Massachusetts,
Museum Purchase, 2004
© yoko yamamoto, all rights reserved

p. 96
Yoko Yamamoto
Rouge, January 8, 1998 (Kagurazaka), from the
series *Diaries of a Kagurazaka Woman, 1983–
2003*, 1998
Olive black gelatin silver print
© yoko yamamoto, all rights reserved

p. 97
Yoko Yamamoto
New Year's Gift, January 10, 1996, from the
series *Diaries of a Kagurazaka Woman, 1983–
2003*, 1996
Gelatin silver print
Peabody Essex Museum, Salem, Massachusetts,
Museum Purchase, 2004
© yoko yamamoto, all rights reserved

p. 98
Yoko Yamamoto
New Year's Party in Kanetanaka, January 18,
1997 (Shinbashi), from the series *Tokyo Geisha
1985–2003*, 1997
Color print
© yoko yamamoto, all rights reserved

p. 99
Yoko Yamamoto
Tossing Fans, April 12, 2003 (Asakusa), from the
series *Tokyo Geisha 1985–2003*, 2003
C print
© yoko yamamoto, all rights reserved

p. 100
Yoko Yamamoto
Praying to *Bishamon* God, November 7, 1990 ,
from the series *Diaries of a Kagurazaka Woman,
1983–2003*, 1990
Gelatin silver print
© yoko yamamoto, all rights reserved

p. 101
Yoko Yamamoto
At Sunset, 1987 (Kagurazaka), from the series
Tokyo Geisha 1985–2003, 1987
C print
© yoko yamamoto, all rights reserved

p. 102
Mihata Jōryū (active 1830–50), calligraphy by
Sōkyū Dōjin
New Year's Dancer, c. 1830–50
Hanging scroll; ink and color on silk
46.6 x 16.5 in. (118.4 x 41.9 cm)
Collection of Robert and Betsy Feinberg

p. 103
Unidentified artist
Three Young Geisha with Musical Instruments,
1880–1900
Hand-colored albumen print
Peabody Essex Museum, Salem, Massachusetts
Photography by Jeffrey Dykes

p. 104
Katsukawa Shunchō (fl. c. 1780–95), calligra-
phy by Rankō
Strolling Along the Riverbank, early 1780s
Hanging scroll; ink and colors on silk
37 7/8 x 13 7/8 in. (96.3 x 35.3 cm)
Private collection

p. 105
Unknown artist
Entertainments at Shinagawa, late 1740s
Woodblock print
10.6 x 16.2 in. (26.9 x 41.1 cm) [sheet]
Honolulu Academy of Arts
Gift of James A. Michener, 1957 (13.990)

p. 106 top left
Unidentified artist
The Kanazawa Geisha Tsunaji and Her
Teacher, Kineya Gosō, c. 1928
Gelatin silver print
Private collection
Photography by Noca Wakihiko

p. 106 top right
Unidentified artist
A Kanazawa Geisha Performing at a Teahouse,
1930s
Gelatin silver print
Private collection
Photography by Noca Wakihiko

p. 106 bottom
Unidentified artist
Child in Dance Performance, Kanazawa, 1930s
Gelatin silver print
Private collection
Photography by Noca Wakihiko

p. 107 left
Suzuki Harunobu (1725–1770)
A Dancing Girl Performing "The Egret
Maiden" for a Young Lord, 1760s
Woodblock print
7 1/4 x 12 3/8 in. (18.4 x 31.4 cm)
Metropolitan Museum of Art
H.O. Havemeyer Collection, Bequest of Mrs.
H.O. Havemeyer, 1929 (JP1645)
Photograph © 1979 The Metropolitan
Museum of Art

p. 101 right
Unidentified artist
Dancer, late 17th century
Hanging scroll; ink and color on silk
21 3/4 x 10 7/8 in. (55.2 x 27.7 cm)
Minneapolis Institute of Arts

p. 108
Unidentified artist
Three Geisha Dancers, Yokohama, c. 1885
Hand-colored albumen print
Peabody Essex Museum, Salem, Massachusetts
Gift of Charles G. Weld
Photography by Jeffrey Dykes

p. 109 top left
Unidentified artist
Dance Fan, early–mid 20th century
Wood, paper, silver leaf, pigment, lead
11 1/2 x 19 3/4 in. (29.2 x 50.2 cm)
Peabody Essex Museum, Salem, Massachusetts
Gift of Lena Bragg; E54255
Photography by Jeffrey Dykes

p. 109 top right
Unidentified artist
Shamisen for Nagauta Performance, early–mid
20th century
Rosewood, catskin, ivory, silk, paper, brass
38 x 8 x 4 in. (96.5 x 20.3 x 10.2 cm)
Courtesy R. Scott Drayer [Sōzan], Yamahatsu,
Kazuemachi, Kanazawa, Japan
Photography by Noca Wakihiko

p. 109 bottom
Unidentified artist
Obi of Nagoya Type Embroidered with Cherry
Blossoms, Drums, and Cock, c. 1930
Silk
148 3/4 x 12 3/8 in. (378 x 31.5 cm)
Private collection
Photography by Noca Wakihiko

p. 110
Yoko Yamamoto
Shadow Shamisen, September 22, 1992
C print
© yoko yamamoto, all rights reserved

p. 111 top
Eishōsai Chōki (active c. 1785–1805)
Geisha Musicians Performing on a River
Pleasure Boat, c. 1796

Woodblock print, panel of pentatych
15 3/8 x 10 1/2 in. (39.1 x 26.7 cm)
Metropolitan Museum of Art
Rogers Fund, 1914 (JP190)
Photograph © 2003 The Metropolitan
Museum of Art

p. 111 bottom
Attributed to Ogawa Kazumasa
Young Geisha Playing Hand Drum, c. 1895
Albumen print
Peabody Essex Museum, Salem, Massachusetts
Photography by Jeffrey Dykes

p. 112 top left
Utagawa Toyokuni (1769–1825)
Geisha and Child Dancer Entertaining the
Daughter of a Lord, from an untitled album
[Twenty-four Scenes of Women], 1816
Board-mounted album leaf; ink and color on silk
15 3/4 x 23 in. (40 x 58.4 cm)
Private collection

p. 112 top right
Utagawa Toyokuni (1769–1825)
Early Morning Lesson, from an untitled album
[Twenty-four Scenes of Women], 1816
Board mounted album leaf; ink and color on
silk
15 3/4 x 23 in. (40 x 58.4 cm)
Private collection

p. 112 bottom
Unidentified artist
Kanazawa Geisha Drums: Taiko and
Zashikidaiko, 20th century
Taiko: Pawlonia wood, cowhide, brass, lacquer,
silk, deerskin;
10.8 x 17.3 x 16.5 in. (27.4 x 43.8 x 41.9 cm)
Zashikidaiko: Zelkova wood, oak, cowhide, silk,
brass, iron;
27.6 x 30.5 x 10.6 in. (69.8 x 77.5 x 26.9 cm)
Courtesy R. Scott Drayer [Sōzan], Yamahatsu,
Kazuemachi, Kanazawa, Japan
Photography by Noca Wakihiko

p. 113 left
Utagawa Toyokuni (1769–1825)
Examining New Hair Ornaments, from an
untitled album [Twenty-four Scenes of
Women], 1816
Board-mounted album leaf: ink and color on silk
15 3/4 x 23 in. (40 x 58.4 cm)
Private collection

p. 113 right
Utagawa Toyokuni (1769–1825)
Choosing Kimono Cloth, from an untitled
album [Twenty-four Scenes of Women], 1816
Board-mounted album leaf: ink and color on silk
15 3/4 x 23 in. (40 x 58.4 cm)
Private collection

p. 114
Hosoda Eishi (1756–1829)
Parody of Ōishi Kuranosuke Feigning De-
bauchery at the Ichiriki Teahouse, c. 1797
Woodblock print, triptych
14 3/8 x 30 in. (36.5 x 76.2 cm)
Metropolitan Museum of Art
Henry L. Phillips Collection, Bequest of Henry
L. Phillips, 1939 (JP2817)

p. 115
Kubo Shunman (1757–1820)
Summer Entertainments at the Shikian
Restaurant, early 1790s
Woodblock print, one panel of a diptych
14 1/4 x 9 7/8 in. (36.2 x 25.3 cm)
Museum of Fine Arts, Boston

William Sturgis Bigelow Collection; 11.14941
Photograph © 2003 Museum of Fine Arts, Boston

p. 116
Torii Kiyonaga (1752–1815)
Cooling off at Nakasu (Nakasū suzumi), from
the series Selection of Current-day Beauties from the
Pleasure Quarters (Tōsei yūri bijin awase), 1783
Woodblock print
15 3/8 x 10 1/2 in. (39.1 x 26.7 cm)
Museum of Fine Arts, Boston
William Sturgis Bigelow Collection; 11.13892

p. 117
Suzuki Harunobu (1725–70)
Two Young Women Playing A Gesture Game, c.
1768–69
Woodblock print
11 1/4 x 8 5/8 in. (28.6 x 21.9 cm)
Metropolitan Museum of Art
Henry L. Phillips Collection, Bequest of Henry L.
Phillips, 1939 (JP2778)
Photograph©2003 The Metropolitan Museum of Art

p. 118
Unidentified artist
Party for a Military Man, Kanazawa, 1930s
Gelatin silver print
Private collection
Photography by Noca Wakihiko

p. 119
Keisai Eisen (1780–1848)
Geisha Changing a Shamisen String, 1820s
From the series, The Six Jeweled Rivers
(Mutamagawa)
Woodblock print
13 5/8 x 9 5/8 in. (sheet)
Peabody Essex Museum, Salem, Massachusetts
Gift of Mrs. Marquis S. Smith, E48624
Photography by Jeffrey Dykes

p. 120
Attributed to Raimund (1839–1911) or Franz (act.
Yokohama 1879–85) von Stillfried
Three Apprentice Geisha (Maiko), c. 1879–82
Hand-colored albumen print
Peabody Essex Museum, Salem, Massachusetts
Photography by Jeffrey Dykes

p. 121
Utagawa Toyokuni (1769–1825)
Whispered Secret at a Wayside Teahouse, from an
untitled album [Twenty-four Scenes of Women], 1816
Board-mounted album leaf; ink and color on paper
15 3/4 x 23 in. (40 x 58.4 cm)
Private collection

p. 122
Torii Kiyonaga (1752–1818)
The Kashima Dance (Kashima odori no tsuzuki)
thought to be from the series Compendium of the
[Yoshiwara] Niwaka Festival (Seirō niwaka zukushi),
1783
Woodblock print
10 1/4 x 7 1/2 in. (26 x 19 cm) [image]
Museum of Fine Arts, Boston
Chinese and Japanese Special Fund; 39.288
Photograph © 2003 Museum of Fine Arts, Boston

p. 124
Kitagawa Utamaro (1754–1806)
Ōmando performance: Oiyo and Takeji from the
Ogie school, from the series Female Geisha Section
of the [Yoshiwara] Niwaka Festival (Seirō niwaka onna
geisha bu), 1783
Woodblock print
15 x 10 in. (38 x 25.3 cm)
Tokyo National Museum
TNM Image Archives; http://TnmArchives.jp/

p. 125
Torii Kiyonaga (1752–1818)
Dragon King Procession, from the series
Compendium of the [Yoshiwara] Niwaka Festival
(*Seirō niwaka zukushi*), 1783
Woodblock print
7 0¼ x 15 in. (26.2 x 38.1 cm) x 10 ¼ in.
(19.1 x 26.1 cm)
Museum of Fine Arts, Boston
Chinese and Japanese Special Funds (39.287)
Photograph © 2003 Museum of Fine Arts,
Boston

p. 126
Kitagawa Utamaro (1754–1806)
Performers in Korean Costume, as Lion
Dancer, and as Sumo Wrestler (*Tōjin, Shishi,
Sumō*), from the series *Female Geisha Section of
the [Yoshiwara] Niwaka Festival* (*Seirō niwaka
onna geisha bu*), 1793
Woodblock print
15 x 10⅜ in. (37.9 x 26.4 cm)
Museum of Fine Arts, Boston
William S. and John T. Spaulding Collection;
21.6383
Photograph © 2003 Museum of Fine Arts,
Boston

p. 127
Kitagawa Utamaro (1754–1806)
Tea Whisk Seller, Firewood Seller, Shrine-
Festival Performer (*Chasen uri, kuroki uri,
Saimon*), from the series *Female Geisha Section
of the Yoshiwara* (*Seirō niwaka onna geisha*),
1793
Woodblock print
14¾ x 10 in. (37.7 x 25.7 cm)
Museum of Fine Arts, Boston
William Sturgis Bigelow Collection; 11.14358
Photograph © 2003 Museum of Fine Arts,
Boston

p. 128
Kitagawa Utamaro (1754–1806)
The Geisha Mine and Ito with Ogie Matsuzō,
1793
Woodblock print
15¼ x 10⅛ in. (38.5 x 25.7 cm)
William Sturgis Bigelow Collection; 11.14373
Photograph © 2003 Museum of Fine Arts,
Boston

p. 129
Kitagawa Utamaro (1754–1806)
Lion Dance (*Shishiren*), 1795
Woodblock print
10⅛ x 7½ in. (25.8 x 19.1 cm) in. (26.2 x 38.1
cm)
Tokyo National Museum
TNM Image Archives; http://TnmArchives.jp/

p. 130
Kitagawa Utamaro (1754–1806)
The Flourishing Harbor of Takase (*Takase
minato no sakae*), from the series *Yoshiwara
Niwaka Festival*, Second Part (*Yoshiwara
niwaka, ni no kawari*), 1798
Woodblock print; triptych
13 x 8 ¾ in. (33 x 22.3 cm) [each panel]
Tokyo National Museum
TNM Image Archives; http://TnmArchives.jp/

p. 131 Kitagawa Utamaro (1754–1806)
The Four Heavenly Kings Reach Mount Ōe
(*Shitenno Ōeyama-iri*), from the series *Niwaka
Performances in the Yoshiwara* (*Yoshiwara
niwaka, ni no kawari*), 1795
Woodblock print
12½ x 8¾ in. (31.9 x 22.1 cm)

Tokyo National Museum
TNM Image Archives; http://TnmArchives.jp/

p. 132
Suzuki Harunobu (1725–70)
The Beauties Ofuji, and Osen, and the Actor
Segawa Kikanojō c.1769
woodblock print
10¼ x 15 in. (26.2 x 38.1 cm)
Tokyo National Museum
Image: TNM Image Archives; Source: http://
TnmArchives.jp/

p. 133 left
Kitagawa Utamaro (1754–1806)
The Geisha Kamekichi of Sodegaura, 1794–95
Woodblock print
9¾ x 15 in. (24.8 x 38.1 cm)
Museum of Fine Arts, Boston
William S. and John T. Spaulding Collection;
21.6409
Photograph © 2003 Museum of Fine Arts,
Boston

p. 133 right
Kitagawa Utamaro (1754–1806)
Three Beauties of the Present Day (*Tōji
sanbijin*): Tomimoto Toyohina, Takashima(ya)
Ohisa, and Naniwaya Okita, 1794
Woodblock print
14⅝ x 9¾ in. (37 x 25 cm)
Museum of Fine Arts, Boston
William S. and John T. Spaulding Collection;
21.6382
Photograph © 2003 Museum of Fine Arts,
Boston

p. 134
Kitagawa Utamaro (1754–1806)
Neck Tug-of-War Between the Wrestler
Tanikaze and Strong Boy Kintarō (*Tanikaze to
Kintarō no kubihiki*), c. 1793
Woodblock print
12 x 17 in. (30.5 x 43.3 cm)
Chiba City Museum of Art
2953001

p. 135
Kitagawa Utamaro (1754–1806)
Seven Lucky Beauties; Their Appearances
Compared (*Shichifuku bijin kiryō kurabe*),
c. 1793–94
Woodblock print
9 x 13 in. (23 x 33.3 cm)
The British Museum
All rights reserved

p. 136
Kitagawa Utamaro (1754–1806)
Young Women of the Present Day Who Have
Made Their Mark (*Tōsei shusse musume*), c.
1795–96
Woodblock print triptych
14⅜ x 9⅝ in. (36.7 x 24.5 cm) [each panel]
Museum of Fine Arts, Boston
William Sturgis Bigelow Collection; 11.14266,
11.14280, 11.14283
Photograph © 2003 Museum of Fine Arts,
Boston

p. 137
Kitagawa Utamaro (1754–1806)
"To," from the series *The Realm of Geisha* (*Gei-
koku to no shirushi*), c. 1796
Woodblock print
10⅛ x 15⅛ in. (26 x 38.5 cm)
Museum of Fine Arts, Boston, Massachusetts
William S. and John T. Spaulding Collection;
21.6469

Photograph © 2004 Museum of Fine Arts,
Boston, Massachusetts

p. 138
Shinoyama Kishin (b. 1940)
Kabuki actor Bandō Tamasaburō in the play
Kanda Matsuri
Photograph courtesy of Shochiku Company

p. 140
Shinoyama Kishin (b. 1940)
Bandō Tamasaburō as the geisha Okō in the
play *Nihonbashi* by Isumi Kyōka
Photograph courtesy of Shochiku Company

p. 141
Unidentified artist
The Kamo River Dances, Pontochō District,
Kyoto, c. 1880–1900
Hand-colored albumen print
8½ x 10⅞ in. (21.5 x 27.4 cm)
Peabody Essex Museum, Salem, Massachusetts
Photography by Jeffrey Dykes

p. 143
Torii Kiyonaga (1752–1818)
Ichikawa Yaozō III and His Geisha Mistress,
c. 1785
Woodblock print
11¾ x 5⅞ in. (29.8 x 14.9 cm)
Metropolitan Museum of Art
The Howard Mansfield Collection, Purchase,
Rogers Fund, 1936 (JP2602)
All rights reserved

p. 144
Scene from the film *Snow Country* (*Yukiguni*),
1957
directed by Toyoda Shirō
Photograph courtesy of Toho Co., Ltd. © 1956
Toho Co., Ltd. All rights reserved

p. 145
Scene from the film *Flowing* (*Nagareru*), 1956
directed by Naruse Mikio
Photograph courtesy of Toho Co., Ltd. © 1956
Toho Co., Ltd. All rights reserved

p. 146
Yamada Isuzu as the geisha Omocha in *Sisters of
Gion* (*Gion no Shimai*), 1936
Directed by Mizoguchi Kenji
Photography courtesy of Shochiku Films

p. 156
Unidentified artist
Imperial Medal for Excellence in Artistic
Performance, 1978
silk, metal
23⅜ x 19 ¾ in. (72.1 x 50.2 cm)
Private collection, Kanazawa, Japan
Photography by Noca Wakihiko

Index

Imperial Medal for Excellence in Artistic Performance, 1978
The Emperor Shōwa (Hirohito) conferred this award on the Kanazawa geisha Sumiko for her achievements in *yokobue* (Japanese flute), her artistic specialty.

Geisha: Beyond the Painted Smile
was produced by Perpetua Press, Santa Barbara
Project Director: Lynda Roscoe Hartigan
Editors: Letitia Burns O'Connor and Jane Oliver
Designer: Dana Levy
Printed in Hong Kong by Toppan Printing Co. (HK) Ltd.